THE NEW Art and Science OF TEACHING

Reading

JULIA A. SIMMS ROBERT J. MARZANO

A joint publication

ASCD

Solution Tree

555 North Morton Street
Bloomington, IN 47404
800.733.6786 (toll free) / 812.336.7700
FAX: 812.336.7790

email: info@SolutionTree.com
SolutionTree.com

Visit **go.SolutionTree.com/instruction** to download the free reproducibles in this book.

Printed in the United States of America

FSC
www.fsc.org
MIX
Paper from responsible sources
FSC® C011935

Library of Congress Cataloging-in-Publication Data

Names: Simms, Julia A., author. | Marzano, Robert J., author.
Title: The new art and science of teaching reading / authors, Julia A. Simms, Robert J. Marzano.
Description: Bloomington, Indiana : Solution Tree Press, [2018] | Includes bibliographical references and index.
Identifiers: LCCN 2018005655 | ISBN 9781945349676 (perfect bound)
Subjects: LCSH: Reading--Research. | Reading comprehension.
Classification: LCC LB1050.6 .S56 2019 | DDC 428.4072--dc23 LC record available at https://lccn.loc.gov/2018005655

Solution Tree
Jeffrey C. Jones, CEO
Edmund M. Ackerman, President

Solution Tree Press
President and Publisher: Douglas M. Rife
Editorial Director: Sarah Payne-Mills
Art Director: Rian Anderson
Managing Production Editor: Kendra Slayton
Senior Production Editor: Suzanne Kraszewski
Senior Editor: Amy Rubenstein
Copy Editor: Miranda Addonizio
Proofreader: Elisabeth Abrams
Text and Cover Designer: Laura Cox
Editorial Assistant: Sarah Ludwig

Visit **go.SolutionTree.com/instruction** to download the free reproducibles in this book.

Table of Contents

Reproducibles are in italics.

About the Authors

Julia A. Simms is the director of content and resources at Marzano Resources. A former classroom teacher, she and her team develop research-based resources and provide support to educators as they implement them. Her areas of expertise include effective instruction, learning progressions and proficiency scales, assessment and grading, argumentation and reasoning skills, and literacy development. She has coauthored eight books including *Coaching Classroom Instruction*, *Vocabulary for the Common Core*, *Questioning Sequences in the Classroom*, and *A Handbook for High Reliability Schools*.

Julia received a bachelor's degree from Wheaton College and master's degrees in educational administration and K–12 literacy from Colorado State University and the University of Northern Colorado.

Robert J. Marzano, PhD, is the cofounder and chief academic officer of Marzano Resources in Denver, Colorado. During his fifty years in the field of education, he has worked with educators as a speaker and trainer and has authored more than forty books and two hundred articles on topics such as instruction, assessment, writing and implementing standards, cognition, effective leadership, and school intervention. His books include *The New Art and Science of Teaching*, *Leaders of Learning*, *Making Classroom Assessments Reliable and Valid*, *A Handbook for Personalized Competency-Based Education*, and *Teacher Evaluation That Makes a Difference*. His practical translations of the most current research and theory into classroom strategies are known internationally and are widely practiced by both teachers and administrators.

Dr. Marzano received a bachelor's degree from Iona College in New York, a master's degree from Seattle University, and a doctorate from the University of Washington.

To learn more about Robert J. Marzano's work, visit marzanoresources.com.

To book Julia A. Simms or Robert J. Marzano for professional development, contact pd@SolutionTree.com.

Introduction

The New Art and Science of Teaching (Marzano, 2017) is a comprehensive model of instruction with a rather long developmental lineage. Specifically, four books spanning two decades precede and inform *The New Art and Science of Teaching* and its use in the field.

1. *Classroom Instruction That Works: Research-Based Strategies for Increasing Student Achievement* (Marzano, Pickering, & Pollock, 2001)
2. *Classroom Management That Works: Research-Based Strategies for Every Teacher* (Marzano, Marzano, & Pickering, 2003)
3. *Classroom Assessment and Grading That Work* (Marzano, 2006)
4. *The Art and Science of Teaching: A Comprehensive Framework for Effective Instruction* (Marzano, 2007)

The first three books address specific components of the teaching process, namely instruction, management, and assessment. The final book puts all three components together into a comprehensive model of teaching. It also makes a strong case for the fact that research (in other words, science) must certainly guide good teaching, but teachers must also develop good teaching as art. Even if they use precisely the same instructional strategies, two highly effective teachers will have shaped and adapted those strategies to adhere to their specific personalities, the subject matter they teach, and their students' unique needs. Stated differently, we can never accurately articulate effective teaching as a set of strategies that all teachers must execute in precisely the same way.

The comprehensive model in the book *The New Art and Science of Teaching* (Marzano, 2017) reflects a greatly expanded and updated version of *The Art and Science of Teaching* (Marzano, 2007). One of the unique aspects of *The New Art and Science of Teaching* is that it focuses on student learning, rather than being teacher focused, as we depict in figure I.1:

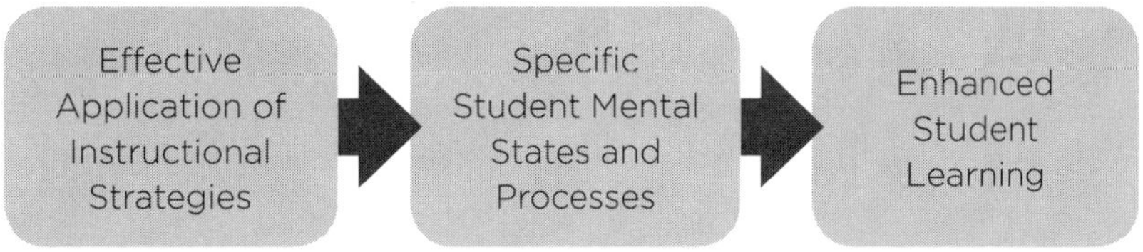

Source: Marzano, 2017, p. 5.

Figure I.1: The teaching and learning progression.

According to figure I.1, the intervening variables between effectively applying an instructional strategy and enhanced student learning are specific mental states and processes in the minds of learners. If teachers do not produce these mental states and processes as a result of employing a given strategy, then that strategy will have little or no effect on students. This implies that teachers should heighten their level of awareness as they use instructional strategies for maximum efficacy.

The Overall Model

At a basic level, the model in *The New Art and Science of Teaching* (Marzano, 2017) is a framework that educators can use to organize the majority (if not all) of the instructional strategies that research and theory identify. The model has several parts: three overarching categories, ten design areas, and forty-three specific elements.

Three Categories

At the highest level of organization, the model has three overarching categories: feedback, content, and context.

1. *Feedback* refers to the all-important information loop teachers must establish with students so that students know what they should be learning about specific topics and their current level of performance on these topics.
2. *Content* refers to the sequencing and pacing of lessons such that students move smoothly from initial understanding to applying knowledge in new and creative ways.
3. *Context* refers to those strategies that ensure all students meet these psychological needs: engagement, order, a sense of belonging, and high expectations.

Embedded in these three overarching categories are more specific categories of teacher actions (design areas).

Ten Design Areas

In *The New Art and Science of Teaching* framework, each of the ten design areas is associated with a specific teacher action, as follows.

1. Providing and communicating clear learning goals
2. Using assessments
3. Conducting direct instruction lessons
4. Conducting practicing and deepening lessons
5. Conducting knowledge application lessons
6. Using strategies that appear in all types of lessons
7. Using engagement strategies
8. Implementing rules and procedures
9. Building relationships
10. Communicating high expectations

Table I.1 shows the ten teacher actions within the three categories and describes the desired student mental states and processes for each. For example, when the teacher conducts a direct instruction lesson (the third design area), the goal is that students will understand which parts of the content are important and how they fit together.

Table I.1: Teacher Actions and Student Mental States and Processes

	Teacher Actions	Student Mental States and Processes
Feedback	Providing and Communicating Clear Learning Goals	1. Students understand the progression of knowledge they are expected to master and where they are along that progression.
	Using Assessments	2. Students understand how test scores and grades relate to their status on the progression of knowledge they are expected to master.
Content	Conducting Direct Instruction Lessons	3. When content is new, students understand which parts are important and how the parts fit together.
	Conducting Practicing and Deepening Lessons	4. After teachers present new content, students deepen their understanding and develop fluency in skills and processes.
	Conducting Knowledge Application Lessons	5. After teachers present new content, students generate and defend claims through knowledge application tasks.
	Using Strategies That Appear in All Types of Lessons	6. Students continually integrate new knowledge with old knowledge and revise their understanding accordingly.
Context	Using Engagement Strategies	7. Students are paying attention, energized, intrigued, and inspired.
	Implementing Rules and Procedures	8. Students understand and follow rules and procedures.
	Building Relationships	9. Students feel welcome, accepted, and valued.
	Communicating High Expectations	10. Typically reluctant students feel valued and do not hesitate to interact with the teacher or their peers.

Source: Marzano, 2017, pp. 5–6.

Each of the ten design areas corresponds with a *design question*. These are a set of questions that help teachers plan units and lessons within those units. Table I.2 shows the design questions that correspond with each design area.

Table I.2: Design Questions

	Design Areas	Design Questions
Feedback	1. Providing and Communicating Clear Learning Goals	How will I communicate clear learning goals that help students understand the progression of knowledge they are expected to master and where they are along that progression?
	2. Using Assessments	How will I design and administer assessments that help students understand how their test scores and grades are related to their status on the progression of knowledge they are expected to master?
Content	3. Conducting Direct Instruction Lessons	When content is new, how will I design and deliver direct instruction lessons that help students understand which parts are important and how the parts fit together?
	4. Conducting Practicing and Deepening Lessons	After presenting content, how will I design and deliver lessons that help students deepen their understanding and develop fluency in skills and processes?
	5. Conducting Knowledge Application Lessons	After presenting content, how will I design and deliver lessons that help students generate and defend claims through knowledge application?
	6. Using Strategies That Appear in All Types of Lessons	Throughout all types of lessons, what strategies will I use to help students continually integrate new knowledge with old knowledge and revise their understanding accordingly?

continued →

Context	7. Using Engagement Strategies	What engagement strategies will I use to help students pay attention, be energized, be intrigued, and be inspired?
	8. Implementing Rules and Procedures	What strategies will I use to help students understand and follow rules and procedures?
	9. Building Relationships	What strategies will I use to help students feel welcome, accepted, and valued?
	10. Communicating High Expectations	What strategies will I use to help typically reluctant students feel valued and comfortable interacting with their peers and me?

Source: Marzano, 2017, pp. 6–7.

Within the ten categories of teacher actions, we have organized sets of strategies in even more fine-grained categories, called *elements*. As teachers think about each design question, they can then consider specific elements within the design area.

Forty-Three Elements

The forty-three elements provide detailed guidance about the nature and purpose of a category of strategies. Table I.3 depicts the elements that correspond to each design area. For example, the design area of *providing and communicating clear learning goals* involves three elements.

- Providing scales and rubrics (element 1)
- Tracking student progress (element 2)
- Celebrating success (element 3)

As a teacher considers how to provide and communicate clear learning goals that help students understand the progression of knowledge he or she expects them to master and where they are along that progression (design question 1), the teacher might think more specifically about providing scales and rubrics, tracking student progress, and celebrating success. These are the elements within the first design area.

Finally, these forty-three elements encompass hundreds of specific instructional strategies.

General and Reading-Specific Strategies

Over 330 specific instructional strategies (embedded in the forty-three elements) have been articulated as a part of the general *The New Art and Science of Teaching* framework. (For detailed descriptions of the strategies articulated in the general model, see Marzano Resources, n.d.) For example, Marzano Resources (n.d.) articulated the following nine strategies for element 24—increasing response rates.

1. Random names
2. Hand signals
3. Response cards
4. Response chaining
5. Paired response
6. Choral response
7. Wait time
8. Elaborative interrogation
9. Multiple types of questions

Teachers can indeed use these nine strategies to increase students' response rates. However, the articulation of these strategies in *The New Art and Science of Teaching* framework does not imply that they are the only strategies that can be used to increase students' response rates. When applying *The New Art and Science of Teaching*

Table I.3: Elements Within the Ten Design Areas

Feedback	Content	Context
Providing and Communicating Clear Learning Goals 1. Providing scales and rubrics 2. Tracking student progress 3. Celebrating success **Using Assessments** 4. Using informal assessments of the whole class 5. Using formal assessments of individual students	**Conducting Direct Instruction Lessons** 6. Chunking content 7. Processing content 8. Recording and representing content **Conducting Practicing and Deepening Lessons** 9. Using structured practice sessions 10. Examining similarities and differences 11. Examining errors in reasoning **Conducting Knowledge Application Lessons** 12. Engaging students in cognitively complex tasks 13. Providing resources and guidance 14. Generating and defending claims **Using Strategies That Appear in All Types of Lessons** 15. Previewing strategies 16. Highlighting critical information 17. Reviewing content 18. Revising knowledge 19. Reflecting on learning 20. Assigning purposeful homework 21. Elaborating on information 22. Organizing students to interact	**Using Engagement Strategies** 23. Noticing and reacting when students are not engaged 24. Increasing response rates 25. Using physical movement 26. Maintaining a lively pace 27. Demonstrating intensity and enthusiasm 28. Presenting unusual information 29. Using friendly controversy 30. Using academic games 31. Providing opportunities for students to talk about themselves 32. Motivating and inspiring students **Implementing Rules and Procedures** 33. Establishing rules and procedures 34. Organizing the physical layout of the classroom 35. Demonstrating withitness 36. Acknowledging adherence to rules and procedures 37. Acknowledging lack of adherence to rules and procedures **Building Relationships** 38. Using verbal and nonverbal behaviors that indicate affection for students 39. Understanding students' backgrounds and interests 40. Displaying objectivity and control **Communicating High Expectations** 41. Demonstrating value and respect for reluctant learners 42. Asking in-depth questions of reluctant learners 43. Probing incorrect answers with reluctant learners

Source: Marzano, 2017, p. 8.

to a specific content area (such as reading), there are additional, reading-specific strategies that teachers can use to increase students' response rates. This book focuses on such strategies. For example, chapter 8 of this book describes the strategy of student-generated questions as a way to increase students' response rates when asking and answering questions about a text. While student-generated questions is not articulated as a strategy in the general *The New Art and Science of Teaching* framework, it is a powerful reading strategy and is clearly associated with increasing students' response rates to questions. Thus, it appears in our discussion of that element in this book. The same logic applies to our treatment of the other forty-two elements: we provide reading-specific strategies for each element of the general *The New Art and Science of Teaching* framework.

Appendix A (page 165) presents an overview of the entire *The New Art and Science of Teaching* framework featuring the categories, design areas, and elements. This can serve as an advance organizer while reading this book.

The Need for Subject-Specific Models

General frameworks like *The New Art and Science of Teaching* certainly have their place in a teacher's understanding of effective instruction. However, a content-specific model of instruction can be a useful supplement to the more general framework in *The New Art and Science of Teaching*. The content-specific model should fit within the context of the general framework, but it should be based on content-specific research and should take into account the unique challenges of teaching a particular content area. For reading, such a content-specific model should address important aspects of reading and reading instruction, such as concepts of print, word recognition, fluency, vocabulary, comprehension, grouping strategies, the role of culture, and the unique needs of English learners and struggling readers, among others. A content-specific model for reading should address these aspects in depth and relate back to the general framework of instruction. We designed this book to provide just such a model. Specifically, in the following chapters, we address the three overarching categories—(1) feedback, (2) content, and (3) context—with their corresponding ten categories of instruction and the embedded forty-three elements that feature specific strategies expressly for reading.

Although this text predominantly provides suggestions to support lesson planning around reading instruction, we encourage readers to explore the foundational book *The New Art and Science of Teaching* (Marzano, 2017). In doing so, they will likely infuse their content areas and grade levels with additional strategies.

This Book

To orient readers, we begin in chapter 1 with an overview of how reading research and instruction have progressed since the middle of the 19th century, followed by a research-based description of how skilled reading develops. Then, we present our reading-specific model of instruction that features five elements—(1) foundational skills, (2) word recognition, (3) fluency, (4) vocabulary, and (5) comprehension—and describe the research supporting each element.

In chapters 2 through 11, we situate that reading-specific model within the broader context of *The New Art and Science of Teaching* framework. Part I, focused on feedback, begins with chapter 2, which describes how teachers can articulate the content to be learned in the reading classroom using learning progressions (called proficiency scales) and use those scales to track students' progress and celebrate their success. In chapter 3, we explain how to assess students' current status relative to the content articulated in the proficiency scales.

Part II addresses content. In chapters 4, 5, 6, and 7, we articulate instructional strategies for teaching the reading content that students need to learn. Chapter 4 focuses on conducting direct instruction lessons, chapter 5 on conducting practicing and deepening lessons, chapter 6 on conducting knowledge application lessons, and chapter 7 on using strategies that appear in all types of lessons.

Part III, concentrated on context, reviews reading-related issues pertaining to student engagement (chapter 8), rules and procedures (chapter 9), building relationships (chapter 10), and communicating high expectations to all students (chapter 11).

Chapter 12 describes a four-step process for developing teachers' expertise. In anticipation of chapter 12, each chapter contains self-rating scales for readers to assess their performance on the elements of the model. By doing this, they can determine their areas of strength and the areas in which they might want to improve relative to *The New Art and Science of Teaching*. All of the self-rating scales in this book have the same format for progression of development. To introduce these scales and help readers understand them, we present the general format of a self-rating scale in figure I.2.

Score	Description
4: Innovating	I adapt strategies and behaviors associated with this element for unique student needs and situations.
3: Applying	I use strategies and behaviors associated with this element without significant errors and monitor their effect on students.
2: Developing	I use strategies and behaviors associated with this element without significant errors but do not monitor their effect on students.
1: Beginning	I use some strategies and behaviors associated with this element but do so with significant errors or omissions.
0: Not Using	I am unaware of the strategies and behaviors associated with this element or know them but don't employ them.

Figure I.2: General format of the self-rating scale.

To understand this scale, it is best to start at the bottom with the Not Using row. Here the teacher is unaware of the strategies that relate to the element or knows them but doesn't employ them. At the Beginning level, the teacher uses strategies that relate to the element, but leaves out important parts or makes significant mistakes. At the Developing level, the teacher executes strategies important to the element without significant errors or omissions but does not monitor their effect on students. At the Applying level, the teacher not only executes strategies without significant errors or omissions, but also monitors students to ensure that they are experiencing the desired effects. We consider the Applying level the level at which one can legitimately expect tangible results in students. Finally, at the Innovating level, the teacher is aware of and makes any adaptations to the strategies for students who require such an arrangement.

Each chapter also contains Guiding Questions for Curriculum Design to support planning and aid in reflection.

Appendix A provides an overview of *The New Art and Science of Teaching* framework. Appendix B features orthography exercises, and appendix C examines reading in the disciplines. Appendix D lists the figures and tables featured in this book. Additionally, please visit **go.Solution Tree.com/instruction** to access the book's three online appendices featuring phoneme charts, vocabulary games, and culturally diverse texts.

In sum, *The New Art and Science of Teaching Reading* is designed to present a reading-specific model of instruction within the context of *The New Art and Science of Teaching* framework. We address each of the forty-three elements from the general model within the context of reading instruction and provide reading-specific strategies and techniques that teachers can use to improve their effectiveness and elicit desired mental states and processes from their students.

CHAPTER 1

Reading Research and a Reading-Specific Model of Instruction

To orient readers, we begin with a brief explanation of how reading research and instruction have progressed since the middle of the 19th century, followed by a research-based description of how skilled reading develops. Then, we present our reading-specific model of instruction. In chapters 2 through 11, we situate that reading-specific model within the broader context of *The New Art and Science of Teaching* framework.

Reading Research

Historically, we can conceptualize reading research and instruction in four chronological phases.

1. Before the 20th century
2. From 1900 to the 1970s
3. From the 1970s to the 1990s
4. From the 1990s to the present

Here, we describe salient features and findings associated with each phase.

Before the 20th Century: Oral Reading Reigns

Before 1900, oral reading was the primary focus of reading instruction. Early reading textbooks, such as William Holmes McGuffey's (1879), were designed to improve a student's oral reading, and in 1892, philosopher William James stated that one could judge the quality of a teacher by the quality of his or her students' oral reading. One reason for this instructional emphasis was a lack of widespread literacy among the American populace; most households had only one person who could read (Hyatt, 1943; Smith, 1965). Therefore, reading in the home, whether for entertainment or information, was typically done aloud.

Recitation lessons were the norm in schools; students listened to the teacher read and then tried to reproduce what they heard. Lyman Cobb (as cited in Smith, 1965) explained that students' goals were:

> Distinct articulation of words pronounced in proper tones, suitably varied to the sense, and the emotions of the mind; with due attention to accent, to emphasis, in its several gradations; to rests or pauses of the voice, in proper places.

Such practices prioritized elocution over comprehension (Hoffman, 1987; Hoffman & Segel, 1983), although teachers sometimes asked students to retell what they had read. Nevertheless, in 1891, Horace Mann claimed that 90 percent of students did not understand what they read.

From 1900 to the 1970s: Meaning Resides in the Text

As the 20th century began, the primacy of oral reading waned. According to P. David Pearson and Gina N. Cervetti (2017), rising literacy rates decreased the demand for oral reading in the home. Immigration, child labor prohibitions, and mandatory school attendance swelled public school enrollment, and an increased emphasis on scientific methods in education gave birth to the standardized testing movement. Silent reading rate and comprehension level moved to the education foreground. Pearson and Cervetti (2017) explain:

> Unlike oral reading, which had to be tested individually and required that teachers judge the quality of responses, silent reading comprehension (and rate) could be tested in group settings and scored without recourse to professional judgement; only stop watches and multiple-choice questions were needed. In modern parlance, we would say that they moved from a "high-inference" assessment tool (oral reading and retelling) to a "low-inference" tool (multiple-choice tests or timed readings). Thus, it fit the demands for efficiency (spawned by the move toward more universal education for all students) and objectivity (part of the emerging scientism of the period). (p. 15)

Educators reasoned that if students could answer questions about a passage, they were able to read it and comprehend it.

Early 20th century educators typically defined comprehension as accessing the *true* meaning of a text. That is, they viewed the meaning of a text as an inherent property of the text itself, and the job of the student (with the teacher's assistance) was to figure it out. Reading "was viewed as a largely bottom-up process in which readers would visually analyze the features of letters, map the sounds onto letters and then onto strings of letters to pronounce words, and listen to the output to achieve understanding" (Pearson & Cervetti, 2017, p. 40). An examination of curriculum materials from this time—William H. Elson and William S. Gray's (1936) well-known Dick and Jane series, for instance—reveals that the dominant approach to teaching reading involved asking questions about a text after students had read it.

From the 1970s to the 1990s: Readers Construct Meaning

Although a few prescient scholars, such as Edmund B. Huey (1908) and Edward L. Thorndike (1917), articulated sophisticated descriptions of reading comprehension in the early 20th century, widespread interest in readers' cognitive processes did not occur until the 1970s. In what is often called the cognitive revolution (Anderson, 2010), reading theorists and researchers turned their attention to the reader (rather than the text) as the maker of meaning. They redefined comprehension as what happens when a reader, influenced and guided by his or her prior knowledge, interprets a text. This shift led to four major areas of inquiry, as shown in table 1.1.

Table 1.1: Areas of Inquiry for Reading Research During the Cognitive Revolution

Area of Inquiry	Question
Knowledge Structures	How is prior knowledge stored in the brain?
Text Structures	How is information stored in a text?
Comprehension Strategies	How do students combine prior knowledge and textual information to make meaning?
Teaching Techniques	How can educators improve students' meaning-making skills?

Here we briefly explain the major ideas associated with each area of inquiry.

Knowledge Structures: Schema Theory

With the acknowledgment that students bring prior knowledge to a text, scientists became interested in how students store that knowledge in their brains and how they access it when reading a text. One of the most prominent models was schema theory. *Schema theory* describes knowledge in the human brain as "little containers [called *schemata*] into which we deposit the particular traces of particular experiences, as well as the 'ideas' that derive from those experiences" (Pearson & Cervetti, 2017, p. 25). Schema theory became popular as a model of reading comprehension in part because it readily explained common phenomena, such as the human propensity to disagree about the interpretation of various texts—books, movies, newspaper articles, and the like. According to schema theory, disagreements arise because each individual approaches a text with a different, and unique, body of prior knowledge and experiences. Richard C. Anderson (1984) describes some of the additional phenomena that schema theory explained.

- **Learning and memory:** For different types of texts, our minds have slots that we expect to fill with certain types of information; information that fits in the slots is that which we easily learn and remember.
- **Identifying important ideas:** The slots in our schemata guide our search for what is important in a text, allowing us to separate main ideas and details.
- **Elaboration and inference:** No text is ever completely explicit; our schemata help us to make educated guesses about how we should fill certain slots.

In sum, schema theory posits that individuals store information about their experiences using particular structures; understanding those structures helps students access and apply knowledge when reading a text.

Text Structures: Kintsch and Meyer

A parallel line of research examined how texts store information, and how text structures interact with knowledge structures to create meaning. Researchers conceptualized structures in texts as "slots" that a writer fills with particular types of information. A reader who knows what to expect from the slots of a specific text structure will more effectively align his or her prior knowledge to the text and is more likely to comprehend it. According to Walter Kintsch (1983), whose model of text comprehension was, and still is, widely accepted:

> Comprehending a text involves the formation of two parallel, complementary structures, the textbase and the situational model. The textbase is a representation of the content of the text, consisting of the elementary propositions derived from the text which are organized into a coherent whole on the basis of some available knowledge structure, e.g. a schema. The situational model is developed in parallel with the text base proper, but it is a richer structure which contains not only the information derived from the text, but also the reader's previous knowledge about the subject matter. (p. 2)

In simpler terms, readers organize information from a text into a structure (the *textbase*) and then combine that with what they already know to create a *situational model*, which they use to make meaning.

Bonnie J. F. Meyer, Carole J. Young, and Brendan J. Bartlett (1989) articulate six specific text structures and investigate the effect of explicitly teaching those text structures on students' comprehension. In numerous studies since 1971, Meyer and her colleagues find that teaching text structures using techniques such as "direct instruction, modeling, scaffolding, elaborated feedback, and adaptation of instruction to student performance" (Meyer & Ray, 2011, p. 127) improves students' comprehension significantly (Meyer, 1971, 1975; Meyer et al., 1989; Meyer et al., 2010; Meyer, Brandt, & Bluth, 1980; Meyer & Freedle, 1979, 1984; Meyer & Poon, 2001; Meyer & Rice, 1982).

Table 1.2 lists the six text structures Meyer and her colleagues identify, examples of texts that typically use each structure, and signal words that alert a reader to the presence of each structure.

Table 1.2: Text Structures

Structure	Definition	Examples	Signal Words
Description	Presents ideas through elaboration of attributes, specifics, or setting information	• Newspaper article	*attributes, characteristics, properties, qualities*
Sequence	Groups ideas based on order or time	• Recipe • History book • Biography	*before, after, earlier, later, initially, finally, previous, following, recent*
Comparison	Relates ideas by highlighting similarities and differences	• Political speech	*comparison, contrast, however, alternatively, similar, different, same, despite, distinction*
Causation	Presents cause and effect relationships between ideas	• Directions • Explanations • Economics text	*result, cause, effect, consequence, thus, reason, explanation*
Problem and Solution	Presents ideas in two parts: a problem to be solved and a solution that eliminates the problem	• Scientific article • Frequently asked questions document	*problem, trouble, difficulty, issue, danger, bad, solution, answer, response, recommend, suggest, reply*
Collection	Relates ideas by simply grouping them together	• To-do list	*and, addition, besides, subsequent, furthermore, another*

Source: Adapted from Meyer et al., 1989; Meyer & Ray, 2011.
Visit ***go.SolutionTree.com/instruction*** *for a free reproducible version of this table.*

Research on knowledge and text structures highlighted and explored a reader's response to a text, rather than meaning inherent in a text. Researchers commonly used metaphors such as *reader as builder* or *reader as creator* to describe this collaboration between reader and text.

Comprehension Strategies: Reciprocal Teaching and Metacognition

Many researchers during the cognitive revolution investigated the processes that readers use to make meaning (such as predicting, questioning, elaborating, inferring, clarifying, visualizing, retelling, or summarizing). They commonly referred to these processes as *comprehension strategies*. Initial research indicated that teaching students to use such strategies improved their comprehension of texts. Moreover, researchers attained even better results when they taught students to use combinations of strategies. The best-known and most-researched combination of strategies from this time is *reciprocal teaching* (Palincsar & Brown, 1984), in which a reader stops regularly while reading a text to engage in four strategies—(1) prediction, (2) questioning, (3) clarification, and (4) summarization—and selects those most appropriate to the comprehension challenges in the text.

Researchers also delved into the *metacognitive strategies* that students use to monitor their comprehension while reading. These processes include:

- **Awareness**—Paying attention to one's thoughts
- **Monitoring**—Recognizing when understanding breaks down
- **Control**—Selecting a strategy to fix the problem
- **Evaluation**—Judging how well one has resolved a problem and if further attention is necessary

Pearson and Cervetti (2017) describe the genesis of metacognitive research as:

> A logical extension of the rapidly developing work on both schema theory and text analysis. These latter two traditions emphasized declarative knowledge, knowing that *X* or *Y* or *Z* is true, but were scant on specifying procedural knowledge, knowing how to engage a strategy for comprehension or memory. This is precisely the kind of knowledge that metacognitive research has emphasized. (p. 26)

The primary metaphor that researchers used to refer to students' use of metacognitive strategies when their comprehension breaks down was *reader as fixer*.

Teaching Techniques: Gradual Release of Responsibility

Researchers also sought to describe effective instructional techniques for teachers to use when teaching comprehension and metacognitive strategies. David Pearson and Margaret Gallagher (1983) proposed an explicit model, called *gradual release of responsibility*, which many educators still use today. In brief, it involves three phases.

1. **Teacher responsibility:** The teacher explains the purpose of a strategy (or set of strategies), how to use it, and when to use it. Then, he or she models its use by thinking aloud, so that students are aware of what is going on in the teacher's mind during reading.
2. **Shared responsibility:** Students engage in guided practice while the teacher provides scaffolding and facilitation.
3. **Student responsibility:** Students use the strategy or strategies independently.

Many studies find that comprehension strategy instruction, using a gradual release of responsibility model (or similar approach), produces measurable gains in students' reading comprehension (see Wilkinson & Son, 2011, for a review). Nevertheless, over the same time period, several notable studies indicated that teachers actually engaged in very little comprehension strategy instruction (for example, Durkin, 1978/1979). Why? Strategies instruction is difficult to learn and difficult to implement effectively. For example, Pamela Beard El-Dinary and Ted Schuder (1993) document the difficulties seven teachers experienced as they learned to implement transactional strategies instruction (a multiple-strategies approach similar to reciprocal teaching). By the end of the year, only two of the seven teachers were still committed to using the approach. More recent studies find similar results (Connor, Morrison, & Petrella, 2004; Hilden & Pressley, 2007; Klingner, Vaughn, Arguelles, Hughes, & Leftwich, 2004; Klingner, Vaughn, Hughes, & Arguelles, 1999; Mason, 2004; Pressley, Wharton-McDonald, Mistretta-Hampton, & Echevarria, 1998; Taylor, Pearson, Clark, & Walpole, 2000; Taylor, Pearson, Peterson, & Rodriguez, 2003, 2005). Pearson and Cervetti (2017) label these implementation challenges the *Achilles heel* of comprehension strategies instruction.

From the 1990s to the Present: Reading Wars and the Common Core

As the 20th century drew to a close, reading research continued to build on the foundation laid in the previous two decades, refining and adding nuance to create a philosophy of reading instruction that researchers often refer to as *whole language*. Kenneth S. Goodman and Yetta Goodman (1985) describe whole language as a "comprehension-centered pedagogy" in which "literacy—reading and writing—is regarded as a natural extension of human language development" (p. 2). Whole language builds on the previously articulated ideas of reader as builder, creator, and fixer of meaning but goes several steps further. In particular, whole language proponents advocate for consideration of context, incorporation of literature, and the addition of critical literacy. Table 1.3 (page 14) elaborates on these three emphases.

Table 1.3: Whole-Language Emphases

Emphasis	Description
Consideration of Context	*Considering context* means recognizing that the situation in which a reader encounters a text affects the meaning of the text. Rand J. Spiro, W. P. Vispoel, John G. Schmitz, Ala Samarapungavan, and A. E. Boerger (1987) advocate for looking at texts from multiple perspectives using the metaphor of crisscrossing a landscape from many different directions in order to fully understand and appreciate it. Following the lead of the influential Louise M. Rosenblatt (1978), Peter Smagorinsky (2001) argues that meaning resides neither in the text nor in the reader, but in a "transactional zone" where text, reader, and context come together (p. 133). Just as text had moved to the background and the reader's response to a text was privileged in the 1970s, the reader moved to the background and context came forward in the 1990s.
Incorporation of Literature	In *Becoming a Nation of Readers*, Richard C. Anderson, Elfrieda H. Hiebert, Judith A. Scott, and Ian A. G. Wilkinson (1985) advocate for an increased amount of independent reading in elementary reading programs. Nancie Atwell, with her popular 1987 book *In the Middle*, inspired many teachers to help students explore literature through reader's workshops. Many basal readers and reading programs paled in comparison to the richness and complexity of authentic literary texts.
Addition of Critical Literacy	Pearson and Cervetti (2017) describe *critical literacy* as a set of practices that "encourage students to analyze texts with attention to the contexts and features of their construction and the ideologies that underlie them, asking, among other things, whose interests are served by particular texts and particular readings of those texts" (p. 34). Such practices require skillful teaching and facilitation of complex analysis in the classroom.

For many reading researchers, theorists, and educators, the whole-language approach represented the leading edge of reading research and instruction.

Nevertheless, throughout the 20th century, there were persistent concerns about students who simply couldn't read. For example, in 1955, Rudolf Franz Flesch wrote the highly controversial *Why Johnny Can't Read—And What You Can Do About It*, a book that advocated for phonics instruction over more holistic, comprehension-based approaches. In 1965, the U.S. federal government passed the Elementary and Secondary Education Act (ESEA) and began infusing significant funding into education in general, and into reading instruction and intervention in particular. Over the next fifty years, the federal government would continue to pour money into reading instruction. With so much money at stake, legislators wanted to know how effective different instructional approaches were at improving students' reading abilities. The following documents and reports attempt to answer those questions and strongly influenced reading policy during this time.

- *A Nation at Risk* (National Commission on Excellence in Education, 1983)
- *Preventing Reading Difficulties in Young Children* (Snow, Burns, & Griffin, 1998)
- *Report of the National Reading Panel* (National Institute of Child Health and Human Development [NICHD], 2000)
- *Reading for Understanding: Toward an R&D Program in Reading Comprehension* (RAND Reading Study Group, 2002)
- *Developing Literacy in Second-Language Learners: Report of the National Literacy Panel on Language-Minority Children and Youth* (August & Shanahan, 2006)
- *Developing Early Literacy: Report of the National Early Literacy Panel* (National Early Literacy Panel, 2008)

While all of these works were influential, none was more so than that of the National Reading Panel (NRP), published in April 2000. The report focuses primarily on five areas related to reading instruction: (1) phonics, (2) phonemic awareness, (3) fluency, (4) vocabulary, and (5) comprehension. For each area, the panel conducted a review of the extant research and makes recommendations for practice.

Many praised the work of the NRP for its rigorous methodology, but others (particularly those who advocated for a whole-language approach) found fault with the areas the NRP chose to focus on. Advocates of whole-language approaches viewed the NRP's emphasis on decoding skills (phonics, phonemic awareness) as a step backward. Although the NRP's report includes comprehension as one of its areas, many researchers and educators believed that there was a subtle repositioning: "Comprehension became the natural consequence of teaching the [alphabetic] code well in the early stages of instruction instead of the primary goal and focus of attention from the very beginning of a child's instructional life in school" (Pearson & Cervetti, 2017, p. 39). A lively debate, often called the *reading wars*, ensued; the crux of the conversation centered on whether a phonics-based approach or a whole-language approach was best for students.

In 2010, the National Governors Association Center for Best Practices and the Council of Chief State School Officers released the Common Core State Standards (CCSS). Although the standards are surrounded by controversy (much of which stems from the false notion that the federal government created the standards), many reading researchers see them as striking a healthy balance between phonics and comprehension. Advocates of whole language, such as Pearson and Cervetti (2017), describe the publication of the CCSS for English language arts standards as a "comeback" for reading comprehension (p. 12) and state that "the CCSS for reading seem to be well grounded in solid theories of reading comprehension" (p. 45).

In their chapter of the fourth volume of the *Handbook of Reading Research*, William E. Tunmer and Tom Nicholson (2011) summarize the benefits and drawbacks of both whole-language approaches and phonics approaches:

> Whole language provides plenty of opportunity for children to read but is weak on teaching the alphabetic principle. . . . Phonics gives lots of practice in learning the alphabetic principle but does not provide much opportunity for putting the alphabetic principle into practice through actual reading of text. (p. 425)

They conclude their comparison of whole language and phonics by suggesting that the most effective reading instruction "draw[s] on key elements of both approaches to provide instruction that best suits the needs of individual children" (Tunmer & Nicholson, 2011, p. 425). In the next section, we elaborate on how we believe teachers can best provide such reading instruction. Here, it suffices to say that the current state of research in reading acknowledges the importance of both phonics and whole-language approaches.

Development-Based Reading Instruction

As we mention previously, Tunmer and Nicholson (2011) assert that effective reading instruction looks different depending on what students already know and are able to do:

> The search for the "best method" of teaching reading is fundamentally misguided, as the most effective approach used with any given child depends crucially on the reading-related knowledge, skills, and experiences the child brings to the task of learning to read. (p. 405)

They use the term *literate cultural capital* to describe the literacy assets that students may or may not have when they begin school. Table 1.4 (page 16) lists literacy activities that children may experience at home or in the community before they come to school, along with the reading-related knowledge or skills that they may learn from such activities.

Table 1.4: Literate Cultural Capital

Literacy Activity	Reading-Related Knowledge and Skills
Seeing parents and other adults reading for entertainment or informational purposes	Understanding the value and purpose of reading
Listening to and participating in conversations	Developing oral language Developing vocabulary knowledge
Playing alphabet games (such as *I Spy*) and reading alphabet books	Building knowledge of letter names and sounds
Playing rhyming games (such as using pig Latin or reading nursery rhymes) and reading rhyming books (such as Dr. Seuss books)	Gaining sensitivity to individual sounds and groups of sounds in spoken words (phonemic and phonological awareness)
Inventing spellings (such as KLR for *color* or FRE for *fairy*)	Developing sensitivity to spelling-sound correspondences (phonics knowledge)
Participating in shared reading experiences	Gaining a basic understanding of concepts and conventions of printed language Gaining a familiarity with decontextualized language Becoming sensitive to the grammatical constraints of written sentences Understanding basic genres of written language Acquiring knowledge about the world and particular topics Using basic meaning-making strategies

Source: Duke & Carlisle, 2011; Purcell-Gates, Duke, & Stouffer, 2016; Tunmer & Nicholson, 2011.

Students who lack literate cultural capital often struggle when learning to read. However, research shows that high-quality teaching *can* compensate for these deficits. Catherine E. Snow, Michelle V. Porche, Patton O. Tabors, and Stephanie R. Harris (2007, as cited in Duke & Carlisle, 2011) find that students from home environments that were rated low (regarding literacy experiences and support) still made expected gains in reading achievement if they were in classrooms that were rated high (regarding literacy instruction) for two consecutive years. In contrast, only 25 percent of students from low-rated home environments made expected gains if they were in a high-rated classroom for one year, and none made expected gains if they were in low-rated classrooms. These findings indicate that high-quality reading instruction is of paramount importance in ensuring that all students learn to read.

As we mentioned previously, the hallmark of high-quality reading instruction is what Victoria Purcell-Gates, and colleagues (2016) call "a diagnostic approach to teaching reading." Such an approach "results in greater reading achievement by learners, is documented as a key element of successful classrooms, and is statistically related to reading achievement (p. 1241).

To implement a diagnostic approach to reading instruction, we believe that teachers must understand how reading skill develops. If a teacher has a mental model of the skills reading requires and an understanding of the continua along which those skills develop, he or she can assess a student's current status for each skill and determine what the student needs to learn next to improve. Such a mental model can also help a teacher understand how various reading skills interact with each other, and the ramifications of low or high skills in particular areas. In figure 1.1, we present a model that teachers might use to conceptualize the development of skilled reading. In the remainder of this introduction, we present research supporting the model.

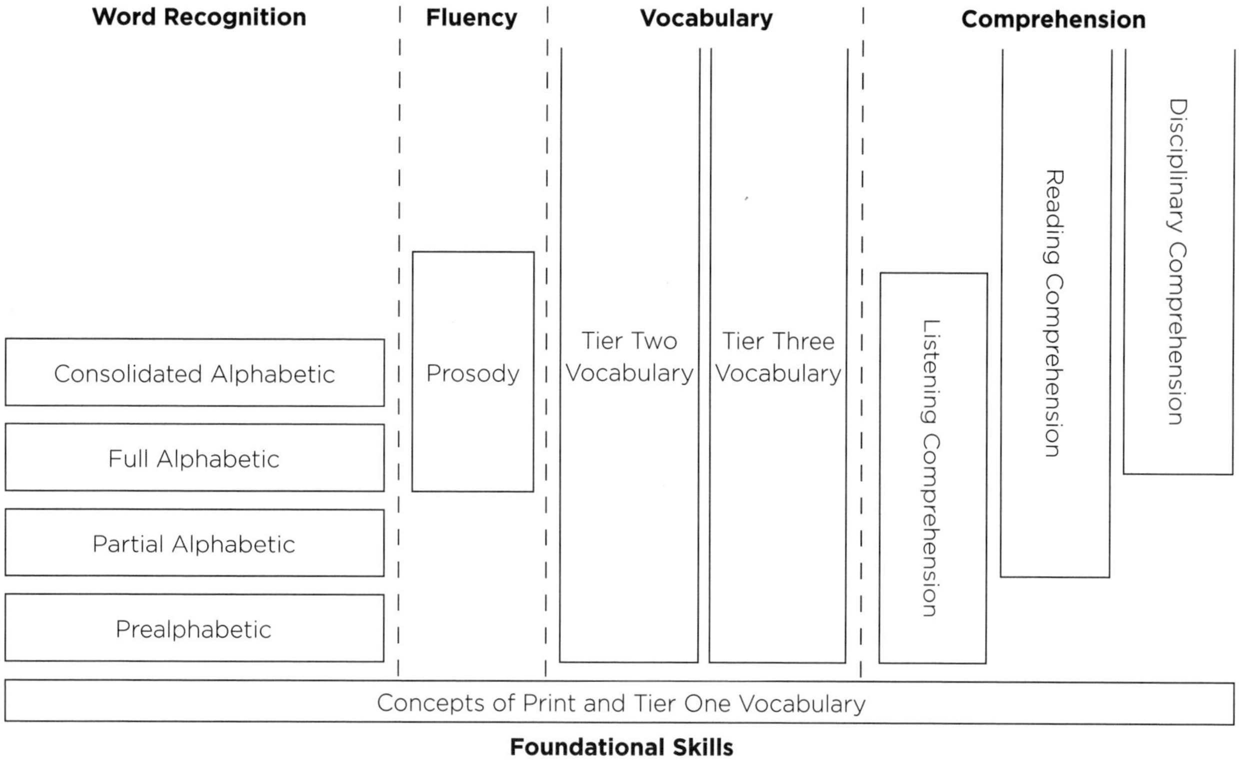

Figure 1.1: Development of skilled reading.

Notice the headings at the top of each column and at the bottom of figure 1.1: foundational skills, word recognition, fluency, vocabulary, and comprehension. Scott Paris and his colleagues (Afflerbach, Pearson, & Paris, 2008; Carpenter & Paris, 2005; Paris, 2005, 2008; Paris, Carpenter, Paris, & Hamilton, 2005; Paris & Luo, 2010) offer a helpful distinction when thinking about these elements: they differentiate between constrained and unconstrained reading skills. *Constrained skills*, such as fluency and word recognition, are those that develop in a fairly linear way and that students can learn to master in a relatively short period of time. We indicate this in figure 1.1 by the closed columns representing word recognition and fluency (on the left side of the figure). *Unconstrained skills*, such as comprehension and vocabulary, develop organically and continually over long periods of time; they have the potential for unlimited growth. These appear in the open columns representing vocabulary and comprehension (on the right of the figure). We also consider foundational skills (at the bottom of the figure), such as concepts of print and tier one vocabulary, to be constrained skills. Readers will note that listening comprehension is an exception; it is represented with a closed column. Research by Nell K. Duke and Joanne Carlisle (2011), which we address in a later section, indicates that listening comprehension improves and is useful up to a point, but then becomes less important than reading comprehension as texts become more complex. Therefore, we represent it with a closed column.

Foundational Skills: Concepts of Print and Tier One Vocabulary

Concepts of print are basic ideas about how print (generally) and books (in particular) work (Clay, 2000, 2013). Table 1.5 (page 18) lists selected concepts of print.

Table 1.5: Selected Concepts of Print

Concept of Print	Description
Book Handling	All books have covers and pages that people read in a specific order.
Vertical Reading Direction	Reading in English goes from the top of the page to the bottom of the page.
Horizontal Reading Direction	Reading in English goes from left to right, line by line.
Page Order	People read book pages in a specific order.
Print Function	The function of print is to carry meaning.
Print-to-Speech Correspondence	One printed word corresponds to one spoken word.
Role of Punctuation in Print	People use punctuation to signal types of sentences and the ends of sentences.
Letter-Word Discrimination in Print	Words and letters are different; people use letters to make words.

Source: Adapted from Zucker, Ward, & Justice, 2009.

Regarding vocabulary, Isabel L. Beck, Margaret G. McKeown, and Linda Kucan (2002) categorize vocabulary terms into three tiers. Tier one terms are those that most native speakers already know because they frequently hear them in oral conversations (for example, *clock*, *happy*, and *baby*). Most native English speakers will acquire tier one terms from oral conversation and will not need instruction in them. However, English learners or students from home environments that lack rich oral language experiences will likely need direct instruction in these words. Robert J. Marzano (2010b) compiled a list of 2,845 of these terms, organized into 420 semantically related clusters; visit **go.SolutionTree.com/instruction** for a list of these terms and their clusters.

Constrained Skills: Fluency and Word Recognition

Fluency is the ability to read accurately and with appropriate expression at an appropriate pace. Most definitions of reading fluency include three components: (1) prosody, (2) accuracy, and (3) automaticity (Kuhn, Schwanenflugel, Meisinger, Levy, & Rasinski, 2010). *Prosody* is the extent to which oral reading sounds like oral speech; it involves the stress placed on syllables, vocal intonation, and pace of reading. *Accuracy* is reading words correctly, and *automaticity* is reading words quickly and without conscious attention to the process (Cunningham, Nathan, & Raher, 2011; Rasinski, Reutzel, Chard, & Linan-Thompson, 2011). Accuracy and automaticity are the twin goals of word recognition development. Figure 1.2 illustrates the relationship between word recognition and the three components of fluency.

Word Recognition + Prosody = Fluency
(Accuracy + Automaticity)

Figure 1.2: Relationship between word recognition and the components of fluency.

As shown in figure 1.2, two components of fluency—accuracy and automaticity—are required for students to effectively read the words on a page. Adding prosody allows students to read the words with expression, proper phrasing, and appropriate intonation. Accordingly, we discuss word recognition (accuracy + automaticity) first and finish with a discussion of prosody.

Automatic word recognition (which implies *accurate word recognition*) is necessary for skilled reading because the brain cannot pay attention to two tasks at once. It must either switch back and forth between tasks, or one of the tasks must become automatic. Reading researchers have been aware of this phenomenon since the late 19th century (for example, see Cattell, 1886; Huey, 1908). In 1974, David LaBerge and S. Jay Samuels articulated their *theory of automatic information processing in reading*. They posit that, in mature readers, surface-level reading processes (such as identifying letters, decoding them, and connecting words to meanings) operate with little to no conscious effort, allowing these readers to focus cognitive resources on making meaning from text (comprehension). Charles A. Perfetti and Thomas Hogaboam (1975) and Michael I. Posner and C. R. R. Snyder (1975) go a step further, claiming that word recognition *has* to become automatic because comprehension can't; understanding a text always requires conscious cognitive control. Later researchers agreed with and extended these theories (see Logan, 1997; Stanovich, 1990), but the fundamental idea remained: "Rapid word recognition frees up mental resources for thinking about the writer's intent and the meaning of the text rather than what word the print represents" (Roberts, Christo, & Shefelbine, 2011, p. 229). Research also indicates that many struggling readers' difficulties stem from a lack of automaticity with word recognition (Fletcher, Lyon, Fuchs, & Barnes, 2007; Vellutino, Fletcher, Snowling, & Scanlon, 2004); these students can't focus on understanding a text because they have dedicated their cognitive resources to figuring out what the words say.

For skilled readers, some researchers call automatic word recognition "the obligatory nature of word recognition" (Roberts et al., 2011, p. 230). In other words, a skilled reader can't resist reading a word; to see a word is to know what it says. Reading "happens automatically without the influence of intention or choice" (Ehri, 2005, p. 135). To illustrate this idea, consider figure 1.3. Try to name the animal in the picture while ignoring the printed word.

Figure 1.3: Picture-word interference task.

For skilled readers, the task in figure 1.3 is difficult because they recognize the printed word automatically; the word creates a cognitive cue that the reader must resist in order to accurately name the animal in the picture. Similarly, *Stroop tasks* (named after the researcher who invented them in 1935) list color words (*red, yellow, blue, green, purple*) printed in nonmatching ink colors (*red* appears in purple ink, *yellow* appears in blue ink, *blue* appears in red ink, and so on). The reader must name the color of the ink while ignoring the printed word; most find this more difficult than picture-word tasks because colored ink is a weaker stimulus than a picture. Tasks such as these provide proof for the idea that skilled readers no longer sound out words but recognize them automatically.

In 2005, reading researcher Linnea C. Ehri synthesized eight theories about the development of automatic word recognition (Chall, 1983; Ehri, 1998, 1999, 2002; Frith, 1985; Gough & Hillinger, 1980; Marsh, Friedman, Welch, & Desberg, 1981; Mason, 1980; Seymour & Duncan, 2001; Stuart & Coltheart, 1988). She concludes that all students learning to read in English progress through four phases of word recognition development: (1) the prealphabetic phase, (2) the partial alphabetic phase, (3) the full alphabetic phase, and (4) the consolidated alphabetic phase. We describe and summarize each in the following sections.

Prealphabetic Phase

During the prealphabetic phase, students read words using visual or context cues. A *visual cue* is a distinctive feature of a word's appearance; for example, a student named *William* might recognize his name because it has "two lines in the middle" (the Ls). A *context cue* is something that typically occurs in a word's immediate environment—for example, the golden arches that often accompany the word *McDonald's*.

Philip B. Gough, Connie Juel, and Priscilla L. Griffith (1992) examined the nature of context cues by teaching preschoolers sets of four words in which one of the words appears with a thumbprint (see figure 1.4 for an example).

stick	frog	 lamp	man

Figure 1.4: Set of words with a thumbprint word.

Students could quickly learn to "read" the thumbprint word (in figure 1.5, *lamp*) with the thumbprint next to it, but when the researchers removed the thumbprint, they no longer knew the word. When the thumbprint appeared by itself, with no print accompanying it, students successfully produced the thumbprint word (*lamp*). When researchers placed the thumbprint next to a different word (for instance, *stick*), almost all of the children produced the original thumbprint word (*lamp*) rather than the new word (*stick*). In essence, these prealphabetic readers were associating the target word's pronunciation and meaning with the thumbprint image, rather than with the letters of the word.

Patricia E. Masonheimer, Priscilla A. Drum, and Linnea C. Ehri (1984) found that preschoolers who could read common signs and labels such as *McDonald's* or *Pepsi* could still read them if letters were altered; for example, if the researchers changed *Pepsi* (shown with its logo) to *Xepsi*, children still read it as *Pepsi*. Even when prompted to look for mistakes, students failed to detect the change. These findings indicate that, during the prealphabetic phase, learners do not associate words with their spellings, but rather with context or visual cues.

Additionally, Brian Byrne (1992) finds that prealphabetic readers attend to print-meaning correspondences, but not to print-sound correspondences. In an experiment, he taught prealphabetic readers that triangle-square meant *little boy* and circle-square meant *big boy* (see figure 1.5). Then he showed them triangle-cross and asked, "Does this say *little fish* or *big fish*?" Most of these prealphabetic readers were able to match the word *little* with the triangle and answer correctly (it says *little fish*).

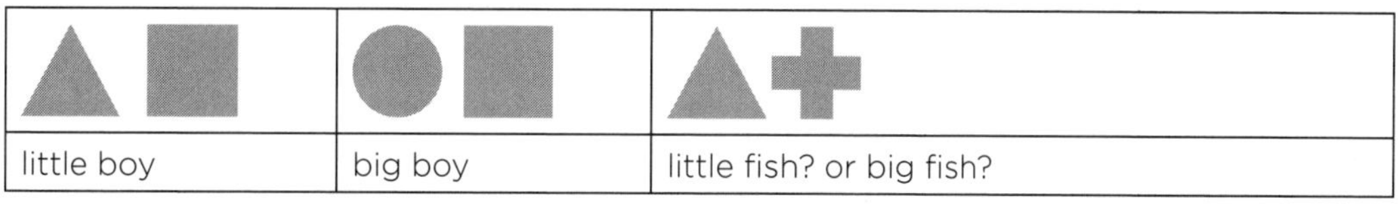

Figure 1.5: Print-meaning correspondence task.

In contrast, when Byrne (1992) taught prealphabetic readers that triangle-square meant *fat* and circle-square meant *bat*, the learners were unable to figure out whether triangle-cross meant *fun* or *bun* (see figure 1.6). That is, they could not isolate the /f/ sound and match it to the triangle.

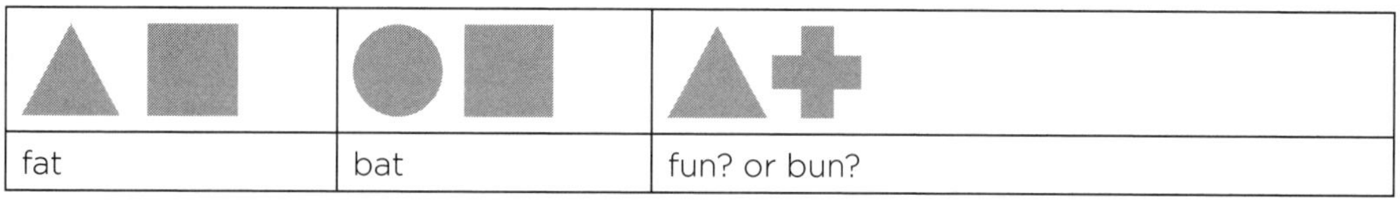

Figure 1.6: Print-sound correspondence task.

Bynre's (1992) findings indicate that prealphabetic readers understand that printed symbols can correspond to spoken words (which have meaning), but they do not understand that printed symbols correspond to spoken sounds (which do not always have meaning by themselves).

Partial Alphabetic Phase

The partial alphabetic phase, according to Ehri (2005), emerges when students begin to form connections between the sounds of letters and the sounds in words. They stop using visual or context cues and start using phonetic (letter-sound) cues to identify words. To make this switch, students must grasp the *alphabetic principle*—the realization that there is a relationship between printed letters and spoken sounds (Purcell-Gates et al., 2016). Students typically begin to grasp the alphabetic principle as they acquire alphabet knowledge and phonological awareness (Paratore, Cassano, & Schickedanz, 2011).

Alphabet knowledge involves knowing the names of the letters and the sound or sounds associated with each letter. Research indicates that students acquire alphabet knowledge in a specific order (Paratore et al., 2011), typically starting with letters in the student's name and letters in frequently encountered words. They usually learn uppercase letters before lowercase letters, and generally distinguish letters with few overlapping features (such as O/E or h/s) before letters with many overlapping features (such as E/F, O/Q, K/X, or m/n). Last of all come letters that differ only in orientation (such as b/d or p/q).

Phonological awareness is the ability to manipulate the sound structure of language, such as by segmenting sentences into words and words into sounds. Like alphabet knowledge, learners follow a typical acquisition sequence for phonological awareness (Paratore et al., 2011). Students typically acquire larger units, such as words and syllables, before smaller units, such as phonemes (single sounds). Interestingly, this is likely because phonemes are not actually articulated as separate units in speech. For example, when you say the word *green*, you blend the phonemes together, making it almost impossible to hear where one ends and the next begins. The National Reading Panel (NICHD, 2000) explains:

> Being able to distinguish the separate phonemes in pronunciations of words so that they can be matched to graphemes is difficult. This is because spoken language is seamless; that is, there are no breaks in speech signaling where one phoneme ends and the next one begins. Rather, phonemes are folded into each other and are coarticulated. Discovering phonemic units requires instruction to learn how the system works. (chapter 2, p. 2)

In other words, because of the coarticulation of phonemes in spoken speech, hearing separate phonemes in speech is a skill that develops as a student learns that words consist of letters, which represent individual sounds. Alphabet knowledge and phonemic discrimination go hand in hand.

To illustrate the difference between the prealphabetic and partial alphabetic phases, Linnea C. Ehri and Lee S. Wilce (1985) conducted a study in which they taught students in both phases to read various invented spellings of words. For example, for the word *giraffe*, one of the spellings they taught was *wBc*, which is visually distinctive (it has a memorable shape—tall in the middle). Another spelling they taught was *JRF*, which is phonetically distinctive (if you say the names or sounds of the letters, it sounds like "giraffe"). Ehri and Wilce (1985) correctly predicted that the prealphabetic readers would remember spellings with strong visual cues (like *wBc*) and partial alphabetic readers would remember spellings with strong phonetic cues (like *JRF*); prealphabetic readers remembered *wBc* as the spelling of *giraffe* while partial alphabetic readers remembered *JRF*. Many other studies have replicated these findings (for example, Bowman & Treiman, 2002; de Abreu & Cardoso-Martins, 1998; Roberts, 2003; Scott & Ehri, 1990; Treiman & Rodriguez, 1999).

Although partial alphabetic readers have begun to use phonetic cues to identify words, they cannot yet accurately and reliably decode text. Ehri (2005) explains:

> During the partial alphabetic phase children might remember how to read *jail* by connecting the first and final letters *J* and *L* to their letter names heard in the words "jay" and "el." Because the middle letters are ignored, the connections formed are only partial; hence the name of the phase. . . . Reading during the partial alphabetic phase is an imperfect process that occurs among beginners who lack full knowledge of the alphabetic system and phonemic segmentation skill. (pp. 143, 145)

In spite of this imperfect decoding, the partial alphabetic phase is critical. Marilyn J. Adams and Maggie Bruck (1993) explain that readers who fail to transition to the partial alphabetic phase (and instead continue to read using context and visual cues) quickly become overwhelmed by the cognitive demands of remembering thousands of words:

> Without the mnemonic support of the spelling-to-sound connections, the visual system must eventually become overwhelmed: the situation in which [these children] are left is roughly analogous to learning 50,000 telephone numbers to the point of perfect recall and instant recognition. (p. 130)

Tunmer and Nicholson (2011) articulate two additional problems with staying in the prealphabetic phase: (1) new words become increasingly harder to acquire, and (2) previously unseen words are unreadable.

New words become increasingly harder to acquire because it becomes more and more difficult to find distinctive visual cues for them. If a student recognizes the word *stop* because it "starts with a squiggle" (the *s* character), that student will likely confuse *stop* with other words that also "start with a squiggle" such as *stove*, *son*, *sand*, or *sheep*. Tunmer and Nicholson (2011) explain that these readers "will make an ever-increasing number of errors and become confused and frustrated unless they discover or are led to discover an alternative strategy for establishing the relationship between the written and spoken forms of the language" (p. 408).

Second, previously unseen words are unreadable for prealphabetic readers because using visual and context cues is not generative; they can't "figure out" a word. Upon encountering a word for the first time, someone must tell them the word, and they must memorize it in order to be able to recognize it again. Tunmer and Nicholson (2011) point out:

> Beginning reading materials typically employ upwards of 1,500 words, each of which must be encountered a first time. Moreover, when a new word does appear in print it does not suddenly begin appearing with great frequency. Approximately 35%–40% of the words used in beginning reading materials appear only once (Jorm & Share, 1983). Thus beginning readers are continually encountering words that they have not seen before and may not set eyes on again for some time. (p. 409)

In sum, even though readers in the partial alphabetic phase do not decode accurately, transitioning from visual or context cues to phonetic cues is critical for later success.

Full Alphabetic Phase

The full alphabetic phase is also called the *cipher stage* (Gough, 1996) because students decipher the code of printed language and begin to accurately read words. During this phase, alphabet knowledge broadens into *phonics knowledge*—familiarity with the sounds associated with spelling patterns. Phonological awareness refines into *phonemic awareness*—the ability to detect and manipulate single sounds (*phonemes*) in spoken words. These progressions facilitate the development of phonological recoding ability.

Phonological recoding ability is the capacity to figure out unknown words by connecting sounds to print (Juel, 1991). The basic process follows these four steps.

1. A student encounters an unknown word in print.
2. The student generates possible pronunciations for the unknown word (using his or her knowledge of letter-sound and spelling-sound relationships).
3. The student searches his or her oral vocabulary for a word that is a close match to one of the possible pronunciations.
4. If the student finds a match, he or she checks to see if that word makes sense in context.

Although there are other ways to decode words (such as from memory, from context, or by creating analogies between unknown and known words), phonological recoding ability is uniquely important for two reasons. First, most obviously, it allows students to figure out words they have never seen before. Second, less obviously, but more importantly, it enables students to self-teach. The *self-teaching hypothesis* (Jorm, 1979; Jorm & Share, 1983; Share, 1995, 1999, 2004, 2008) suggests that once students can successfully sound out words, the best way for them to improve their reading is through independent reading. This is because, ultimately, skilled reading requires extensive and implicit knowledge of English orthography, which is impossible to teach directly.

Orthography refers to the representation of the sounds of a language by written or printed symbols. According to Roberts and colleagues (2011), "English has one of the most opaque or deep orthographies of all the world's languages and is characterized by complex and variable relationships between spoken and written language" (p. 230). Orthographic knowledge includes familiarity with various spellings for various sounds, the ability to properly pronounce speech sounds, and an understanding of the proper formation of plurals and affixed words, permissible spelling patterns, and exceptions to rules. English orthography also includes:

> Knowledge of correspondences between single letters or digraphs (e.g., *sh*, *oa*) and single phonemes, correspondences between groups of letters (e.g., *tion*) and groups of phonemes (e.g., /shun/), and polyphonic spelling patterns (e.g., *ear* as in *bear* and *hear*,

> *own* as in *clown* or *flown*) . . .[,] knowledge of more complex conditional rules whose application depends on position-specific constraints or the presence of "marker" letters . . . [,and] morphophonemic rules that speakers of English know implicitly, such as that regular noun plural inflection is realized as /s/ when it follows a voiceless stop consonant, as in *cats*, and as /z/ when it follows a voiced phoneme, as in *dogs*. (Tunmer & Nicholson, 2011, p. 414)

Exercises 1 through 5 in appendix B (page 169) provide further insight into the complexities of English orthography.

In sum, English orthography entails a vast amount of detailed and highly variable information, most of which skilled readers access and apply quickly and without conscious attention. It is impossible for educators to directly teach such a volume of information to such a depth in the time available for reading instruction; "there are simply too many letter-sound relationships for children to acquire by direct instruction, probably several hundred" (Tunmer & Nicholson, 2011, p. 414). Therefore, students must learn the bulk of English orthography implicitly during independent reading (Adams, 1990; Adams & Bruck, 1993; Bowey & Muller, 2005; Cunningham, 2006; Cunningham, Perry, Stanovich, & Share, 2002; de Jong & Share, 2007; Ehri, 1992, 1997, 2005; Gough & Walsh, 1991; Harm & Seidenberg, 1999; Hulme, Snowling, & Quinlan, 1991; Kyte & Johnson, 2006; Perfetti, 1992; Share, 1995, 1999, 2004; Sprenger-Charolles, Siegel, & Bonnet, 1998; Tunmer & Chapman, 1998, 2006; Wessling & Reitsma, 2000). Cunningham and colleagues (2011) explain:

> The detailed orthographic representations necessary for fast, efficient word recognition are primarily self-taught during independent reading. Phonological recoding (i.e., decoding via translation of a printed letter string into its spoken form) is the mechanism or self-teacher that enables a reader to independently acquire an autonomous orthographic lexicon. . . . A successful decoding encounter with an unfamiliar word provides the reader with an opportunity to acquire word-specific orthographic information, such as order and identity of letters. This exhaustive grapheme-by-grapheme decoding (en route to a correct pronunciation) will result in the formation of well-specified orthographic representations. . . . The ability to independently decode novel strings through phonological recoding, such that rich orthographic representations can be formed, stored, and used, is perhaps the most valuable skill for learning orthographic representations of words. (pp. 265, 277)

To sum up, phonological recoding (sounding words out) is a critical skill because it enables independent reading. In turn, implicit learning during independent reading is the only way for students to acquire the comprehensive and implicit understanding of English orthography that they need to be skilled readers.

While it is not feasible to teach all of the phonics patterns in English directly, research shows that teaching a systematic progression of them helps jump-start phonological recoding (Gough, 1996; NICHD, 2000; Thompson, Fletcher-Flinn, & Cottrell, 1999; Tunmer & Nicholson, 2011). Catherine E. Snow and Connie Juel (2005) explain that "phonics may be useful to children not because of the specific letter-sound relations taught, but because a phonics approach gives children the chance to discover the alphabetic principle, and provides practice looking closely at word spelling" (p. 516). In chapter 4, we provide research-based guidelines regarding which phonics patterns to teach and what order to teach them in.

Consolidated Alphabetic Phase

By the time students enter the consolidated alphabetic phase, word recognition has moved from "a highly demanding, intentional process requiring constant, laborious symbol-sound translation to a less demanding, direct process which incorporates the automatic recognition of letters and immediate identification of specific words" (Cunningham et al., 2011, p. 260). Readers in the consolidated alphabetic phase are reading large amounts of text independently, and they now process words in larger chunks. Ehri (2005) explains, "As a result of practice reading many words, the reader processes increasingly larger units as these units recur, from features to letters to spelling patterns to whole words, referred to as unitization" (p. 151). For example, consolidated alphabetic phase readers recognize the unit *–ing* and read it as a whole, rather than as individual sounds. Ehri (2005) additionally points out:

> Knowing larger blends contributes to the learning of sight words by reducing the memory load. For example, connections to learn the word *interesting* are much easier to form if the four syllabic spellings, *IN*, *TER*, *EST*, *ING*, are known as units than if the word is analyzed as 10 graphophonemic units. (p. 150)

Also, Ehri and Wilce (1983) find that readers in the consolidated phase could read words as rapidly as they could name numbers, indicating that words were stored in memory and accessed as whole units, rather than sequences of letters or syllables.

As students engage in unitization, they also begin to learn that different word parts carry meaning. They can use these *morphemes* to determine the meanings of unfamiliar words, which students can now read but may not possess in their oral vocabularies. For example, a student might encounter the word *reworked* for the first time in text. By studying the morphemes in the word—*re* meaning "to do again," *work* meaning "an effortful activity," and *ed* meaning "in the past"—the student can reason that it means that someone worked on something again in the past. According to Purcell-Gates and colleagues (2016), students who know more about morphemes and are more aware of them in text exhibit stronger reading comprehension than students without such knowledge and awareness.

Prosody

As we mentioned previously, fluency comprises word recognition (accuracy + automaticity) and prosody; *prosody* centers on the rhythmic and tonal features of speech and involves three major elements (Kuhn & Schwanenflugel, 2017; Rasinski et al., 2011).

1. **Stress:** The prominence the speaker places on particular words and syllables
2. **Intonation:** The rise and fall of vocal pitch
3. **Duration:** The length of time the speaker employs in pronouncing a word or part of a word and patterns of pausing between words, phrases, and sentences

Research indicates that there is a relationship between prosody and comprehension. Melanie R. Kuhn and Paula J. Schwanenflugel (2017) find that "as children develop good reading prosody, they also develop better reading comprehension skills" (p. 320). Rebekah G. Benjamin and Paula J. Schwanenflugel (2010) find that good readers actually make greater prosodic distinctions as texts become more complex and difficult. James V. Hoffman (2017) cites extensive research indicating that prosody assists the reader in constructing meaning from a text (Allington, 1983; Rasinski, Blachowicz, & Lems, 2006; Rasinski & Hoffman, 2005; Schrieber, 1980, 1987).

There are at least three possible reasons for the relationship between prosody and comprehension. First, Andreas Lind, Lars Hall, Björn Breidegard, Christian Balkenius, and Petter Johansson (2014) suggest that the auditory feedback from their own voices helps readers clarify and specify the information they read. Second, Lyn Frazier, Katy Carlson, and Charles Clifton Jr. (2006) suggest that prosody helps to preserve information in working memory, giving the brain more time to make connections between this information and prior knowledge. Finally, Kuhn and Schwanenflugel (2017) hypothesize, "Good readers might link ideas in working memory using a prosodic packaging that is more optimal for comprehension" (p. 320). Although research has not yet completely explained the relationship between prosody and comprehension, it does indicate that prosody plays a mediating role between automatic word recognition and comprehension.

Unconstrained Skills: Comprehension and Vocabulary

Comprehension and vocabulary, as unconstrained skills, develop continually over long periods of time and have the potential for unlimited growth. Regarding comprehension, Duke and Carlisle (2011) write:

> Comprehension is a quintessential growth construct. As adults, we might still be developing our ability to comprehend some kinds of text (e.g., the IRS manual) and some content (e.g., studies in neuropsychology), and we might be refining the practices we use to comprehend text (e.g., searching text ever more effectively). (p. 200)

Unlike constrained skills, which develop along a fairly predictable progression, unconstrained skills develop more organically. Again, Duke and Carlisle (2011) explain:

> While it is clear that comprehension develops, it is also clear that there is not a single path to comprehension development. This is largely because there are myriad reader factors, text factors, and context factors that all impact reading comprehension. . . . Comprehension is affected by individual differences in students' capabilities and experiences as they interact with the quality of the opportunities they have at home and school to develop language and literacy. . . . There is no single set of stages or linear trajectory on which readers can be placed. (p. 215)

Vocabulary functions similarly. For example, it would be impossible to articulate a progression of words that all students learn in a fixed order (or even phases of word learning that students advance through). Therefore, in this section, rather than presenting developmental progressions, we first define vocabulary and comprehension and then present research and instructional considerations for both areas.

Vocabulary

As we explained previously, vocabulary knowledge is a critical element of reading. A student's ability to use phonological recoding to read an unfamiliar word hinges on whether the unfamiliar word is in his or her oral vocabulary. As the National Reading Panel (NICHD, 2000) states:

> Benefits in understanding text by applying letter-sound correspondences to printed material come about only if the target word is in the learner's oral vocabulary. When the word is not in the learner's oral vocabulary, it will not be understood when it occurs in print. (chapter 4, p. 3)

Tunmer and Nicholson (2011) add:

> Children with poorly developed vocabulary knowledge will have trouble identifying and assigning appropriate meanings to unknown printed words, especially partially decoded or irregularly spelled words, if the corresponding spoken words are not in their listening vocabulary (Ricketts, Nation, & Bishop, 2007). This in turn will limit the development of their phonological recoding skills, as additional spelling-sound relationships can be induced from words that have been correctly identified. (p. 421)

As we discussed, instruction in tier one vocabulary terms is foundational and critical for students (usually English learners) who do not know such terms; tier one vocabulary instruction should occur immediately and intensively as soon as possible for these learners. However, all students (including those receiving instruction for tier one terms) need direct instruction in terms from tiers two and three. Terms in both tiers occur infrequently in print; thus, students are unlikely to learn their meanings through repeated exposure. Tier two terms are general and appear in all disciplines and content areas (*analyze, inquire, rescind*); tier three terms are specific to one discipline or content area (*quadrilateral, federalism, valence, allegory*).

Once students have achieved automatic word recognition, their vocabularies appear to be the limiting factor in their comprehension. Andrew Biemiller (2005, 2012; Biemiller & Slonim, 2001) finds that after third grade, most students could decode 25 to 30 percent more words than they could understand: "From third grade on, the main limiting factor for the majority of children is vocabulary, not reading mechanics (i.e., decoding print into words)" (Biemiller, 2012, p. 34). Robert J. Marzano, Katie Rogers, and Julia A. Simms (2015) synthesize research to articulate the following five characteristics of effective vocabulary instruction.

1. **Presenting individual terms and their descriptions in rich contexts** (Graves, 2000; NICHD, 2000; Stahl & Fairbanks, 1986): Teachers select terms to teach and provide context-rich descriptions of them (rather than dictionary definitions). These descriptions can include using the term in sentences, providing pictures associated with the term, and explaining synonyms and antonyms of the term.
2. **Asking students to generate information about terms** (Anderson & Reder, 1979; Graves, 2000; Nagy, 2005; NICHD, 2000; Scott, Jamieson-Noel, & Asselin, 2003; Stahl & Clark, 1987; Stahl & Fairbanks, 1986; Vogel, 2003): Teachers prompt students to generate their own descriptions of terms. Such descriptions should involve both words and pictures.
3. **Using multimedia methods (words, pictures, animations, and so on) to introduce and practice terms** (Mayer, 2001; Mayer & Moreno, 2002; NICHD, 2000; Neuman, Newman, & Dwyer, 2011; Sadoski & Paivio, 2001): Teachers strive to incorporate multisensory activities and experiences into vocabulary instruction. Engaging as many senses as possible when learning a term solidifies it more rigorously in memory.
4. **Asking students to relate new terms to words they already know** (Anderson & Reder, 1979; Booth, 2009; Chi & Koeske, 1983; Entwisle, 1966; Glaser, 1984; Levelt, Roelofs, & Meyer, 1999; Scott et al., 2003; Stahl & Murray, 1994; Stahl & Nagy, 2006; Tinkham, 1997): Teachers help students create mental networks of concepts by pointing out how new words connect to previously learned words. As with multisensory activities, explicit connections between terms solidify them in memory.
5. **Providing multiple exposures to new terms and opportunities to use those terms in the classroom** (Beck et al., 2002; Beck, Perfetti, & McKeown, 1982; Bowman, Donovan, & Burns, 2001; Brophy & Good, 1986; Daniels, 1994, 1996; Dole, Sloan, & Trathen, 1995; Hoffman, 1991; Leung, 1992; McKeown, Beck, Omanson, & Pople, 1985; McKeown, Beck, & Sandora, 2012; NICHD, 2000; Pressley, Allington, Wharton-McDonald, Block, & Morrow, 2001; Rosenshine, 1986; Scott et al., 2003; Sénéchal, 1997; Snow et al., 1998; Stahl & Fairbanks, 1986; Wharton-McDonald, Pressley, & Hampston, 1998): Teachers review previously taught terms on a regular basis, asking students to discuss them, extend their understanding of them, and play games with them. Each subsequent exposure to a term solidifies it more firmly in memory.

Marzano and colleagues (Marzano, 2004, 2010b; Marzano et al., 2015; Marzano & Pickering, 2005; Marzano & Simms, 2013) have designed a six-step process that incorporates each of these elements of effective vocabulary instruction.

1. **Provide a description, explanation, or example of the new term:** State the new term, ask students what they already know about it, and provide information that communicates and clarifies its meaning.
2. **Ask students to restate the description, explanation, or example in their own words:** Prompt students to think about how they might describe the new term to a friend or use the new term in their personal lives. Students should record their responses in a vocabulary notebook or academic journal.

3. **Ask students to construct a picture, symbol, or graphic representing the term or phrase:** Students should create a visual representation for the term. This might be a sketch of the object a term refers to, a symbol for the term, an example of the term, a cartoon with a character using the term, or a graphic for the term.
4. **Engage students periodically in activities that help them add to their knowledge of previously taught terms:** At various times over the next few days or weeks, students should identify similarities and differences between terms and examine the morphology of terms.
5. **Periodically ask students to discuss previously taught terms with one another:** At various times over the next few days or weeks, students should talk to each other about terms they've learned and try to refine or revise their descriptions of terms (recorded during step 2) as a result of their discussion.
6. **Involve students periodically in games that allow them to play with previously taught terms:** At various times over the next few days or weeks, students should play word games with terms they've learned.

Comprehension

The RAND Reading Study Group (2002) defines comprehension as "the process of simultaneously extracting and constructing meaning through interaction and involvement with written language" (p. 11). Duke and Carlisle (2011) elaborate:

> Meaning does not reside in the oral or written text, which Spiro (1980) calls but "a skeleton, a blueprint for the creation of meaning" (p. 245). . . . The reader accesses the meaning of words in text, processes the syntax of clauses and sentences, relates clauses and sentences to one another to build local coherence (e.g., by inferring what pronouns refer to), and relates larger pieces of text to build global coherence (e.g., by inferring how one portion of the text is relevant to another), in the end building a situation model of the text (Kintsch, 1998; Perfetti, 2007). This typically no longer includes memory of the specific clauses or sentences within the text, but rather is the overall meaning made of the text through the interaction of reader, text, and context factors. (p. 200)

Additionally, Cynthia Shanahan (2017) points out:

> Competent readers do not use a universal approach to reading. Depending on the level of prior knowledge, the kind of text, and the purpose for reading, individuals alter their attention to different structural, rhetorical, and linguistic characteristics and think in varied ways about the elements they encounter. (p. 479)

Research indicates that skilled readers perform the comprehension-related actions listed in table 1.6 before, during, and after reading.

Comprehension strategies are "goal-oriented processes that readers and writers use to construct meaning" (Conley, 2017, p. 407). Research has shown that educators can teach comprehension strategies and that such instruction has positive effects on reading comprehension (Dole, Duffy, Roehler, & Pearson, 1991; Gambrell & Bales, 1986; Haller, Child, & Walberg, 1988; Mahdavi & Tensfeldt, 2013; Palincsar & Brown, 1984; Pressley, 2002, 2006; Pressley et al., 1992; Trabasso & Bouchard, 2002). Ian A. G. Wilkinson and Eun Hye Son (2011) elaborate:

> There is now no doubt that instruction in small repertoires of comprehension strategies, when implemented well, produces robust effects on measures of comprehension, including standardized tests (e.g., Anderson, 1992; Brown et al., 1996; Collins, 1991). . . . There are at least two alternative explanations for the effect of teaching strategies. One alternative explanation is that teaching strategies promote students' active engagement with

Table 1.6: Comprehension-Related Actions

Before Reading	• Know why they are reading and set goals for reading. • Know how they will use the knowledge gained from reading. • Know many word meanings (vocabulary). • Know a lot about the world (prior knowledge). • Preview a text to determine its genre and structure. • Skim a text to determine which parts to process before reading closely.
During Reading	• Recognize words on the page automatically. • Read text fluently. • Look for important information (in words or pictures) and pay more attention to it. • Try to relate important points to one another. • Use what they already know (prior knowledge) to make predictions. • Relate new content to prior knowledge. • Use strategies such as predicting, imaging, questioning, summarizing, clarifying, inferring, and connecting to prior knowledge to construct meaning and interpret the text. • Remember information from a text using strategies such as reviewing, summarizing, paraphrasing, and questioning. • Monitor their understanding and the alignment of their understanding to their reading goal or goals. • Revise their prior knowledge and interpretation of a text as they read. • Rate the quality of a text and its usefulness for accomplishing the purpose for reading. • Interact with the text on both personal and intellectual levels as they read. • Engage in an internal dialogue or responsive conversation with the author of the text. • Evaluate the author's purposes, intentions, and goals based on assumptions, worldviews, and beliefs that are overt or covert in a text.
When Comprehension Breaks Down	• Become even more active. • Adjust reading speed and level of concentration depending on the purpose and importance of reading. • Change comprehension strategies. • Puzzle out unfamiliar words, phrases, or concepts, especially when they seem important to interpreting the text. • Reread or use other strategies to try to regain a hold on the text (such as reviewing, questioning, summarizing, evaluating, or considering alternative interpretations).
After Reading	• Continue to build and reflect on their understanding of the text. • Assess how a text has affected or will affect their knowledge, attitudes, and behavior.
General	• Have a repertoire of comprehension strategies and know when and how to use them and combine them. • Have a repertoire of metacognitive strategies to monitor their reading processes. • Employ different processes in different ways, and to different degrees, depending on why they are reading and what they are reading, both with respect to disciplinary context and genre.

Sources: Cho & Afflerbach, 2017; Purcell-Gates et al., 2016; Wharton-McDonald & Erickson, 2017.

Visit ***go.SolutionTree.com/instruction*** *for a free reproducible version of this table.*

> text. Kintsch and Kintsch (2005) noted that a feature of all strategies is that they promote the active construction of meaning during reading, and the linking of the text with reader's prior knowledge and experience (see also Willingham, 2007). Another alternative explanation is that strategies are vehicles that enable students to engage in dialogue about text. (pp. 364–365)

The most effective comprehension instruction is explicit and utilizes a gradual release of responsibility model (see Purcell-Gates et al., 2016, for supporting research).

Comprehension instruction should begin before students have developed automatic word recognition. That is, it should start as soon as they begin school, even before they can read text independently. Duke and Carlisle (2011) state that "we should be concerned about the development of reading comprehension from very early on, long before children can read text themselves" (p. 217). Paratore and colleagues (2011) advise that "curricula intended to guide both parents and teachers in their interactions with young children must be as relentlessly focused on developing vocabulary and language knowledge as they are on developing code knowledge" (p. 123). As we show in figure 1.1 (page 17), comprehension instruction before students have reached the full alphabetic phase will largely focus on developing students' listening comprehension. Duke and Carlisle (2011) explain that developing comprehension skills through listening and then asking students to transfer those skills to their reading make sense because both listening and reading comprehension focus on making meaning from language:

> Comprehension refers to the listener or reader's understanding of the message expressed by the speaker or writer. . . . In this respect, listening comprehension and reading comprehension are not different—both are focused on accessing the meaning of a message communicated by someone else. (p. 199)

Once students can use phonological recoding to read texts themselves, they can apply their existing listening comprehension strategies and skills to text they read themselves.

As students mature in their comprehension abilities and read more difficult texts, research shows that listening comprehension actually becomes less important because it is less effective as texts increase in complexity. Again, Duke and Carlisle (2011) explain:

> In the years when students are first learning to read, they typically can comprehend more challenging passages when listening than when reading, because of limitations in their word recognition. By the middle school years, the pattern is often reversed: students' performance on challenging passages is better by reading than by listening. This is because readers can pace themselves, reread sentences, and carry out other strategic activities to construct their understanding of the text. Such activities are not possible when listening to passages of the kind that are typically used in written texts. (p. 202)

Also, as students mature in their reading comprehension skills, they are increasingly expected to read texts in order to learn from them, especially in the content areas of social studies, science, and mathematics. Teachers can facilitate such disciplinary reading by making certain that students understand the norms of the discipline in which they are reading and the specific strategies that experts in those disciplines typically use. For an analysis of disciplinary reading and recommendations regarding strategies to use with social studies, science, and mathematics texts, please see appendix C (page 177).

Summary

In this chapter, we assert that there is no one best way to teach reading; the most effective method depends on what a student already knows and can do. An effective reading teacher uses his or her understanding of how reading develops to assess a student's current status and select instructional strategies that will move him or her closer to the goal of skilled reading.

In chapters 2–11, we connect our model of reading development to the ten design areas of *The New Art and Science of Teaching* framework. We begin in chapter 2 with providing and communicating clear learning goals. There, we explain how teachers can use learning progressions, or *proficiency scales*, to articulate what students should know and be able to do as a result of reading instruction, track students' progress, and celebrate success. We also make recommendations about how teachers of science, social studies, and mathematics can integrate high-quality reading instruction into their existing content-area instruction.

PART I

Feedback

CHAPTER 2

Providing and Communicating Clear Learning Goals

The New Art and Science of Teaching framework begins by addressing how teachers will communicate with students about what they need to learn. This design area also includes elements related to tracking students' progress and celebrating their success. Together, these three elements—(1) providing scales and rubrics, (2) tracking student progress, and (3) celebrating success—create a foundation for effective feedback. Here we describe how each element might manifest in a reading classroom.

Element 1: Providing Scales and Rubrics

Scales and rubrics articulate what students should know and be able to do as a result of instruction. The content in a scale or rubric should come from a school or district's standards. As an example of how teachers might do this, Simms (2016) led a team of analysts at Marzano Research (since renamed Marzano Resources) to organize standards from a wide range of sources into topics and articulate proficiency scales (also called learning progressions) for those topics in English language arts, mathematics, science, and social studies (a project called *The Critical Concepts*). Of the topics they articulated for English language arts, some pertain to reading and others pertain to writing; we list those related to reading in table 2.1.

Table 2.1: *Critical Concepts* K–12 Reading Topics

Measurement Topic	K	1	2	3	4	5	6	7	8	9–10	11–12
Decoding	X	X	X	X	X						
Phonological Awareness	X	X									
Print Concepts	X										
Analyzing Text Organization and Structure	X	X	X	X	X	X	X	X	X	X	X
Text Features	X	X	X								

continued →

Measurement Topic	K	1	2	3	4	5	6	7	8	9–10	11–12
Analyzing Main Ideas (K–2) Analyzing Ideas and Themes (3–12)	X	X	X	X	X	X	X	X	X	X	X
Analyzing Claims and Reasons (K–2) Analyzing Claims, Evidence, and Reasoning (3–12)	X	X	X	X	X	X	X	X	X	X	X
Analyzing Narratives	X	X	X	X	X	X	X	X	X	X	X
Analyzing Point of View (1–7) Analyzing Point of View and Purpose (8–12)		X	X	X	X	X	X	X	X	X	X
Analyzing Style and Tone											X
Comparing Texts	X	X	X	X	X	X	X	X	X	X	X
Analyzing Words	X	X	X	X	X						
Analyzing Language		X	X	X	X	X	X	X	X	X	X

Source: Adapted from Simms, 2016.

While the topics in table 2.1 (and their corresponding proficiency scales, which we describe in the following section) align to grade levels using standards documents as a guide, teachers may need to make adjustments for the specific needs of individual students. For example, the first three topics in table 2.1—(1) decoding, (2) phonological awareness, and (3) print concepts—represent fluency and word recognition. The standards align these topics to the early elementary grades (with decoding continuing until grade 4). However, following the recommendations in the introduction, teachers should determine a student's current level of development relative to automatic word recognition. If students are at a level far enough above or below the content that the standards articulate for their grade level, they may need word recognition and fluency instruction that does not necessarily align with these designated standards.

For example, if a kindergarten student is already able to fluently read text, including multisyllabic words (such as *interesting*), he or she is likely in the full or consolidated alphabetic phase, and instruction in the content articulated for decoding, phonological awareness, and print concepts at kindergarten and first grade will be unnecessary. Such a student should spend as much time as possible reading text, practicing comprehension skills, and learning new vocabulary terms in order to make as much progress as possible in the time available. Modifications of this sort will likely require teachers to document the changes and obtain approval from parents and guardians, but they are necessary to avoid wasting students' time by teaching them skills they have already mastered.

Alternatively, if a student in sixth grade is not able to phonologically recode reliably enough to read connected text, that student is likely at the pre- or partial alphabetic phase and needs intensive instruction in the alphabetic principle, phonemic and phonological awareness, and phonics, even though the standards do not articulate such content at sixth grade. Again, such modifications will likely require documentation and approval by parents and guardians but are critical to ensure that such a student doesn't spend further time missing out on the benefits of independent reading.

Returning to table 2.1, the next eight topics relate to comprehension and the final two relate to vocabulary (analyzing words and analyzing language). Fitting the idea that learners develop unconstrained skills more organically than constrained skills, the content of these ten topics spirals, slowly building on and extending the knowledge and skills that previous grade levels highlight. Therefore, while it may still be necessary to use an alternative proficiency scale based on a student's current level of knowledge and skill, it is not likely to happen as often as with skills related to word recognition and fluency.

Finally, any discussion of learning goals related to reading must address the fact that reading is both a content area (often referred to, with writing, as English language arts, or ELA) and a medium for learning in other content areas (for example, students read to learn in science, social studies, and mathematics). When teaching and assessing reading skills (as opposed to content knowledge), we recommend that science, social studies, and mathematics teachers use some of the same proficiency scales English language arts teachers use. Based on our synthesis of research regarding the strategies that experts in social studies, science, and mathematics use to read (see appendix C, page 177), we make the following recommendations.

- A social studies teacher might use reading proficiency scales for topics such as analyzing text organization and structure; analyzing claims, evidence, and reasoning; analyzing point of view and purpose; analyzing style and tone; and comparing texts.
- A science teacher might use reading proficiency scales for topics such as analyzing text organization and structure; analyzing claims, evidence, and reasoning; analyzing ideas and themes; and analyzing language.
- A mathematics teacher might use proficiency scales for topics such as analyzing text organization and structure and analyzing claims, evidence, and reasoning.

Scores given by content-area teachers and scores given by an ELA teacher to a student for a particular reading topic might be combined to determine the student's final score for that topic. For example, a science teacher and an ELA teacher might both use the proficiency scale for analyzing claims, evidence, and reasoning to assign a student the scores shown in figure 2.1 over the course of six weeks.

	9/18	9/22	9/28	10/6	10/19	10/26
ELA Teacher	2.0		2.5	2.5		3.0
Science Teacher		1.5	2.0		2.5	

Figure 2.1: Sample scores for analyzing claims, evidence, and reasoning.

The ELA teacher could confer with the science teacher before assigning a final score to the student for the topic of analyzing claims, evidence, and reasoning, using the science teacher's observations and assessments to influence her decision about the student's status. To clarify, content-area teachers should use their own proficiency scales (focused on their particular content) to score students on social studies, mathematics, or science content. But they could use the ELA teacher's proficiency scale to score students relative to their content-area reading skills.

We recommend that teachers use the scale in figure 2.2 to rate their current level of effectiveness with providing scales and rubrics.

Score	Description
4: Innovating	I adapt behaviors and create new strategies for unique student needs and situations.
3: Applying	I provide scales and rubrics, and I monitor the extent to which my actions affect students' performance.
2: Developing	I provide scales and rubrics, but I do not monitor the effect on students.
1: Beginning	I use the strategies and behaviors associated with this element incorrectly or with parts missing.
0: Not Using	I am unaware of strategies and behaviors associated with this element.

Figure 2.2: Self-rating scale for element 1—Providing scales and rubrics.

Element 2: Tracking Student Progress

Tracking student progress in the reading classroom is similar to tracking student progress in any content area: the student receives a score based on a proficiency scale, and the teacher uses the student's pattern of scores to "provide each student with a clear sense of where he or she started relative to a topic and where he or she is currently" (Marzano, 2017, p. 14). For each topic at each applicable grade level, teachers should construct a proficiency scale (or learning progression). Such a scale allows teachers to pinpoint where a student falls on a continuum of knowledge, using information from assessments. A generic proficiency scale format appears in figure 2.3.

4.0	**More complex content**
3.5	In addition to score 3.0 performance, partial success at score 4.0 content
3.0	**Target content**
2.5	No major errors or omissions regarding score 2.0 content, and partial success at score 3.0 content
2.0	**Simpler content**
1.5	Partial success at score 2.0 content, and major errors or omissions regarding score 3.0 content
1.0	With help, partial success at score 2.0 content and score 3.0 content
0.5	With help, partial success at score 2.0 content but not at score 3.0 content
0.0	Even with help, no success

Figure 2.3: Generic format for a proficiency scale.

The proficiency scale format in figure 2.3 is designed so that the only descriptors that change from one scale to the next are those at the 2.0, 3.0, and 4.0 levels. Those levels articulate target content, simpler content, and more complex content. Teachers draw target content from standards documents; simpler content and more complex content elaborate on the target content. For example, figure 2.4 shows a proficiency scale for comparing texts at the eighth-grade level (bold text indicates the target content drawn from standards documents).

4.0	The student will: • Compare the techniques two different types or genres of texts use to communicate similar themes (for example, read "A Poison Tree" by William Blake and "The Cask of Amontillado" by Edgar Allan Poe and compare the literary devices in both pieces and their portrayals of revenge).
3.5	In addition to score 3.0 performance, students have partial success at score 4.0 content.
3.0	The student will: **1—Describe the faithfulness of a live or filmed production to a source text** (for example, describe how certain elements of the plot changed in the film adaptation of Louisa May Alcott's *Little Women* and how these changes affect the themes present in the film). **2—Describe how a work of fiction draws on character types, patterns of events, and themes from classic texts** (for example, describe the common archetype of the underdog and explain how this character type is developed in texts such as Howard Pyle's *The Merry Adventures of Robin Hood* or Charles Dickens's *Oliver Twist* and how it relates to the biblical narrative of David and Goliath). **3—Describe the advantages and disadvantages of expressing ideas in various media** (including genres such as poetry, prose, and drama; for example, describe how the same story could be written as a script or a book, and describe how each form requires the writer to use different techniques to convey a theme).
2.5	The student has no major errors or omissions regarding score 2.0 content and partial success at score 3.0 content.
2.0	1—The student will recognize or recall specific vocabulary (for example, *adaptation*, *observation*, *production*) and perform basic processes such as the following: • Summarize observations gained while watching a film or live production. • Identify the characters, setting, and plot in both an original text and its adaptation. • Compare different plot elements from an original text and its adaptation. • Note any characters or events that are missing from or added to an adaptation of a text. 2—The student will recognize or recall specific vocabulary (for example, *archetype*) and perform basic processes such as the following: • Classify a well-known character from a text or film as a specific character archetype (such as the hero, the mentor, the underdog, or the villain). • Identify a well-known story that follows an archetypal pattern of events (such as quest, revenge, or transformation). • Identify a text that conveys a thematic archetype (such as love conquers all, greed as downfall, loss of innocence, and coming of age). 3—The student will recognize or recall specific vocabulary (for example, *free verse*, *sestina*, *sonnet*) and perform basic processes such as the following: • Describe the techniques a particular genre uses to communicate a story or idea. • Describe how a reader or viewer interacts with a particular medium. • Compare elements that differ between genres or media.
1.5	The student has partial success at score 2.0 content and major errors or omissions regarding score 3.0 content.
1.0	With help, the student has partial success at score 2.0 content and score 3.0 content.
0.5	With help, the student has partial success at score 2.0 content but not at score 3.0 content.
0.0	Even with help, the student has no success.

Source: Simms, 2016.

Figure 2.4: Proficiency scale for comparing texts at grade 8.

The three elements at the 3.0 level are closely related and therefore grouped together into a single topic. The 2.0 level articulates simpler content for each of these three elements, and the 4.0 level articulates a task that students might use to demonstrate that they can make in-depth inferences and applications of the content that go beyond what teachers explicitly taught. For further guidance regarding the construction and use of proficiency scales, see *Formative Assessment and Standards-Based Grading* (Marzano, 2010a) and *Making Classroom Assessments Reliable and Valid* (Marzano, 2018). By clearly articulating different levels of performance relative to the target content, both teachers and students can describe and track students' progress. A line graph or bar graph of the data can be used to show students' growth over time.

From the perspective of reading instruction, there is a special consideration that reading teachers may want to incorporate into their tracking. Recall from the discussion of word recognition and comprehension in chapter 1 that reading researchers caution against waiting until students are able to decode to begin comprehension instruction (Duke & Carlisle, 2011). Rather, students should work on their comprehension through listening to texts until they are able to read independently. Because of this dynamic, students who are unable to read text independently may be making significant progress in *listening comprehension*, but a proficiency scale that measures *reading comprehension* may not reflect that growth. To monitor listening comprehension growth (while acknowledging that the ultimate goal is for the student to comprehend while reading independently), the teacher might maintain a tracking chart with two lines for each comprehension-related proficiency scale: one for listening comprehension and one for reading comprehension, as we show in figure 2.5.

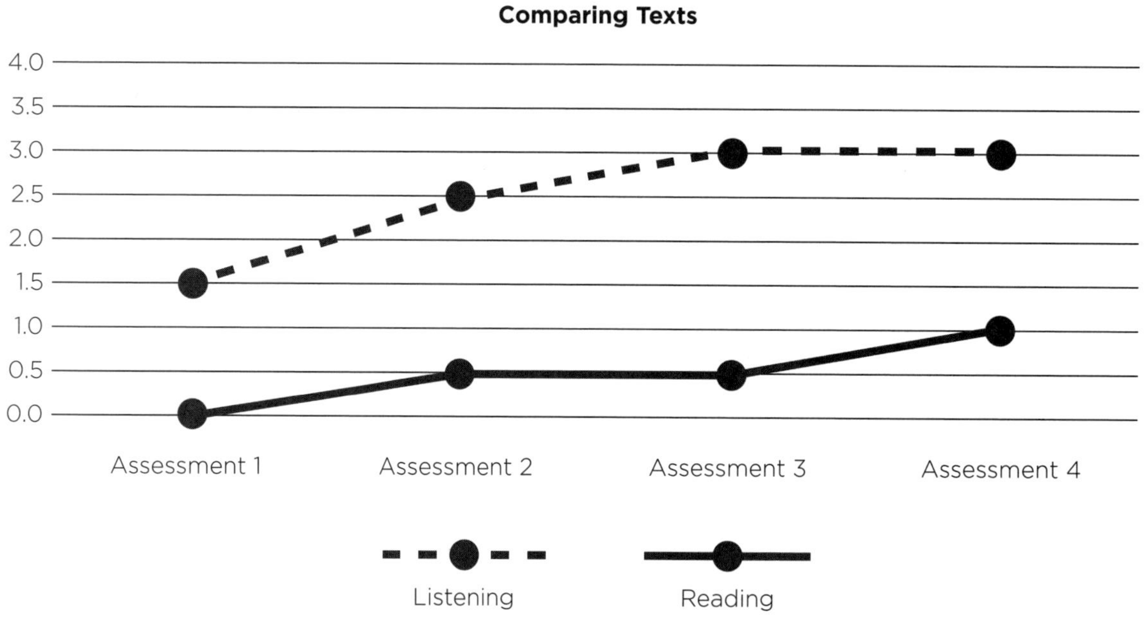

Figure 2.5: Sample listening and reading comprehension tracking chart for comparing texts.

Such an approach allows students to see their progress while recognizing that their eventual goal is to comprehend while reading independently.

We recommend that teachers use the scale in figure 2.6 to rate their current level of effectiveness with element 2, tracking student progress.

Score	Description
4: Innovating	I adapt behaviors and create new strategies for unique student needs and situations.
3: Applying	I track student progress, and I monitor the extent to which my actions affect student learning.
2: Developing	I track student progress, but I do not monitor the effect on student learning.
1: Beginning	I use the strategies and behaviors associated with this element incorrectly or with parts missing.
0: Not Using	I am unaware of strategies and behaviors associated with this element.

Figure 2.6: Self-rating scale for element 2—Tracking student progress.

Element 3: Celebrating Success

Celebrating success in the reading classroom should focus on students' progress on proficiency scales. That is, teachers should celebrate students for their growth on the proficiency scales. This may differ from what teachers traditionally celebrate in the classroom. For instance, a teacher might be used to celebrating how many books a student has read, or how many words per minute a student is able to read, or the level of text that a student is able to read independently. While there may be benefits to these types of celebrations, they are not as conducive to reliable measurement as progress on a proficiency scale.

To illustrate, consider the celebration of the number of books a student has read since the beginning of the year. Such a metric does not take into account a number of important factors, such as the length of each book, the difficulty of each book, or the literary value of each book. One student might read three *Harry Potter* books while another reads fifty books by Sandra Boynton. Clearly, counting the number of books fails to capture the nuances of this situation. Similarly, consider words per minute: one student might read one hundred words per minute but not remember or comprehend anything of what she read. Another student might read fifty words per minute but be able to chat intelligently about the content. Again, the words-per-minute metric fails to capture important data. Finally, think about text level. A student reading a high-reading-level book simply because it is "difficult" is not necessarily reading it for a meaningful purpose. And there are many high-quality picture books with complex characters and sophisticated plots that are easy to read. Add to such inconsistencies the inherent complexities of measuring text levels (see Graesser, McNamara, & Louwerse, 2011; McNamara, Graesser, McCarthy, & Cai, 2014), and it becomes clear that reading level is not necessarily a reliable indicator of a student's reading skill. For these reasons, we recommend celebrating students' growth and final status using proficiency scales.

Figure 2.7 presents the self-rating scale for element 3, celebrating success.

Score	Description
4: Innovating	I adapt behaviors and create new strategies for unique student needs and situations.
3: Applying	I celebrate success, and I monitor the extent to which my actions affect students.
2: Developing	I celebrate success, but I do not monitor the effect on students.
1: Beginning	I use the strategies and behaviors associated with this element incorrectly or with parts missing.
0: Not Using	I am unaware of strategies and behaviors associated with this element.

Figure 2.7: Self-rating scale for element 3—Celebrating success.

GUIDING QUESTIONS FOR CURRICULUM DESIGN

When teachers engage in curriculum design, they consider this overarching question for communicating clear goals and objectives: *How will I communicate clear learning goals that help students understand the progression of knowledge I expect them to master and where they are along that progression?* Consider the following questions aligned to the elements in this chapter to guide your planning.

- **Element 1:** How will I design scales and rubrics?

- **Element 2:** How will I track progress?

- **Element 3:** How will I celebrate success?

Summary

Providing and communicating clear learning goals involves three elements: providing scales and rubrics, tracking student progress, and celebrating success. In the reading classroom, teachers may need to adjust the scales or rubrics they use with a student depending on the student's current level of skill. They may also decide to track different, but related, types of progress (such as listening versus reading comprehension) and should ensure that celebrations focus on appropriate measurements.

CHAPTER 3

Using Assessments

The second design area from *The New Art and Science of Teaching* framework involves the use of effective assessments—particularly, using informal assessments of the whole class (element 4) and formal assessments of individual students (element 5). Together, these two elements allow teachers to monitor student progress, provide useful feedback, and ensure that all students are moving toward mastery of the content. Here we describe how each element might manifest in a reading classroom.

Element 4: Using Informal Assessments of the Whole Class

Informal assessments in the reading classroom look different depending on what skills teachers are assessing. Consider the five areas from our model of reading development (see chapter 1, page 17): (1) foundational skills, (2) word recognition, (3) fluency, (4) vocabulary, and (5) comprehension.

Regarding foundational skills, teachers can informally assess the whole class's concepts of print by passing out a book to each student and asking the class to complete a series of tasks in unison, such as the following.

- "Point to the front cover of your book."
- "Point to the back cover of your book."
- "Turn to the title page."
- "Turn to the page that you would start reading on."
- "Point to a word."
- "Point to a picture."
- "Point to the [first, second, third] word that you would read."
- "Find a word you can read in your book. Read it to a partner."

As students complete these tasks, the teacher might circulate around the room, estimating how many students in the class are familiar with concepts of print. This appraisal allows the teacher to determine if he or she should teach concepts of print to the whole class or only to individual students who need such instruction.

Teachers can also informally assess tier one vocabulary. One of the easiest ways to do so is to use fill-in-the-blank, selected-response items and have students use voting technologies or response techniques to simultaneously signal their answers. The teacher should read these items aloud since he or she is assessing vocabulary knowledge, not reading skill. Figure 3.1 shows several such items, along with how we recommend the teacher read the item to the class.

Question	What the Teacher Reads
Shelly tried really hard. She said, "I ______ do it." 1. am 2. can 3. have 4. now	Shelly tried really hard. She said, "I am do it." "I can do it." "I have do it." "I now do it."
Sarah's best friend moved across the country. She went ______ away. 1. close 2. down 3. far 4. up	Sarah's best friend moved across the country. She went close away. She went down away. She went far away. She went up away.
Mrs. Smith reminded her students, "Please ______ your hand if you have a question." 1. find 2. spare 3. wring 4. raise	Mrs. Smith reminded her students, "Please find your hand if you have a question." "Please spare your hand if you have a question." "Please wring your hand if you have a question." "Please raise your hand if you have a question."

Figure 3.1: Tier one fill-in-the-blank items.

Regarding informal assessments of word recognition, we caution teachers against *round-robin reading*, wherein the teacher calls on each student, in turn, to read a passage of text aloud while other students follow along silently. Steven A. Stahl (2004) raises two major objections to this practice: (1) being forced to read aloud can have negative effects on a struggling reader's self-concept, and (2) listening to others read aloud limits the time each student actually spends reading, thus wasting valuable practice time. A better approach to informally assess word recognition is to ask the class (or segments of the class) to read chorally using a big book or text projected on a screen (Gambrell, Wilson, & Gnatt, 1981). Such shared reading practices have beneficial effects on students' accuracy, prosody, vocabulary, and comprehension, in addition to providing information to the teacher about the class's word recognition skill (Gambrell et al., 1981).

Regarding the prosodic component of fluency, teachers might ask students to pair up and take turns reading short passages of text to one another. As mentioned previously, it is important to keep passages brief to avoid wasting time that students could otherwise spend practicing reading. The listening partner could rate the reading partner's performance using a scale such as the one in figure 3.2.

4	Sounds just like talking
3	Sounds a lot like talking
2	Sounds a little bit like talking
1	Doesn't sound much like talking

Figure 3.2: Informal fluency rating scale.

After each student in the pair has taken a brief turn reading, the teacher might ask each student to report his or her rating. Using anonymous reporting (for example, with electronic devices) avoids making students with low ratings uncomfortable.

Teachers can assess vocabulary and comprehension using a wide variety of questions and techniques. With early elementary students (who may have trouble writing an answer down), the teacher might ask the class to act out the meaning of a term or their interpretation of a character's emotions. With upper elementary or secondary students, the teacher could ask the class to use response devices (electronic or otherwise) to answer questions related to text organization and structure; text features; main ideas and themes; claims, evidence, and reasoning; narratives; point of view and purpose; or style and tone. Vocabulary questions could focus on specific terms or on larger segments of language (such as metaphors or idioms).

Figure 3.3 presents the self-rating scale for element 4, using informal assessments of the whole class, so teachers can gauge their professional performance.

Score	Description
4: Innovating	I adapt behaviors and create new strategies for unique student needs and situations.
3: Applying	I use informal assessments of the whole class to determine students' proficiency with specific content, and I monitor the extent to which students respond to assessment-guided feedback and instruction.
2: Developing	I use informal assessments of the whole class to determine students' proficiency with specific content, but I do not monitor the effect on students.
1: Beginning	I use the strategies and behaviors associated with this element incorrectly or with parts missing.
0: Not Using	I am unaware of strategies and behaviors associated with this element.

Figure 3.3: Self-rating scale for element 4—Using informal assessments of the whole class.

Element 5: Using Formal Assessments of Individual Students

When formally assessing individual students' reading knowledge and skills, it is also useful to think in terms of the five areas from our model of reading development: (1) foundational skills, (2) word recognition, (3) fluency, (4) vocabulary, and (5) comprehension.

Relative to foundational skills, teachers can use observational interviews to determine how well a student understands concepts of print. Many such checklists are available online. For example, the Teachers College Reading and Writing Project (2006) at Columbia University offers an excellent assessment tool based on the work of Marie M. Clay (2000); in figure 3.4 (page 46) we show an adapted version aligned to the foundational print concepts listed in the introduction. To administer such an assessment, the teacher selects a book that has a distinct layout of print and illustrations, good spacing of words, and multiple lines of text (for example, Judith Viorst's [1972] *Alexander and the Terrible, Horrible, No Good, Very Bad Day* or Don Freeman's [1976] *Corduroy*). The teacher might begin by saying to the student, "I'm going to read you this story, and I want you to help me. It is called __________."

Concept of Print	Description	Assessment Tasks
Book organization	All books have covers and pages that people read in a specific order.	Hand the student the book, holding it vertically with the spine facing the student. Ask: • "Where is the front of the book?" • "Where is the back of the book?" • "Please open the book to where the story begins."
Print function	The function of print is to carry meaning.	With the book open to page 1, say to the student: • "Please show me the picture." • "Please show me the words."
Page orientation	Reading in English goes from the top of the page to the bottom of the page.	With the book open to page 1, say to the student: • "Please show me where to start reading." (If the student's response is vague, say, "Where exactly? Please point with your finger.") Point to the first word, read it, and then ask: • "Where do I read after this?"
Print direction	Reading in English goes from left to right, line by line.	Turn to a page with at least two lines of text. Read the top line and keep your finger on the last word. Ask: • "Where do I read after this?"
Page order	People read book pages in a specific order.	Point to the last word on the left page and ask: • "Where do I read after this?" Point to the last word on the right page and ask: • "Where do I read after this?"
One-to-one correspondence	One printed word corresponds to one spoken word.	Point to the first word on a new page (before reading it) and say to the student: • "Please point to each word as I read this line."
Role of punctuation	Writers use punctu-ation to signal types of sentences and the ends of sentences.	Point to a period (trace it with a pencil) and ask: • "What is this?" • "What is it for?"
Letter-word discrimination	Words and letters are different; writers use letters to make words.	Give the student two strips of paper and demonstrate how they slide together and apart on a page in the book. On the same page, say to the student: • "Please show me one letter." • "Please show me one word." • "Please show me the first letter in a word." • "Please show me the last letter in a word."

Source: Adapted from Teachers College Reading and Writing Project, 2006.

Figure 3.4: Concepts of print assessment tasks.

*Visit **go.SolutionTree.com/instruction** for a free reproducible version of this figure.*

Regarding tier one vocabulary, we recommend using a list of terms organized along a continuum. That is, the terms' arrangement indicates the order in which educators might teach them. There are a number of characteristics that teachers could use to arrange terms, such as difficulty, frequency, and so on. As previously mentioned, Marzano (2010b) identified 2,845 tier one terms and organized them into 420 semantically related clusters. He ordered the clusters in terms of the *basicness* of the words they contain (for a description of the index used to rate terms, see *Teaching Basic and Advanced Vocabulary*, Marzano, 2010b). A teacher could use the assessment available at **go.SolutionTree.com/instruction** to determine which cluster or clusters of words a student should focus on first.

Relative to word recognition, we recommend that the goal of formal assessment be to determine what phase of word recognition development the student is currently in. Use the flowchart in figure 3.5 to make this determination.

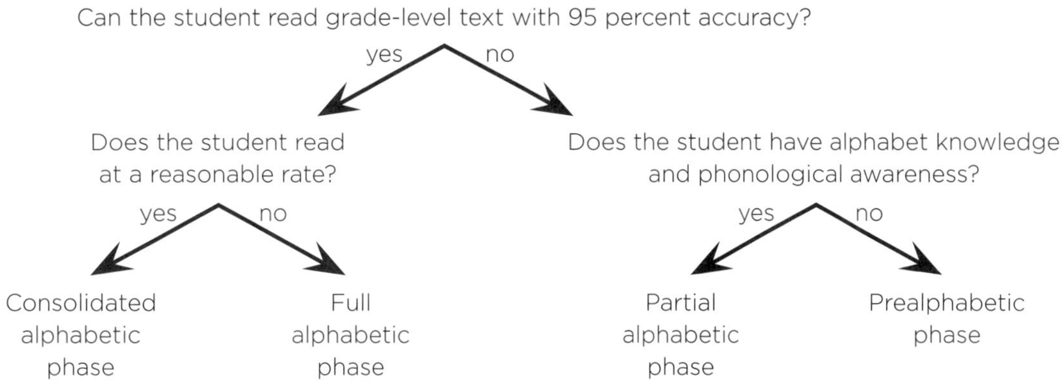

Figure 3.5: Flowchart for formal assessments of word recognition skill.

There are a variety of assessment tools available (online and in curricular resources) that teachers can use to answer the questions in figure 3.5. For example, a teacher can use a running record to determine if the student can read grade-level text with 95 percent accuracy. A count of words read in a minute could determine if the student reads at a reasonable rate. When assessing alphabet knowledge, we recommend asking the student to both give the names and make the sounds of upper- and lowercase letters. According to Paratore and colleagues (2011), "Phonological awareness progresses from larger to smaller speech units" (p. 116), beginning with words and syllables and moving toward phonemic awareness, in which students can manipulate individual *phonemes*, the smallest units of sound in English speech, as shown in figure 3.6.

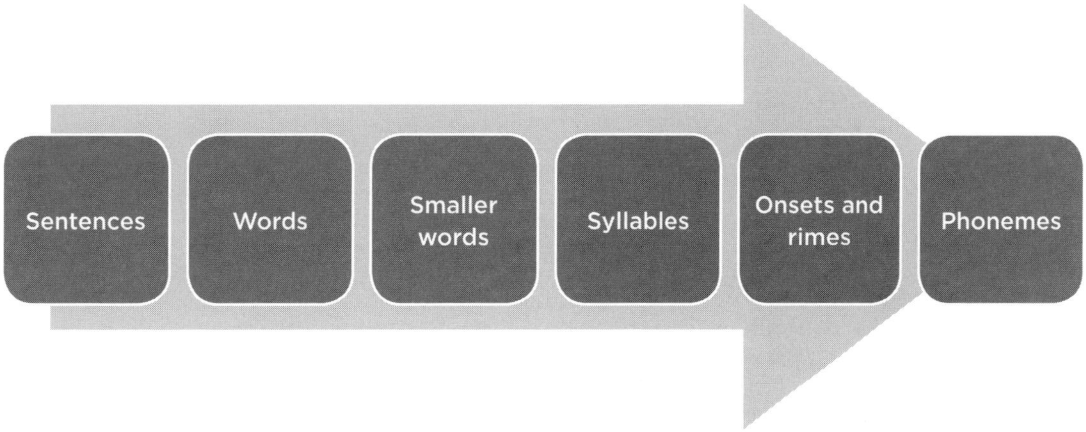

Figure 3.6: Continuum of phonological awareness.

Table 3.1 (page 48) lists assessment activities to help determine where a student falls on such a continuum.

Table 3.1: Phonological Awareness Assessment Activities

Speech Segment	Sample Assessment Tasks
Breaking Sentences Into Words	Provide a sentence (such as *The boy ate two pieces of pizza*) and ask the student how many words are in the sentence (seven).
Breaking Words Into Smaller Words	**Blending:** Provide two words (such as *book* and *shelf*) and ask the student what word they make together (*bookshelf*). **Segmenting:** Provide a compound word (such as *cowboy*) and ask the student what word is left after taking away one of the words (taking away *cow* leaves *boy*).
Breaking Words Into Syllables	Provide a multisyllabic word (such as *remember*) and ask the student how many syllables it contains (three).
Breaking Syllables Into Onsets and Rimes	**Blending:** Provide an onset and a rime and ask the student what word they make together. For example, /l/ and /ight/ make *light*. **Segmenting:** Provide a single-syllable word and ask the student to break it into onset (initial consonant, blend, or digraph) and rime (the vowel and any other phonemes in the syllable). For example, the word *cool* breaks down into /c/ and /ool/.
Breaking Onsets and Rimes Into Phonemes	**Blending:** Provide a group of phonemes and ask the student what word they make together. For example, /s/, /u/, and /n/ make *sun*. **Segmenting:** Provide a single-syllable word and ask the student to break it into sounds. For example, the word *dig* breaks into /d/, /i/, and /g/.

Source: Adapted from Foorman et al., 2016; Paratore et al., 2011.

Visit ***go.SolutionTree.com/instruction*** *for a free reproducible version of this table.*

Regarding fluency, Justin Miller and Paula J. Schwanenflugel's (2006) research indicates that qualitative rubrics or rating scales are the best options to guide assessment. Figure 3.7 depicts such a rubric.

4	Well-phrased, expressive reading
3	Good phrasing and expression most of the time, with a few instances of monotonic, word-by-word reading
2	Monotonic, word-by-word reading most of the time, with a few instances of good phrasing and expression
1	Monotonic, word-by-word reading

Figure 3.7: Formal fluency rating scale.

To use such a rubric, the teacher listens to the student read for at least sixty seconds before consulting the rating scale and assigning a score.

Relative to vocabulary, teachers can assess students' understanding of terms both *obtrusively* (instruction stops for assessment to happen) and *unobtrusively* (assessment occurs in the course of instruction). As an example of unobtrusive assessment, the teacher might notice that a student has used a term correctly in his or her speaking or writing; the teacher records such information as evidence of the student's vocabulary knowledge. If the student uses a term incorrectly, the teacher also records this information. Teachers might also refer to students' academic notebooks (records of students' learning in a particular course or content area, containing notes and other information) or vocabulary notebooks (records of previously learned vocabulary terms and students' descriptions of those terms) to gauge their level of understanding for specific terms or groups of terms.

When designing obtrusive vocabulary assessments, Robert J. Marzano and Debra J. Pickering (2005) recommend using open-ended items rather than multiple-choice or selected-response options:

> A multiple-choice or matching test might not be a valid assessment, especially if words within the test items are unfamiliar to the student. We recommend constructing tests with open-ended questions that allow the students to show what they understand about the terms. (pp. 33–34)

A teacher could ask students to explain a term in their own words, draw a picture or other graphic representation of a term, or write a short dialogue between two characters using the term so that its meaning is clear. Katherine A. D. Stahl and Marco A. Bravo (2010) offer other examples of open-ended vocabulary assessments; examples of each appear in figures 3.8, 3.9, and 3.10 (page 50).

Write terms that describe **actions related to argumentation**:	Write terms that describe **actions related to logical reasoning**:
Write terms that describe **actions related to problem solving**:	Write terms that describe **actions related to making comparisons**:

Figure 3.8: Open-ended assessment for tier two cognitive terms.

Write the causes, consequences, and human responses to the terms that appear in the left column.			
Term	**Causes**	**Consequences**	**Human Responses**
Flood			
Earthquake			
Hurricane			
Volcanic eruption			
Severe weather			
Drought			
Tsunami			

Figure 3.9: Open-ended assessment for tier three science vocabulary terms.

In the list of words that follows, put a circle around those that have something to do with **data distributions**. For each word you circled, write a short explanation of how it relates to the topic.
arc ______
box plot ______
central value ______
confidence interval ______
deviation ______
directrix ______
exponential function ______
factorial ______
histogram ______
intercept ______
interquartile range ______
logarithm ______
mean absolute deviation ______
measure of central tendency ______
normal distribution ______
outlier ______
parabola ______
parametric equation ______
quartile ______
radius ______
rectilinear figure ______
trigonometric function ______
vertex ______

Figure 3.10: Open-ended assessment for tier three mathematics vocabulary terms.

Finally, teachers can use student self-reports to assess vocabulary knowledge. Students might rate their understanding of a term using a scale such as the one in figure 3.11.

4	I understand even more about the term than I was taught.
3	I understand the term, and I'm not confused about any part of what it means.
2	I'm a little uncertain about what the term means, but I have a general idea.
1	I'm very uncertain about the term. I really don't understand what it means.

Source: Marzano & Pickering, 2005, p. 32.

Figure 3.11: Vocabulary self-rating scale.

Students can keep track of their ratings in their academic or vocabulary notebooks and should update their ratings as their understanding of terms deepens over time.

Finally, comprehension assessment can take a variety of forms. For example, recall the list of reading topics from table 2.1 (pagse 35–36). Teachers can pair those related to comprehension with specific questions, as shown in figure 3.12.

Comprehension Topic	Sample Assessment Questions
Analyzing Text Organization and Structure	• What words in this text signal different structures? • What relationships between ideas are in this text? • What substructures are in this text? • What is the overall structure of this text? • How does the structure help you understand this text?
Text Features	• What features are present in this text? • What does each feature contribute to the meaning of the text?
Analyzing Main Ideas; Analyzing Ideas and Themes	• What is most important in this text? • What details support the most important elements of this text? • What is the best summary of this text? • How well did the author convey the important elements of this text?
Analyzing Claims and Reasons; Analyzing Claims, Evidence, and Reasoning	• What does the author of this text want me to think? • What evidence does the author give? • What reasoning does the author use? • How relevant is the author's information? • How credible is the author's information?
Analyzing Narratives	• Who are the characters in this text? • What do the characters in this text think and feel? • How does the setting (when and where) affect the characters in this text? • What happens in this text?
Analyzing Point of View; Analyzing Point of View and Purpose	• Who is speaking in this text? • Why was this text written? • What is an alternative point of view that someone might take about this topic?
Analyzing Style and Tone	• What style of writing does the author use in this text? • What is the tone of this text? • What techniques is the author using to achieve this text's tone?
Comparing Texts	• What other texts is this text like? • How is this text different from similar texts? • How do similarities to other texts affect this text's meaning? • How do differences between this text and similar texts affect this text's meaning?

Figure 3.12: Comprehension topics and questions.

*Visit **go.SolutionTree.com/instruction** for a free reproducible version of this figure.*

The teacher could use questions such as those in figure 3.12 in a written assessment or as part of a probing discussion or interview with a student.

Figure 3.13 (page 52) presents the self-rating scale for element 5, using formal assessments of individual students, so teachers can gauge their professional performance.

Score	Description
4: Innovating	I adapt behaviors and create new strategies for unique student needs and situations.
3: Applying	I use formal assessments of individual students to determine students' proficiency with specific content, and I monitor the extent to which students respond to assessment-guided feedback and instruction.
2: Developing	I use formal assessments of individual students to determine students' proficiency with specific content, but I do not monitor the effect on students.
1: Beginning	I use the strategies and behaviors associated with this element incorrectly or with parts missing.
0: Not Using	I am unaware of strategies and behaviors associated with this element.

Figure 3.13: Self-rating scale for element 5—Using formal assessments of individual students.

GUIDING QUESTIONS FOR CURRICULUM DESIGN

This overarching question can guide teachers when using assessments: *How will I design and administer assessments that help students understand how their test scores and grades relate to their status on the progression of knowledge I expect them to master?* Consider the following questions aligned to the elements in this chapter to guide your planning.

- **Element 4:** How will I informally assess the whole class?

- **Element 5:** How will I formally assess individual students?

Summary

Using assessments involves two elements: (1) informal assessments of the whole class and (2) formal assessments of individual students. In the reading classroom, teachers can structure these informal and formal assessments around the five areas of our reading-specific model of instruction: (1) foundational skills, (2) word recognition, (3) fluency, (4) vocabulary, and (5) comprehension.

PART II
Content

CHAPTER 4

Conducting Direct Instruction Lessons

The third design area in *The New Art and Science of Teaching* framework involves addressing content in the classroom through direct instruction lessons. During direct instruction, teachers should chunk content into appropriately sized segments (element 6), provide opportunities for students to process the content in each segment (element 7), and prompt students to record and represent content in a variety of modes (notes, pictures, diagrams, and so on; element 8). Together, these elements facilitate direct instruction that highlights the important parts of new content and how those parts fit together. Here we describe how each element might manifest in a reading classroom.

Element 6: Chunking Content

Chunking content involves creating small, understandable increments of information or skills that students can hold in their working memory. Here we discuss how teachers might break down specific content from the five elements of our model of reading development into such segments.

As indicated previously, we can split foundational skills into concepts of print and tier one vocabulary knowledge. From there, we can further chunk concepts of print into the two types of knowledge we show in table 4.1: (1) book-related knowledge and (2) print-related knowledge. A teacher might choose to focus on either book-related concepts or print-related concepts during a specific read-aloud.

Table 4.1: Types of Knowledge Related to Concepts of Print

	Concept of Print	Description
Book-Related Knowledge	Book Handling	All books have covers and pages that people read in a specific order.
	Vertical Reading Direction	Reading in English goes from the top of the page to the bottom of the page.
	Horizontal Reading Direction	Reading in English goes from left to right, line by line.
	Page Order	People read book pages in a specific order.

continued →

	Concept of Print	Description
Print-Related Knowledge	Print Function	The function of print is to carry meaning.
	Print-to-Speech Correspondence	One printed word corresponds to one spoken word.
	Role of Punctuation in Print	Punctuation signals types of sentences and the ends of sentences.
	Letter-Word Discrimination in Print	Words and letters are different; people use letters to make words.

During direct instruction, teachers can organize tier one vocabulary into chunks known as semantic categories. A *semantic category* is simply a group of words that are all related in some way. Research has found that teaching terms in semantic, or meaning-related, groups mirrors the way the brain stores terms. William E. Nagy and Elfrieda H. Hiebert (2011) explain:

> The picture of the mental lexicon that emerges from various research paradigms is that of a richly interconnected network, reflecting a variety of types of relationships among word meanings. . . . If words are stored in groups, they should be taught in groups. (p. 393)

As mentioned previously, Marzano (2010b) organized his list of tier one terms into 420 semantic groupings called *clusters* that he further ordered in terms of basicness. We might consider each of these semantic groups a chunk. If a teacher is using another list, he or she could sort the terms into groups of related words.

Relative to word recognition instruction, there are three categories of knowledge that facilitate students' development: (1) alphabet and phonics knowledge, (2) phonological and phonemic awareness, and (3) morphology. We group alphabet and phonics knowledge together because alphabet knowledge develops into phonics knowledge; students begin by learning the sounds and names of individual letters (alphabet knowledge) but then transition to learning that groups of letters also represent specific sounds or groups of sounds (phonics knowledge). We group phonological and phonemic awareness together for the same reason; students move seamlessly from one to the other.

Within each category, chunks look slightly different. Teachers can best chunk alphabet and phonics knowledge according to letters (for alphabet knowledge) and spelling patterns (for phonics knowledge). They can break down phonological and phonemic awareness according to the size of the sound segment they are addressing (word, syllable, onset and rime, or phoneme). And they can divide morphology into four subcategories (prefixes, suffixes, roots, and contractions), which they can best chunk according to the specific prefix, suffix, root, or type of contraction they are teaching.

As we explain in chapter 1, we can conceptualize the prosodic element of fluency in three chunks.

1. **Stress:** The prominence the speaker places on particular words and syllables
2. **Intonation:** The rise and fall of vocal pitch
3. **Duration:** The length of time the speaker employs in pronouncing a word or part of a word and patterns of pausing between words, phrases, and sentences

Although students need to use the three in combination to read fluently, there are instructional advantages to thinking of each as a separate chunk. For example, during one read-aloud, the teacher might model duration and ask students to notice where she sped up or slowed down while reading. During a different read-aloud, the teacher might intentionally place stress on various words or syllables, and ask students to notice which words she read with more emphasis. Finally, the teacher might ask students to notice the rising and falling volume of her voice (intonation) during a third read-aloud.

Vocabulary instruction using the six-step process we outline in chapter 1 (see pages 27–28) can occur in three phases.

1. Introducing new terms (step 1 of the six-step process)
2. Asking students to record and represent new terms (steps 2 and 3)
3. Asking students to practice using new terms in various contexts (steps 4, 5, and 6)

Consider each new term as one chunk of content; the six-step process gives students plenty of opportunities to process the terms multiple times, reviewing and revising their knowledge after each opportunity. We elaborate on step 2 of the process in our discussion of element 7, processing content (pages 58–63); step 3 in our discussion of element 8, recording and representing content (pages 63–67); step 4 in our discussion of element 10, examining similarities and differences (pages 71–75); step 5 in our discussion of element 11, examining errors in reasoning (pages 76–79); and step 6 in our discussion of element 30, using academic games (pages 131–132).

Finally, we recommend chunking comprehension instruction by focusing on one comprehension-related topic at a time. Following Simms's (2016) analysis, a teacher might use the following list of topics to chunk comprehension content.

- Analyzing text organization and structure
- Analyzing text features
- Analyzing ideas and themes
- Analyzing claims, evidence, and reasoning
- Analyzing narratives
- Analyzing point of view and purpose
- Analyzing style and tone
- Comparing texts

Chunking comprehension content in this way facilitates instruction that prompts students to think about which groups of strategies they should use for each topic (for example, Which strategies do I need to use to analyze the main ideas and themes of this text?).

We recommend that teachers use the scale in figure 4.1 to rate their current level of effectiveness in regard to chunking content.

Score	Description
4: Innovating	I adapt behaviors and create new strategies for unique student needs and situations.
3: Applying	I chunk content, and I monitor the extent to which my actions affect students.
2: Developing	I chunk content, but I do not monitor the effect on students.
1: Beginning	I use the strategies and behaviors associated with this element incorrectly or with parts missing.
0: Not Using	I am unaware of strategies and behaviors associated with this element.

Figure 4.1: Self-rating scale for element 6—Chunking content.

Element 7: Processing Content

Processing content in the reading classroom involves giving students opportunities to think about each chunk of information the teacher provides before progressing on to the next chunk. Here we describe strategies that the teacher might use to help students process the chunks of content we describe in the previous section.

Relative to foundational skills, a technique called print referencing gives students opportunities to process instruction pertaining to concepts of print. Developed by Laura M. Justice and colleagues (Ezell & Justice, 2000; Justice & Ezell, 2002, 2004; Justice, Kaderavek, Fan, Sofka, & Hunt, 2009; Zucker et al., 2009), *print referencing* uses verbal and nonverbal cues to call students' attention to print concepts. Verbal and nonverbal cues include the following.

- **Questions**, such as, "How many words are on this page?"
- **Requests**, such as, "Show me where I would start reading on this page."
- **Comments**, such as, "These words are exactly the same."
- **Nonverbal techniques**, such as pointing to print and tracking it with a finger while reading

Table 4.2 lists specific ways that a teacher could use print-referencing techniques to call students' attention to specific concepts of print.

Table 4.2: Print-Referencing Techniques

	Concept of Print	Description	Use Print Referencing to Draw Attention to . . .
Book-Related Concepts	Book Handling	All books have a title, covers, and pages.	• The front and back covers of the book: "How do we hold the book? How will we open it? How will we hold the book when we are finished reading?" • The title on the cover: "This is the title of the book. It is like the book's name." • The title page: "This is the title page. It tells us the name of the book again and when the book was published."
	Vertical Reading Direction	Reading in English goes from the top of the page to the bottom of the page.	• The order in which people read words on a page: "The writing starts here, at the top of the page. I will read this top line first, then this line, and then this last line."
	Horizontal Reading Direction	Reading in English goes from left to right, line by line.	• Direction of normal print: "When I read I go this way" (while sweeping finger under print). • Print with unusual orientations or shapes to convey meaning: "These words are printed at an angle so they'll look like they're splashing into the water."
	Page Order	People read book pages in a specific order.	• First and last pages: "What page do we read first? What page do we read next? What page do we read last?"

	Concept of Print	Description	Use Print Referencing to Draw Attention to . . .
Print-Related Concepts	Print Function	The function of print is to carry meaning.	• Special typefaces that convey meaning: "These words are red because he's angry." • Print that appears in speech bubbles: "These are the fox's words in this bubble—he's talking." • Words in illustrations: "This jar has the word *cookies* on it."
	Print-to-Speech Correspondence	One printed word corresponds to one spoken word.	• Individual words: "Let's count the words on this page. Who can show me just one word?" • Words of different lengths: "Which word is longer—*vegetable* or *soup*?"
	Role of Punctuation in Print	Punctuation signals types of sentences and the ends of sentences.	• Periods: "This period tells me that the sentence is ending and my voice should pause." • Question marks: "This question mark tells me that the boy is asking a question. My voice should go up." • Exclamation points: "This exclamation point tells me that the woman is excited. My voice should be excited."
	Letter-Word Discrimination in Print	Words and letters are different; people use letters to make words.	• Individual letters: "This is the letter G. It is in the word *grow* and *garden*." • Letters that make words: "This is the word *sun*. *S-u-n* spells *sun*."

Source: Adapted from Zucker et al., 2009, pp. 64–65.
Visit ***go.SolutionTree.com/instruction*** *for a free reproducible version of this table.*

Relative to tier one vocabulary, Marzano (2010b) recommends that after teachers have introduced each word, they engage students in activities that require them to articulate their own description of the term. Linguistic activities of this sort might involve writing a description for the term, identifying synonyms or antonyms for the term, or using the term in a sentence. We discuss nonlinguistic techniques for processing terms in the next section.

Relative to alphabet and phonics knowledge, students should receive time to process after learning about each letter or pattern. Such processing might involve finding examples and nonexamples, answering questions, or discussing a particular chunk of content. Barbara Foorman and colleagues (2016) recommend that teachers introduce consonants first, followed by short vowels, then long vowels in words with the VC*e* pattern, and finally long vowels spelled as vowel teams. Such a progression leads directly into phonics instruction; Foorman and colleagues (2016) also suggest that teachers begin phonics instruction by teaching consonant patterns (such as blends, digraphs, trigraphs, and silent-letter combinations). Vowel patterns and syllable-construction patterns should follow (see table 4.3, page 60).

Table 4.3: Consonant, Vowel, and Syllable-Construction Patterns

Category	Pattern	Examples
Consonant Patterns	Blends (two or more consecutive consonants that retain their individual sounds)	*scr, st, cl, ft*
	Consonant digraphs and trigraphs (multiletter combinations that stand for one phoneme)	*th, sh, ch, ph, ng* *tch, dge*
	Silent-letter combinations (two letters; one represents the phoneme, and the other is not pronounced)	*kn, wr, gn, rh, mb*
Vowel Patterns	Vowel teams (a combination of two, three, or four letters standing for a single vowel sound)	*ea, oo, oa, igh, eigh*
	Vowel diphthongs (complex speech sounds or glides that begin with one vowel and gradually change to another vowel within the same syllable)	*oi, ou*
	r-controlled vowels or bossy *r*'s (vowels making a unique sound when followed by *r*)	*ar, er, ir, or, ur*
	Long *e*	*ee, ie, ea, e_e, ey, ei, y, ea*
	Long *a*	*a_e, ai, ay, a_y, ei, ea, ey*
Syllable-Construction Patterns	Closed syllables (a short vowel spelled with a single vowel letter and ending in one or more consonants)	*in-sect* *stu-dent*
	VC*e* (a long vowel spelled with one vowel + one consonant + silent *e*)	*com-pete* *base-ball*
	Open syllables (ending with a long vowel sound, spelled with a single vowel letter)	*pro-gram* *tor-na-do*
	Vowel team (multiple letters spelling the vowel)	*train-er* *neigh-bor-hood*
	Vowel-*r* (vowel pronunciation changing before */r/*)	*char-ter* *cir-cus*
	Consonant-*le* (unaccented final syllable containing a consonant before *l* followed by a silent *e*)	*drib-ble* *puz-zle*

Source: Foorman et al., 2016, p. 25.

Similarly, students should receive time to process after learning about each sound segment associated with phonological and phonemic awareness (word, syllable, onset/rime, or phoneme, see figure 3.6, page 47).

Relative to morphology, Thomas G. White, Joanne Sowell, and Alice Yanagihara (1989) identified the most frequently used prefixes and suffixes in English. Table 4.4 shows the results of their work.

Table 4.4: Frequently Occurring Prefixes and Suffixes

Prefix	Percentage of All Prefixed Words	Suffix	Percentage of All Suffixed Words
un-	26	*-s, -es*	31
re-	14	*-ed*	20
in-, im-, ir-, il- (meaning "not")	11	*-ing*	14
dis-	7	*-ly*	7
en-, em-	4	*-er, -or* (indicating agency)	4
non-	4	*-ion, -tion, -ation, -ition*	4

Prefix	Percentage of All Prefixed Words	Suffix	Percentage of All Suffixed Words
in-, *im-* (meaning "in" or "into")	4	*-ible*, *-able*	2
over- (meaning "too much")	3	*-al*, *-ial*	1
mis-	3	*-y*	1
sub-	3	*-ness*	1
pre-	3	*-ity*, *-ty*	1
inter-	3	*-ment*	1
fore-	3	*-ic*	1
de-	2	*-ous*, *-eous*, *-ious*	1
trans-	2	*-en*	1
super-	1	*-er* (indicating comparison)	1
semi-	1	*-ive*, *-ative*, *-itive*	1
anti-	1	*-ful*	1
mid-	1	*-less*	1
under- (meaning "too little")	1	*-est*	1

Source: Adapted from White et al., 1989.

White and colleagues (1989) also articulate a process that teachers can use to introduce the most common prefixes and suffixes and give students time to process them. The teaching sequence they recommend, which includes opportunities for processing, appears in figure 4.2.

Teaching Prefixes	Teaching Suffixes
Lesson 1: Present examples and nonexamples of words with prefixes (*unkind* and *refill* have prefixes [*un-* and *re-*]; *uncle* and *reason* do not have prefixes). **Lesson 2:** Explain and give examples of the negative meanings of *un-* and *dis-* ("not" as in *unlike* and *disagree*). **Lesson 3:** Explain and give examples of the negative meanings of *in-*, *im-*, and *non-* ("not" as in *incompetent*, *impossible*, and *nonconforming*). **Lesson 4:** Explain and give examples of both meanings of *re-* ("again" as in *rebuild* or *revise* and "back" as in *recover* or *relapse*). **Lesson 5:** Address the less common meanings of *un-* and *dis-* ("do the opposite" as in *unbutton* or *disown*) and *in-* and *im-* ("in" or "into" as in *inquire* or *implant*). **Lesson 6:** Explain and give examples of *en-* and *em-* ("in" or "into" as in *encircle* and *embrace*), *over-* ("above" or "beyond" as in *overreact*), and *mis-* ("bad" or "wrong" as in *mistrust* or *mistrial*).	**Lesson 1:** Present examples and nonexamples of words with suffixes (*employee* and *natural* have suffixes [*-ee* and *-al*]; *bee* and *charcoal* do not). **Lesson 2:** Present words with suffixes whose spellings do not change when the suffix is added (such as *monkeys*, *foxes*, *walking*, *higher*, *jumped*, *softly*, *laughable*, *comical*, and *windy*). **Lesson 3:** Illustrate each of the three major spelling changes that can occur with suffixes: • Consonant blending (*bigger*, *running*, *skipped*, and *sunny*) • Change from *y* to *i* (*married*, *skies*, *happily*, *classifiable*, and *filthiness*) • Deleted silent *e* (*riding*, *gated*, *baker*, *advisable*, *natural*, and *wheezy*) **Lesson 4:** Provide examples of inflectional endings (*-s*, *-es*, *-ed*, *-ing*) and derivational suffixes (*-ly*, *-er*, *-ion*, *-able*, *-al*, *-y*, *-ness*).

Source: Adapted from White et al., 1989.

Figure 4.2: Recommended sequences for teaching affixes.

Research shows that repeated reading is an extremely effective way to provide opportunities for students to process information related to fluency. Janette Klingner and colleagues (2016) state that "repeated reading that includes modeling and corrective feedback is noted to be the most recommended instructional method for improving reading fluency" (p. 667). *Repeated reading*, according to David J. Chard, Leanne R. Ketterlin-Geller, Scott K. Baker, Christian Doabler, and Chanisa Apichatabutra (2009), involves reading a short passage multiple times. Reader's theater is one strategy that incorporates repeated reading; students rehearse a script, speech, or poem by reading through it multiple times. Teachers should not expect them to memorize it or dramatize the content. Rather they focus on reading smoothly and with proper expression. Reader's theater culminates with an opportunity for students to read their pieces in front of the class or to record their readings for others to listen to asynchronously.

Relative to vocabulary, students process terms during steps 2 and 3 of the six-step process. One of the critical elements of direct vocabulary instruction is multiple encounters with and exposures to new terms. This is because "knowing a word is not an all-or-nothing phenomenon. Word learning happens incrementally; with each additional encounter with a word, depth of understanding accrues" (Stahl & Bravo, 2010, p. 567). Stahl and Stahl (2012) explain that when students first learn a word, they usually overgeneralize its meaning. Subsequent encounters help to refine the meaning into a "more constrained and particular usage" that incorporates "the boundaries and nuances of that particular word" (pp. 73–74). As we note in our discussion of tier one vocabulary, a teacher should give students opportunities to process their understanding of each new term after introducing it. Students might do this linguistically through writing a description, identifying synonyms or antonyms, or by using the term in a sentence. We provide nonlinguistic methods for processing new terms in the next section.

As we explain in the introduction, research shows that teaching students to use small sets of comprehension strategies is an excellent way to facilitate their processing of texts. Shanahan and colleagues (2010) review the research on different multiple-strategy formats and summarize those with the strongest research base. Table 4.5 lists the multiple-strategy formats they recommend.

Table 4.5: Multiple-Strategy Formats for Comprehension Instruction

Multiple-Strategy Format	Description	Typical Strategies Taught
Reciprocal Teaching	Students take turns leading a conversation on the text using four strategies. First, the teacher describes all of the strategies in succession. Then the teacher models each strategy and explains why the strategy helps students understand the text. Finally, students take turns leading the conversation. This method usually occurs with students in small groups.	Predicting Clarifying Questioning Summarizing
Transactional Strategy Instruction	The teacher focuses on a few strategies at a time, concentrating on improving students' memory, comprehension, and problem-solving skills. First, the teacher selects from a large menu of strategies to explicitly teach (see list at right). The teacher then explicitly teaches the strategies by explaining strategy use and processes, modeling the strategy using teaching think-alouds, assisting in practicing the strategy, and applying the strategy to reading and writing. Teachers should gradually release responsibility to the students (see page 13 for information on gradual release of responsibility). Teachers may use these strategies to motivate students to involve themselves in the text and to stimulate a class discussion about the text.	Activating prior knowledge Predicting Questioning Visualizing Summarizing Monitoring Clarifying Goal setting Text structure

Multiple-Strategy Format	Description	Typical Strategies Taught
Informed Strategies for Learning	The teacher combines a variety of reading-comprehension strategies to show students that the strategies they learn are useful and necessary for being able to read with understanding. To begin, the teacher can explicitly teach several strategies that will help students understand what they read. For example, teachers can model how they monitor their own understanding by stopping periodically and asking themselves whether they understand what they just read. When combining this strategy with others, teachers can display a bulletin board linking each strategy to a picture or themed metaphor (for example, various road signs) representing how to put each into practice (in the previous example, a stop sign might remind students to stop and monitor their own understanding). The board serves as a reminder during lessons and while students read independently. Teachers encourage students to be aware of what they are reading, and students continually monitor and evaluate their own understanding.	Activating prior knowledge Drawing inferences Visualizing Summarizing Monitoring
Concept-Oriented Reading Instruction	The teacher teaches comprehension strategies in the context of learning about an overarching concept, typically in the natural sciences, in order to engage students and motivate them to learn. The teacher introduces one strategy per week, systematically integrating the strategies in later weeks. Teachers can bring in other instructional practices, including hands-on activities, collaborative learning activities, and offering students some choice in and control over what they learn.	Activating prior knowledge Questioning Summarizing Text structure

Source: Adapted from Shanahan et al., 2010.

We recommend that teachers use the scale in figure 4.3 to rate their current level of effectiveness with processing content.

Score	Description
4: Innovating	I adapt behaviors and create new strategies for unique student needs and situations.
3: Applying	I engage students in processing content, and I monitor the extent to which my actions affect students.
2: Developing	I engage students in processing content, but I do not monitor the effect on students.
1: Beginning	I use the strategies and behaviors associated with this element incorrectly or with parts missing.
0: Not Using	I am unaware of strategies and behaviors associated with this element.

Figure 4.3: Self-rating scale for element 7—Processing content.

Element 8: Recording and Representing Content

Depending on the type of reading content, there are numerous ways to help students form internal representations of their learning. Teachers might ask students working on print concepts to create their own books, with covers, titles, title pages, pages, text on the pages (which a reader should read in a specific order), and illustrations. Although students working on print concepts will probably not be able to use real letters, words, or spellings, such an activity provides an opportunity to use their new knowledge about how print and books work to create their own products.

Relative to tier one vocabulary, Marzano (2010b) recommends that the teacher provide students with different representational options depending on the type of term.

- **Nouns:** Students can sketch or find a picture of the noun (such as a *sled*).
- **Verbs:** Students can sketch or find a picture of someone doing the verb (for example, two people *discussing* something).
- **Adjectives:** Students can sketch or find a picture of something that illustrates the defining characteristics of the adjective (such as someone being *polite*).
- **Adverbs:** Students can sketch or find a picture of someone acting in the manner described by the adverb (like someone walking *away*).
- **Conjunctions:** Students can compose a sentence that uses the conjunction and then sketch or find a picture that illustrates the content of their sentence (for example, "*Since* I was tired, I went to bed early" accompanied by a picture of the student sleeping).
- **Prepositions:** Students can compose a phrase that uses the preposition and then sketch or find a picture that illustrates the content of their phrase (such as, "*across* the bridge" accompanied by a picture of someone walking across a bridge).
- **Interjections:** Students can sketch or find a picture of a situation in which an onlooker might respond with the interjection (for example, a picture of someone receiving an award for the term *wow*).
- **Pronouns:** Students can compose a sentence that uses the pronoun and then sketch or find a picture that illustrates the content of their sentence (such as, "The candy is *mine*" accompanied by a picture of the student holding a piece of candy).

These strategies can help students record and represent tier one terms that may otherwise be difficult to capture nonlinguistically.

Because word recognition content is fundamentally based on segmenting and blending parts of language, an excellent instructional technique for recording and representing such content is Elkonin boxes (named for their creator, D. B. Elkonin, 1973). This strategy uses a set of boxes, such as the one in figure 4.4, to represent how individual letters and sounds come together to create meaningful language parts.

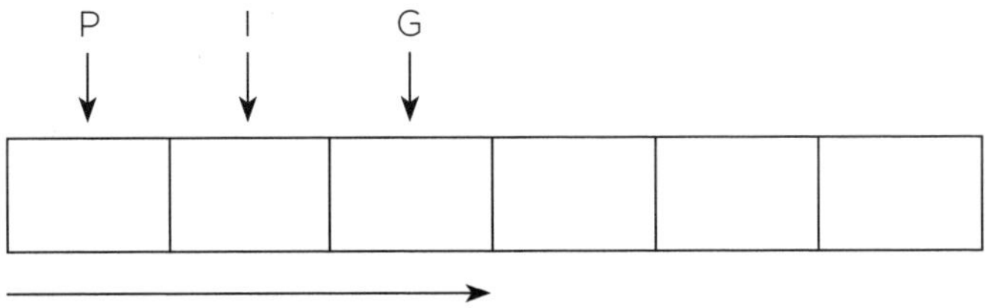

Figure 4.4: Elkonin box activity.

The National Reading Panel (NICHD, 2000) finds that "teaching children to manipulate phonemes using letters produced bigger effects than teaching without letters" (chapter 2, p. 4). Therefore, we recommend that teachers use movable letters or letter tiles with Elkonin boxes (rather than discs or other unlettered plastic pieces). Foorman and colleagues (2016) explain how to use Elkonin boxes for instruction:

> Have students repeat the word slowly, pulling one . . . letter tile down into the box for each unique sound that they say. Then, have students run their finger under the boxes from left to right as they blend the individual sounds together and say the word. . . . Once students have learned to connect several sounds to print, repeat this exercise, having

> them write the corresponding letters in the boxes, rather than pulling down discs or letter tiles. (p. 18)

Teachers can use Elkonin boxes for all levels of phonological awareness. A teacher could write the words of a sentence on cards and have students practice breaking the sentence into words. Similarly, the teacher could make cards for the two words that make up a compound word, the onset and rime of a one-syllable word, or spelling patterns that represent single phonemes (for example, *igh* for /ī/). Essentially, the teacher creates cards for whatever sized phonological unit the student needs to focus on.

Students can record and represent their prosodic learning using voice recordings. Roxanne F. Hudson, Holly B. Lane, and Paige C. Pullen (2005) explain:

> Hearing one's own voice on audiotape can be an eye-opening experience. . . . Having the opportunity to record, listen, and rerecord can be a powerful method for increasing reading fluency. This approach promotes independent judgment and goal setting, along with ownership of the process. (p. 711)

If recording technology or equipment is not available, a teacher could also have students use whisper phones or phonics phones. These are simply PVC pipe elbows connected to create a telephone shape. When students read into one end (as if talking on the phone), their voice is amplified for their ears only, giving them feedback about how they sound while reading.

Representing vocabulary terms is the focus of step 3 of the six-step process. Table 4.6 lists various options for representing different types of terms.

Table 4.6: Representation Options for Vocabulary Terms

Representation Option	Sample Term	Sample Picture
Sketch the actual object. If a term is concrete and easy to depict, simply sketch a picture of it.	*Punnett square*	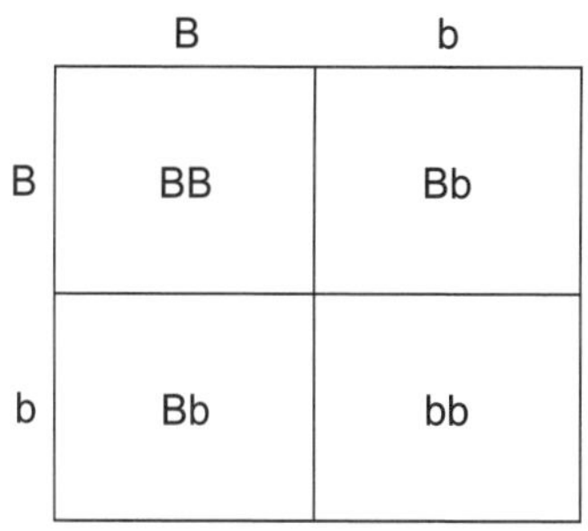
Sketch a symbol for the term. If a term is abstract, sketch a symbol that represents the term.	*inequality*	< >
Sketch an example of the term. If the term is abstract, sketch an example of the term.	*primary source*	

continued →

<table>
<tr><th>Representation Option</th><th>Sample Term</th><th>Sample Picture</th></tr>
<tr><td>Sketch a cartoon or vignette with a character using the term.
If a term is abstract, use speech bubbles to show how a character in a cartoon might use the term.</td><td>algebra</td><td>

</td></tr>
<tr><td>Sketch a graphic for the term.
If a term is abstract, sketch a graphic that depicts the meaning of the term.</td><td>logical</td><td>
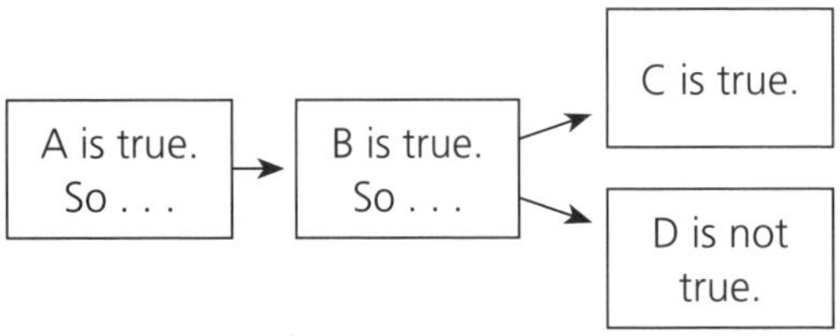

</td></tr>
</table>

To help students represent their comprehension of a text, Simms and Marzano (2018) have developed a set of knowledge maps (based on Meyer & Ray's [2011] list of text structures described in chapter 1, page 12) that students can use to record and represent their comprehension of texts. Linda M. Phillips and Anat Yarden (2017) explain why structure-based maps and organizers are so powerful:

> Knowledge of the structure of texts affords students a mental grasp of the organization and representation of concepts and ideas, and enhances their ability to identify, sequence, integrate, and judge content. . . . Knowledge of text structure improves the identification and memory of relevant information. (pp. 430, 433)

Knowledge maps are images that correspond to various structures that students will encounter in texts and while learning. Simms and Marzano's (2018) set of maps corresponds to the following fourteen areas.

1. Basic relationships
2. Description
3. Sequence
4. Causation
5. Problem–solution
6. Comparison
7. Collection
8. Classification
9. Argumentation
10. Reasoning
11. Systems
12. Episode
13. Metaphor
14. Analogy

After reading a text, ask students to look at the knowledge maps and decide which one best fits the information they are learning or communicating. In many cases, multiple maps may apply. For example, many stories can fit into a sequence or a causation structure (since they occur chronologically, and since one event often causes another event). Lists are often embedded in comparison or description structures. The important part of using knowledge maps in the classroom is not finding one correct structure for a set of information, but rather discussing the pros and cons of using different structures to remember or communicate information. Throughout chapters 5, 6, and 7, we highlight (and give images of) various knowledge maps that are especially relevant to specific instructional elements.

Figure 4.5 presents the self-rating scale for recording and representing content.

Score	Description
4: Innovating	I adapt behaviors and create new strategies for unique student needs and situations.
3: Applying	I have students record and represent content, and I monitor the extent to which my actions affect students' performance.
2: Developing	I have students record and represent content, but I do not monitor the effect on students.
1: Beginning	I use the strategies and behaviors associated with this element incorrectly or with parts missing.
0: Not Using	I am unaware of strategies and behaviors associated with this element.

Figure 4.5: Self-rating scale for element 8—Recording and representing content.

GUIDING QUESTIONS FOR CURRICULUM DESIGN

This design question pertains to conducting direct instruction lessons: *When content is new, how will I design and deliver direct instruction lessons that help students understand which parts are important and how the parts fit together?* Consider the following questions aligned to the elements in this chapter to guide your planning.

- **Element 6:** How will I chunk the new content into short, digestible bites?

- **Element 7:** How will I help students process the individual chunks and the content as a whole?

- **Element 8:** How will I help students record and represent their knowledge?

Summary

Conducting direct instruction lessons involves three elements: (1) chunking content, (2) processing content, and (3) recording and representing content. In the reading classroom, teachers should consider how to apply each of these elements to foundational skills such as concepts of print and tier one vocabulary, to constrained skills such as fluency and word recognition, and to unconstrained skills such as vocabulary and comprehension.

CHAPTER 5

Conducting Practicing and Deepening Lessons

Once students have grasped the important ideas and structure of new content, they need to deepen their understanding of concepts and develop fluency with new skills and processes. This is the focus of the fourth design area in *The New Art and Science of Teaching* framework. To support such practice and deepening, teachers can use structured practice sessions (element 9), help students examine similarities and differences in content (element 10), and prompt students to examine possible errors in reasoning relative to specific content (element 11). Here we describe how each element of this design area might manifest in a reading classroom.

Element 9: Using Structured Practice Sessions

As students practice and deepen their new knowledge related to reading, foundational skills are subsumed into other areas. Students practice and apply print concepts in the context of word recognition, fluency, and comprehension; the later phases of tier one vocabulary instruction are identical to steps 4, 5, and 6 of the process for teaching tier two and three terms (see pages 27–28 for a description of the steps). Therefore, in this and the following chapters, we address foundational skills in the context of word recognition, fluency, vocabulary, and comprehension.

Relative to word recognition, students' practice should focus on achieving phonological recoding ability. The chief skill involved in phonological recoding (once students can identify the sounds being made by different letters in a word) is blending. According to Foorman and colleagues (2016), *blending* is "reading a word systematically from left to right by combining each successive letter or combination of letters into one sound" (p. 23). They suggest that educators teach blending using two strategies: (1) chunking and (2) sounding out.

In the *chunking* approach to blending, students add each sound in a word to the previous sound before going on to the next sound. For example, a student chunking the word *green* would begin with the /g/ sound and add the /r/ sound to make /gr/. After practicing the /gr/ sound and remembering it, the student would add the long e sound to make /grē/. Finally, the student would add the /n/ sound and say /grēn/. In the *sounding out* approach to blending, students say the sound of each letter or letter combination one by one until they reach the end of a word; then they say all the sounds together quickly. For example, a student sounding out the word *green* would say /g/ first, then /r/, then /ē/, and last /n/. Then, he or she would say all the sounds in order quickly: /grēn/.

While teaching blending, Foorman and colleagues (2016) recommend that teachers listen specifically for students who add a strong /uh/ to the end of stopped consonant sounds (that is, they pronounce /p/, /b/, /t/, /d/, /k/, and /g/ as /puh/, /buh/, /tuh/, and so on). It is important for teachers to help these students make the /uh/ as small as possible for sounds that require it (the voiced consonants /b/, /d/, and /g/) and eliminate it entirely for sounds that do not require it (/p/, /t/, and /k/). Doing so will make it easier for students to recognize words when blending the sounds together.

Fluency practice can occur in many different ways. Some of the best ways involve the teacher and students reading at the same time, such as with *choral reading*. During choral reading, Foorman and colleagues (2016) recommend that the teacher carefully monitor to make sure that all students are participating, rather than simply copying their peers. If a teacher suspects that a student in the group is simply following along orally with the group (rather than reading the text himself), she might meet with him for a session of simultaneous reading. *Simultaneous reading* is similar to choral reading, but only involves the teacher and one student. In both situations, Foorman and colleagues (2016) suggest that the teacher "read with expression in a quiet voice and set a pace that reflects students' word-reading abilities, slowing down a bit for words that present particular challenges" (p. 36).

Steps 4, 5, and 6 of the six-step vocabulary process provide structured practice with the vocabulary terms the teacher has introduced during steps 1, 2, and 3 (or during the introductory phase, for tier one terms). Step 4 involves engaging students in activities that help them add to their knowledge of the terms in their vocabulary notebooks. This can take the form of identifying similarities and differences (through comparison activities, classification activities, or by creating metaphors and analogies) or through examining word roots and affixes. We elaborate on activities teachers can use during step 4 in the next section on element 10, examining similarities and differences. Step 5 involves having students discuss terms with one another to refine or revise their understanding of those terms. This might involve asking students to make connections between terms using semantic mapping or similar organizers. Alternatively, the teacher might ask students to meet in small groups and discuss terms. We elaborate on activities teachers can use during step 5 in our discussion of element 11, examining errors in reasoning. Finally, step 6 entails involving students in games that allow them to play with terms. These games can be as simple as inventing puns and jokes that involve new terms or as complex as activities based on popular games such as *Pictionary* or *Jeopardy!* We elaborate on games that students can play with terms in our discussion of element 30, using academic games, in chapter 8 (pages 131–132).

Relative to comprehension, we suggest that the teacher engage in regular read-alouds and use a think-aloud protocol such as the one in figure 5.1 to model how to think about the text. As students gain skill with the different comprehension-related topics in the protocol, the teacher can ask students to participate in the think-aloud, sharing their own thoughts and analyses. Eventually, students might use steps 2 and 3 (noticing and thinking) from figure 5.1 to scaffold their independent thinking about a text.

Figure 5.2 presents the self-rating scale to guide teachers in addressing element 9, using structured practice sessions.

Preparatory Question: Why am I reading this text? [purpose]
Step 1: Teacher Read Through [print concepts, fluency, and prosody] • Read with expression and feeling, but no commentary. • Pause about two seconds after finishing the words on a page.
Step 2: Noticing • What information is in the words, pictures, and figures? [text features] • How did the writer organize this text? [text organization and structure] ◆ Sequence ◆ Description ◆ Comparison ◆ Causation ◆ Problem and solution ◆ Collection • Who is talking in this text? [point of view]
Step 3: Thinking • What other texts is this text like? [comparing texts] • What do specific words and phrases mean? [words and language] • Who feels what and where?* [analyzing narratives] • What does the text mean? What ideas are the most important? [main idea and themes] • What does the author want me to think? [claims, evidence, and reasoning]

** Include if the text is a narrative.*

Figure 5.1: Think-aloud protocol.

Visit ***go.SolutionTree.com/instruction*** *for a free reproducible version of this figure.*

Score	Description
4: Innovating	I adapt behaviors and create new strategies for unique student needs and situations.
3: Applying	I use structured practice sessions, and I monitor the extent to which my actions affect students.
2: Developing	I use structured practice sessions, but I do not monitor the effect on students.
1: Beginning	I use the strategies and behaviors associated with this element incorrectly or with parts missing.
0: Not Using	I am unaware of strategies and behaviors associated with this element.

Figure 5.2: Self-rating scale for element 9—Using structured practice sessions.

Element 10: Examining Similarities and Differences

As students develop alphabet knowledge, examining similarities and differences between and among letters is an excellent way to learn to discriminate between them. Purcell-Gates and colleagues (2016) state that the most effective alphabet instruction "cycles repeatedly and rapidly through the alphabet, involves explicit teaching, examines letters in the context of text as well as in isolation, and considers name, sound, recognition, and formation/writing" (p. 1248). Research has clearly shown that teaching alphabet knowledge is most effective when teachers use letter names, letter sounds, and images of letters together when introducing and discussing letters (Jones & Reutzel, 2012; Phillips & Piasta, 2013). Alphabet puzzles, magnetic letters, and alphabet books all provide excellent opportunities for students to interact with upper- and lowercase letters in different fonts and sizes and allow them to compare and detect the minor physical differences in letters. Paratore and colleagues (2011) explain:

> Interesting and playful experiences that allow for comparing a variety of letters in their conventional forms . . . and in different fonts . . . are important supports for letter-name learning and likely more motivation than isolated letter instruction, such as introducing one letter a week or teaching letters via flash cards. (pp. 118–119)

Handwriting programs also provide excellent opportunities for students to learn about and examine how various upper- and lowercase letters are alike and different.

To practice identifying similarities and differences between phonemes, students might sort cards with pictures on them into piles of pictures that share the same first sound, middle sound, or final sound (Foorman et al., 2016). Additionally, the National Reading Panel (NICHD, 2000) recommends the following activities, which allow students to compare phonemes in a number of different contexts.

> - **Phoneme identity**, which requires recognizing the common sound in different words, for example, "Tell me the sound that is the same in bike, boy, and bell." (/b/)
> - **Phoneme categorization**, which requires recognizing the word with the odd sound in a sequence of three or four words, for example, "Which word does not belong? Bus, bun, rug." (rug) (chapter 2, p. 10)

Rhyming texts such as poems, songs, and nursery rhymes are also engaging and give students practice comparing and contrasting phonological segments.

Relative to fluency, partner reading can help a student compare his or her reading to the reading of another student. Timothy V. Rasinski and colleagues (2011) explain:

> Reading with a tutor, partner, buddy, or peer appears to have beneficial effects for developing students' reading fluency. Students increase their engagement in reading practice when they select their partners and when the texts to be practiced are of appropriate difficulty for the pair of students. Research demonstrates that reading practice assisted by older students working with younger students is also effective. (p. 303)

Students could use a plus-delta protocol to comment on each other's reading. In such a structure, students take turns telling each other what they did well and what they still might work on relative to their fluency.

Step 4 of the six-step vocabulary process helps students review and refine their understanding of vocabulary terms by examining their similarities and differences. Two tools that teachers can use to facilitate this comparison process are the knowledge maps for metaphors and analogies.

Metaphor structures compare two items. Students can use a metaphor knowledge map to analyze a metaphor, such as *love is a rose*, or to compose a metaphor for a concept, such as *leadership*. Figure 5.3 shows a metaphor knowledge map.

To analyze a metaphor such as *love is a rose*, students might match characteristics of each item that have abstract attributes in common. For example, on the left side, a student would write *love* in the item circle. Then the student might indicate that a characteristic of love is that it can be lost easily. In the right side of the metaphor map, a student writes *rose* in the item circle. A characteristic is that a rose can be damaged easily. In the abstract sense, both are fragile, which the student notes in the middle column.

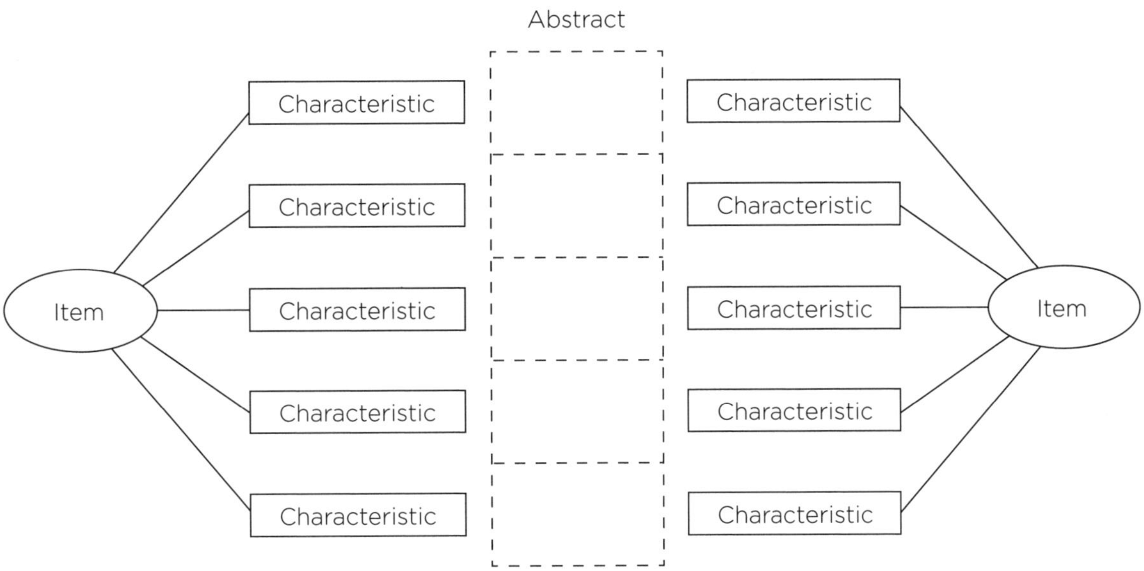

Figure 5.3: Metaphor knowledge map.

Visit ***go.SolutionTree.com/instruction*** *for a free reproducible version of this figure.*

To compose a metaphor, students might begin by articulating the characteristics of one item. For example, a good leader:

- Is able to see things others can't see
- Faces difficult situations bravely
- Doesn't give up easily
- Likes big challenges
- Adapts to changing conditions and circumstances
- Trains people to take his or her place

In the abstract, one might state those characteristics as *great vision*, *fearless*, *tenacious*, *high-achiever*, *flexible*, and *reproduces himself or herself*. The student then tries to think of another item that possesses those same abstract characteristics. In this case, he or she might think of an eagle, which has the following characteristics that correspond to the abstract characteristics of a good leader.

- Is able to see things that other birds can't see
- Will fight birds and animals much larger than itself
- Doesn't fly away from storms, just flies higher
- Flies up to altitudes of ten thousand feet
- Adapts to changing wind currents and weather conditions
- Raises young eagles, teaching them to fly and hunt

Creating metaphors for vocabulary terms deepens students' understanding of terms and allows them to make connections between terms that they otherwise might not realize.

An *analogy* structure features pairs of items that are connected by a particular type of relationship. Figure 5.4 (page 74) shows an analogy knowledge map.

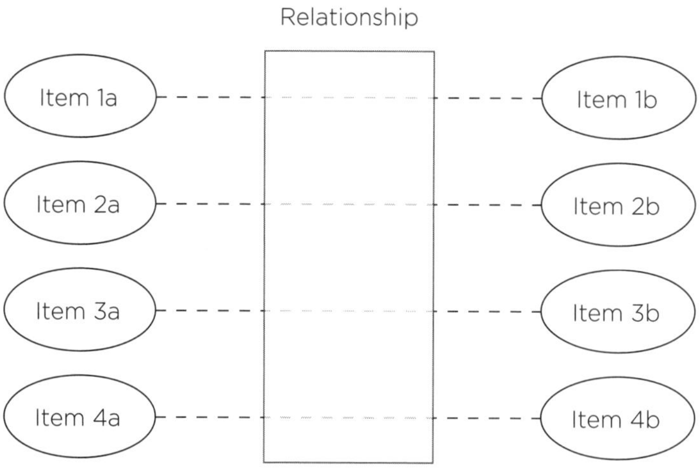

Figure 5.4: Analogy knowledge map.

Visit ***go.SolutionTree.com/instruction*** *for a free reproducible version of this figure.*

For example, a movie might affect your emotions in the way that a roller coaster affects your body. In this case, there is a causal relationship between the movie and your emotions and the roller coaster and your body; one causes the other to feel shaken up and disoriented. Following are nine types of relationships that an analogy might feature as well as examples of each.

1. **Function:** As a sword is the weapon of a warrior, the pen is the weapon of a writer; as a detective investigates crimes, a doctor diagnoses diseases.
2. **Time and sequence:** As a caterpillar emerges from its cocoon, she stepped out of her comfort zone.
3. **Synonyms:** Twelve is to a dozen as three is to a trio.
4. **Antonyms:** Hot is to cold as day is to night.
5. **Shared category:** Knife is to fork as pen is to pencil.
6. **Category and member:** Eating utensil is to fork as writing utensil is to pencil.
7. **Size:** Ant is to elephant as cottage is to mansion.
8. **Whole-part:** Foot is to human as wheel is to car.
9. **Cause:** Movie is to emotions as roller coaster is to body.

To analyze an analogy, the student might begin by identifying the relationship being represented and write it in the center box of the analogy knowledge map. For example, if the student was asked to analyze the sports analogy *pitcher is to catcher as quarterback is to receiver*, he might begin by identifying a function relationship in which the first element throws something and the second element catches it. The student would then write *pitcher*, *catcher*, *quarterback*, and *receiver* in the circles marked item 1a, 1b, 2a, and 2b. Finally, the student could compose additional analogies for the same type of function relationship by adding terms to the circles marked 3a, 3b, 4a, and 4b (for example, a *bowler* and *wicket-keeper* have the same relationship in cricket). Creating analogies for vocabulary terms stimulates students' creative thinking, which deepens and refines students' knowledge about and understanding of terms.

Finally, comparing texts is one of the topics Simms (2016) identifies as critical to reading instruction. A teacher might use the comparison knowledge map to structure such tasks. A *comparison* structure uses several characteristics to compare several items. Figure 5.5 shows the comparison knowledge map.

	Item	Item	Item	Similarities	Differences
Characteristic					
Characteristic					
Characteristic					

Summary

Figure 5.5: Comparison knowledge map.

Visit ***go.SolutionTree.com/instruction*** *for a free reproducible version of this figure.*

For example, students could compare versions of the Cinderella story from around the world.

- **African:** *Mufaro's Beautiful Daughters: An African Tale* by John Steptoe
- **Native American:** *The Rough-Face Girl* by Rafe Martin
- **Asian:** *Yeh-Shen: A Cinderella Story From China* by Ai-Ling Louie
- **European:** *Tattercoats: An Old English Tale* by Flora Annie Steel
- **Central American:** *Adelita: A Mexican Cinderella Story* by Tomie dePaola

Students can compare these different versions (which would be the items in figure 5.5) according to characteristics such as:

- Cinderella's family members
- Mistreatment of Cinderella
- Important ball or dance
- Role of a shoe or slipper
- Identity of the prince
- Ending of the story

Using the comparison knowledge map, as opposed to simpler visuals (such as a Venn diagram), prompts students to make defensible, substantive comparisons based on concrete characteristics.

Figure 5.6 presents the self-rating scale for examining similarities and differences.

Score	Description
4: Innovating	I adapt behaviors and create new strategies for unique student needs and situations.
3: Applying	I engage students in examining similarities and differences, and I monitor the extent to which students deepen their knowledge.
2: Developing	I engage students in examining similarities and differences, but I do not monitor the effect on students.
1: Beginning	I use the strategies and behaviors associated with this element incorrectly or with parts missing.
0: Not Using	I am unaware of strategies and behaviors associated with this element.

Figure 5.6: Self-rating scale for element 10—Examining similarities and differences.

Element 11: Examining Errors in Reasoning

Examining errors in reasoning looks different depending on the grade level of reading instruction. At lower grade levels, examining errors might focus on errors of word recognition. At upper grade levels, students might focus on analyzing the claims, evidence, and reasoning in texts to identify weak or unsupported claims and explain why they may not be credible.

Relative to word recognition, there are a number of approaches a teacher can take if a student makes a word recognition error. Foorman and colleagues (2016) recommend initially asking students if the word they produced by sounding out "makes sense" or is a "real word" (p. 25). To go deeper, a teacher can analyze what led the student to read a word wrong. Miscue analysis (Goodman, 1965, 1967) involves figuring out what type of cues a student was using when he or she read a word incorrectly. There are three types of cues that students might rely on when reading words (McKenna & Picard, 2006).

1. **The letters within the word:** If a student says "pony" when the text says *horse*, the student has failed to examine the letters within the word (instead, the student is likely paying attention to semantic cues).
2. **The semantic content of the word's context:** If a student says, "The cowboy rode a house" when the text says *The cowboy rode a horse*, the student has failed to pay attention to the semantic content of the word's context (instead, he or she is likely paying attention to letter and syntax cues, albeit imperfectly).
3. **The syntax of the sentence in which the word is found:** If a student says, "The cowboy rode a hopping" when the text says *The cowboy rode a horse*, the student has failed to pay attention to the syntax of the sentence (instead, he or she is likely paying attention to letter cues, albeit imperfectly).

As we explain in chapter 1, the best cues for students to rely on are those the letters in a word provide. When a student uses the letters of a word to create possible pronunciations and then searches his or her mental lexicon for a word that matches one of the pronunciations (phonological recoding), the student learns a great deal of information implicitly about the English orthographic system. Semantic and syntactic cues can support the use of letter cues, but readers should use them to confirm, not identify, a word.

Relative to fluency, teachers may notice that students who feel pressure to read quickly adopt a guessing strategy when faced with an unfamiliar word. As explained previously, the benefits of phonological recoding (and the drawbacks of guessing) make it imperative that teachers prevent such a habit. Foorman and colleagues (2016) recommend that "if students adopt a guessing strategy to identify words, rather than taking the time to use the strategies they have been taught, [the teacher should] temporarily reduce or suspend fluency practice, and increase activities designed to support word-reading accuracy" (p. 37). Teachers might use a strategy called echo reading in such a situation. *Echo reading* involves the teacher reading a section of text aloud and the student then reading the same section of text aloud. Slightly more advanced is *alternated reading*, in which the teacher and the student take turns reading a continuous section of text.

The focus of step 5 of the six-step vocabulary process is that students discuss terms with each other. Often, such discussions highlight errors in understanding about terms that students might have. For example, a student who thinks that *disinterested* means *uninterested* might realize in a conversation with a peer that it actually means *unbiased*. Whole-class discussions can also be helpful. Stahl and Nagy (2006) explain, "Children benefit from the contributions of other children. . . . In open discussions, children are often able to construct a good idea of a word's meaning from the partial knowledge of the entire class" (p. 69). One activity Marzano and colleagues (2015) describe that can stimulate both whole-class and partner discussions of terms is semantic mapping.

To begin the semantic mapping process, the teacher chooses a term to be the focus of the activity—for example, *figurative language*. This should be something that the teacher introduced previously that students have described and depicted in their vocabulary notebooks, both linguistically and nonlinguistically. Ask students to generate a list of words associated with the focus term. For *figurative language*, students might come up with the following list.

- Alliteration
- Allusion
- Analogy
- Euphemism
- Figure of speech
- Hyperbole
- Idiom
- Imagery
- Irony
- Metaphor
- Onomatopoeia
- Oxymoron
- Paradox
- Personification
- Proverb
- Simile
- Symbolism

Then, students work individually or in small groups to generate categories that the terms fit into and create a semantic map that shows how the terms relate to each other, as shown in figure 5.7.

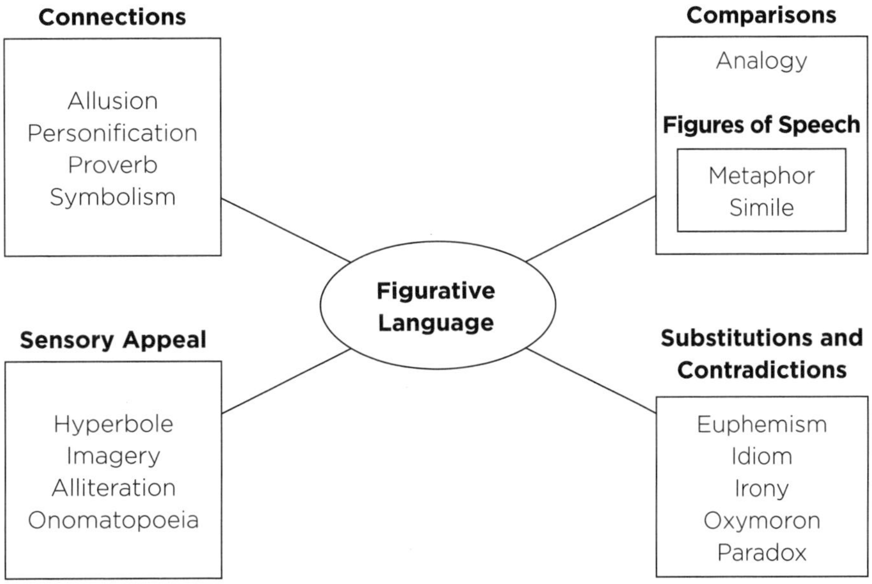

Figure 5.7: Semantic map for *figurative language*.

As we show in figure 5.7, students first created four categories for the terms they generated: *connections*, *comparisons*, *sensory appeal*, and *substitutions and contradictions*. Then they sorted each term into the appropriate category. In some cases, a term was related to a category through another term; for example, *metaphor* and *simile* are figures of speech, which is a type of comparison. The semantic map in figure 5.7 makes this indirect relationship clear. Finally, students explain their semantic maps. If they worked individually to create them, students might explain their maps to a partner. If they worked in groups, each group might pair with another group and take turns explaining their work to each other.

In brief, semantic mapping involves four steps.

1. Choose a focus term.
2. Ask students to generate a list of words associated with the focus term.
3. Have students work individually or in groups to create categories for the generated words and a semantic map that shows how the terms relate to each other and the focus term.
4. Prompt students to explain their semantic maps to their peers.

The final step of this process is critical. Steven A. Stahl and Sandra J. Vancil (1986) find that constructing semantic maps without discussing them is not effective. To facilitate discussions of semantic maps, or even individual terms, teachers can use a variety of strategies that actively engage students and allow them to practice and deepen their knowledge of new terms.

Relative to comprehension, students can use the reasoning knowledge maps to examine the reasoning found in texts. There are two types of reasoning structures: inductive and deductive. *Inductive reasoning* structures begin with a set of concepts (from the same category) and a series of questions (about the concepts). Figure 5.8 shows the inductive reasoning knowledge map.

Category of Concepts	Question	Question	Question	**Conclusions About Questions**
Concept	Observation	Observation	Observation	
Concept	Observation	Observation	Observation	
Concept	Observation	Observation	Observation	
Conclusions About Concepts				**Claim**

Figure 5.8: Inductive reasoning knowledge map.

Visit ***go.SolutionTree.com/instruction*** *for a free reproducible version of this figure.*

The goal of inductive reasoning is to make a claim. Students apply each question to each concept and write their observations in the appropriate cells. Then they draw conclusions about each concept, conclusions about each question, and finally formulate a claim. For example, a student reading a narrative text might select three characters to insert in the concept spaces. For questions, the student might ask about the characters' backgrounds, motives, and actions relative to a particular event in the text. After filling out the knowledge map, the student could generate conclusions and finally a claim about the characters relative to the target event.

Deductive reasoning structures begin with a situation and a possibly applicable generalization or principle. Under certain conditions, a student can use the generalization or principle to predict or make a claim about what will happen in the situation. Figure 5.9 shows the deductive reasoning knowledge map.

Situation

Possibly Applicable Generalization or Principle	
Conditions That Must Be Met for Generalization or Principle to Apply	**Condition Met?**
Condition	
Condition	
Condition	

Claim

Figure 5.9: Deductive reasoning knowledge map.

Visit ***go.SolutionTree.com/instruction*** *for a free reproducible version of this figure.*

For example, while reading a text, students might stop and use the deductive reasoning knowledge map to predict what will happen next, using their understanding of archetypal plot patterns and knowledge of the author's other works.

Figure 5.10 contains the self-rating scale for element 11, examining errors in reasoning.

Score	Description
4: Innovating	I adapt behaviors and create new strategies for unique student needs and situations.
3: Applying	When content is informational, I engage students in activities that require them to examine their own reasoning or the logic of information as presented to them, and I monitor the extent to which students are deepening their knowledge.
2: Developing	When content is informational, I engage students in activities that require them to examine their own reasoning or the logic of information as presented to them, but I do not monitor the effect on students.
1: Beginning	I use the strategies and behaviors associated with this element incorrectly or with parts missing.
0: Not Using	I am unaware of strategies and behaviors associated with this element.

Figure 5.10: Self-rating scale for element 11—Examining errors in reasoning.

GUIDING QUESTIONS FOR CURRICULUM DESIGN

This design question focuses on practicing and deepening lessons: *After presenting content, how will I design and deliver lessons that help students deepen their understanding and develop fluency in skills and processes?* The following questions, which align to each of the elements in this chapter, can guide teachers to plan instruction.

- **Element 9:** How will I help students engage in structured practice?

- **Element 10:** How will I help students examine similarities and differences?

- **Element 11:** How will I help students examine errors in reasoning?

Summary

Conducting practicing and deepening lessons involves three elements: (1) structured practice sessions, (2) examining similarities and differences, and (3) examining errors in reasoning. In the reading classroom, this practice allows students to move ahead through the phases of word recognition and to increase their reading fluency. Students deepen their understanding of vocabulary terms as they engage in word-related activities, discussions, and games and enhance their understanding of comprehension topics through think-alouds, textual comparisons, and textual analysis.

CHAPTER 6

Conducting Knowledge Application Lessons

The fifth design area in *The New Art and Science of Teaching* framework involves activities that require students to apply the content they have learned to unique situations. Specifically, as students engage in cognitively complex tasks (element 12), teachers provide resources and guidance (element 13) to help them generate and defend claims (element 14). Here we describe how each element of this design area might manifest in a reading classroom.

Element 12: Engaging Students in Cognitively Complex Tasks

Reading itself is a cognitively complex task. Each time a student encounters a new text, he or she must apply learning in that unique situation to make meaning. However, reading is also a skill necessary to perform many of the types of cognitively complex tasks that *The New Art and Science of Teaching* describes: decision making, problem solving, investigation, experimentation, and invention. Here, we discuss the reading-related factors that teachers should take into account when engaging students in cognitively complex tasks that require students to read texts.

Relative to word recognition, teachers must consider the level of text that a student can read independently and ensure that students have access to appropriately leveled texts on topics related to their cognitively complex tasks. In a review, Jennifer P. Cheatham and Jill H. Allor (2012) point out that, for students who are still acquiring the alphabetic principle, decodable texts (which use regularly spelled words that typically follow a distinct and limited set of letter-sound relationships or spelling patterns) are a "key characteristic in ensuring that students develop the alphabetic principle that is necessary for successful reading" (p. 2242). Purcell-Gates and colleagues (2016) agree, stating, "Texts that provide fewer multisyllabic words and repeat them more frequently may be more facilitative of students' word-reading development" (p. 1249). However, some teachers have concerns that decodable texts, which the National Reading Panel (NICHD, 2000) describes as often featuring "pigs doing jigs and cats in hats," may be "too stilted and boring" to cultivate excitement about reading in students (chapter 2, p. 137). To address such concerns, and in cases where appropriate decodable texts are not available on a particular topic, Foorman and colleagues (2016) suggest that if a book contains sound-spelling patterns or other complex words that students will not likely be able to successfully sound out, the teacher should:

> Identify a few [words] that are repeated often within the text, are meaningful, and that students will encounter in future texts or settings. Introduce these non-decodable words to students in advance of reading the new text, including their spelling and meaning. Teaching non-decodable words expands students' reading opportunities beyond decodable texts. (p. 30)

One of the advantages of cognitively complex tasks is that they require students to engage in wide reading, which has benefits for fluency. *Wide reading* is similar to repeated reading in that it involves reading a text multiple times. However, it is different from repeated reading because it involves fewer repetitions and more texts. Rasinski and colleagues (2011) explain:

> Wide reading involves reading a range of new books with fewer repetitions than [are] found in traditional implementations of repeated reading practice. In repeated reading practice, a single text may be read and reread for multiple days. In wide reading, repeated reading of text is usually confined to a single day, lesson or sitting before moving onto a new book the next day. Wide reading, like repeated reading, also incorporates assisted reading facilitated by teachers and peers into the lesson structure. (p. 297)

Kuhn (2000, 2004, 2005; Kuhn et al., 2006) finds that wide reading may have advantages over repeated reading. Specifically, he found that students who engage in wide reading experience the same improvements as students who engage in repeated reading relative to word recognition and prosody, but the students who engage in wide reading demonstrate larger gains in comprehension. Foorman and colleagues (2016) recommend a balance between the two approaches, since repeated reading also has advantages over wide reading:

> To support oral reading fluency, give students assignments for both repeated reading—in which they read the same text multiple times for mastery—and wide reading—in which they read many different texts. In repeated reading, students are less likely to practice incorrect word reading or to guess unknown words. They are repeatedly exposed to the same words, which should help students recognize them more efficiently. Wide reading, on the other hand, exposes students to more diverse vocabulary and word knowledge. (p. 36)

In sum, giving students multiple opportunities to engage with a wide variety of authentic texts supports development in many reading-related areas, including fluency.

Relative to vocabulary, a specific type of cognitively complex task is particularly relevant: *definitional investigation*. In general, the goal of any investigation task is to clear up confusion about ideas or events. In definitional investigation (Marzano & Pickering, 1997), students construct a precise definition for a concept without a generally agreed-upon definition (such as *civil disobedience*). Students might use the following questions to drive their investigation of a term or concept.

- What are the important features of this term?
- What are the defining characteristics of this term?

Teachers can provide students with a process to guide them as they engage in definitional investigation. Such a process might involve the following six steps.

1. **Clarify the topic:** What term, idea, or concept do I want to explain?
2. **Examine information:** What do people already know about this term, idea, or concept?
3. **Summarize what is known:** What is the best way to express what is already known?
4. **Explain confusions or contradictions:** What is unclear about this term, idea, or concept?
5. **Develop a resolution:** How can I clear up the confusion or contradiction?
6. **Provide support and evidence for your resolution:** Why is my solution the best one?

Teachers can ask secondary students to identify the topic and find information for their investigation independently. For elementary students, the teacher might provide topics for them to choose from and relevant information for them to use during their investigation.

Finally, relative to comprehension, many cognitively complex tasks require students to capture and organize information, either to solve a problem or to analyze a system of variables or interacting factors (such as in investigation, experimental inquiry, or invention tasks). In such cases, the knowledge maps for problem solving and systems analysis can be quite useful.

A *simple problem-solution* structure presents a problem and several potential solutions, indicating the best solution. Figure 6.1 shows the simple problem-solution knowledge map.

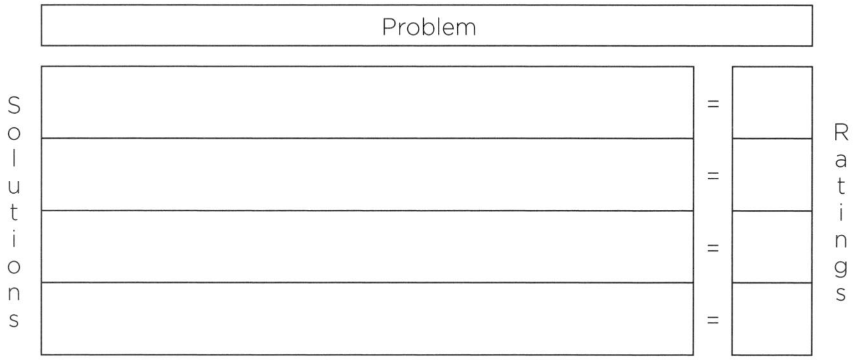

Figure 6.1: Simple problem-solution knowledge map.

Visit ***go.SolutionTree.com/instruction*** *for a free reproducible version of this figure.*

A classic fiction example of a simple problem-solution structure is *The Three Little Pigs*, as we show in figure 6.2.

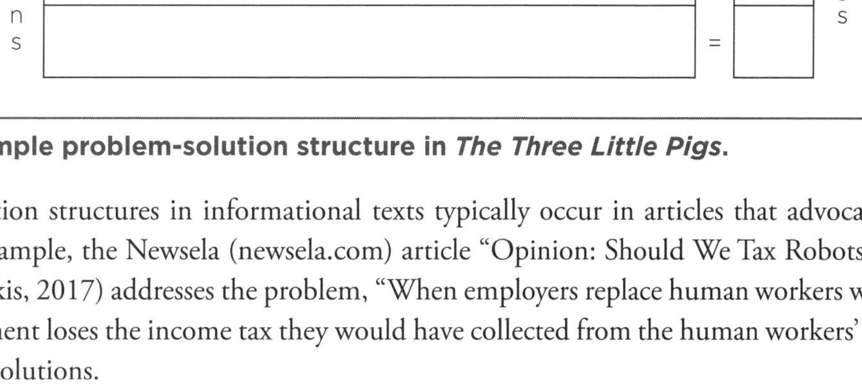

Figure 6.2: Simple problem-solution structure in *The Three Little Pigs*.

Problem-solution structures in informational texts typically occur in articles that advocate for a specific solution. For example, the Newsela (newsela.com) article "Opinion: Should We Tax Robots That Take Our Jobs?" (Varoufakis, 2017) addresses the problem, "When employers replace human workers with robot workers, the government loses the income tax they would have collected from the human workers' wages." It offers three potential solutions.

1. Estimate what a human worker would make doing the same job as a robot and charge the employer a tax based on the robot's hypothetical salary.
2. Charge employers a one-time sales tax when they buy a robot to replace a human.

3. Transfer some ownership of a company that uses robots instead of human workers to the government and use profits from the government-owned part of the company to replace the income tax that would have been collected from a human worker.

The author of the article, Yanis Varoufakis, a former finance minister of Greece and now a professor of economics at the University of Athens, advocates for solution three.

A *complex problem-solution* structure adds criteria that are used to evaluate the solutions. Figure 6.3 shows the complex problem-solution knowledge map.

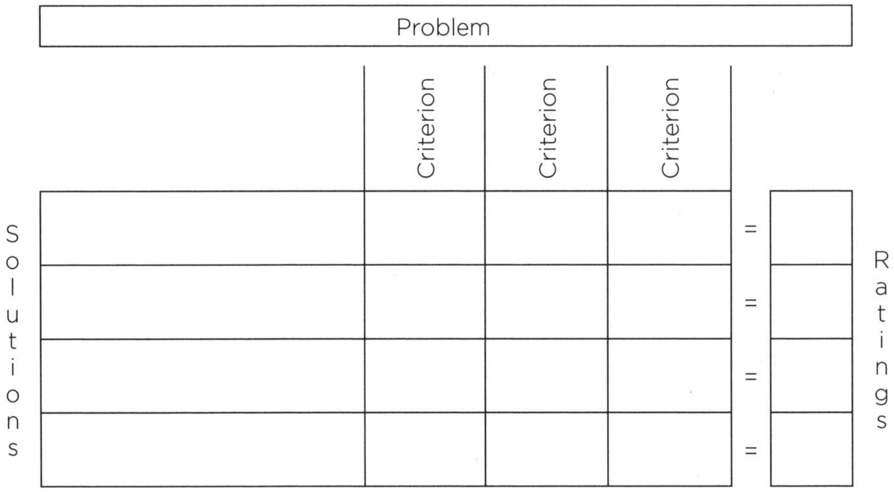

Figure 6.3: Complex problem-solution knowledge map.

Visit ***go.SolutionTree.com/instruction*** *for a free reproducible version of this figure.*

For example, the Newsela article "Environmentalists Are Not in Favor of Government-Planned Fish Farms" (Associated Press, 2017) addresses the problem of commercial fishing threatening fish populations worldwide. It offers three potential solutions.

1. Establish man-made fish farms on land.
2. Establish fish farms close to shore using natural and man-made elements.
3. Establish off-shore fish farms in the open ocean.

It also offers criteria for judging each solution.

- Impact on the environment
- Impact on the U.S. economy
- Legislative approval

An *advanced problem-solution* structure weights each of the criteria. Figure 6.4 shows the advanced problem-solution knowledge map.

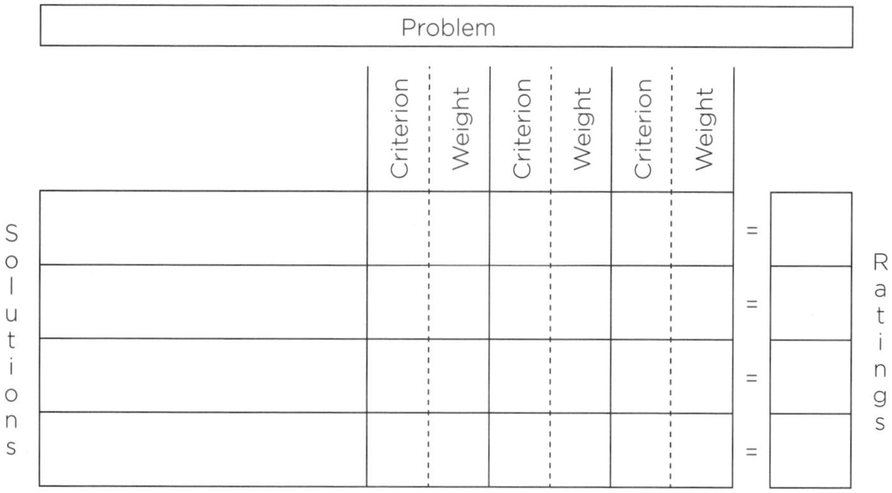

Figure 6.4: Advanced problem-solution knowledge map.

Visit ***go.SolutionTree.com/instruction*** *for a free reproducible version of this figure.*

In the previous example addressing the threat of commercial fishing to worldwide fish populations, a student might assign the following weights to each of the criteria.

- Impact on the environment—2 (somewhat important)
- Impact on the U.S. economy—1 (least important)
- Legislative approval—3 (most important)

Using maps such as these can structure students' cognitively complex tasks and help them arrive at substantive solutions and conclusions.

Cognitively complex tasks might also involve analyzing systems. There are four structures that fall under the category of systems: (1) process, (2) cycle, (3) flowchart, and (4) complex system. A *process* is a set of steps that does not repeat. For example, most recipes are processes in which the cook follows a set of steps to arrive at a final product. Figure 6.5 shows the process system knowledge map.

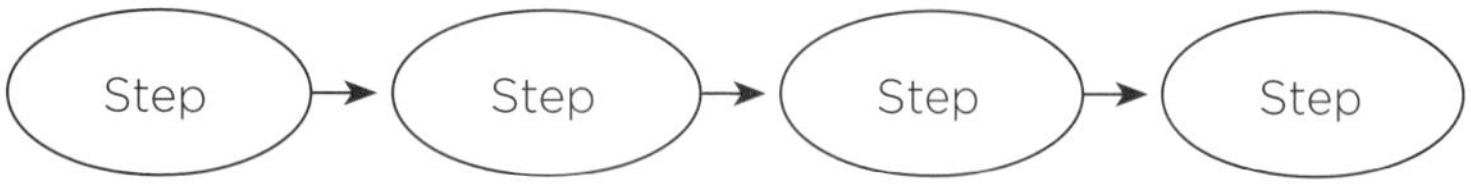

Figure 6.5: Process system knowledge map.

Visit ***go.SolutionTree.com/instruction*** *for a free reproducible version of this figure.*

A *cycle* is a set of steps that repeats. For example, the life stages of many insects occur in cycles. A butterfly lays an egg, it hatches, the caterpillar eats and then forms a chrysalis, emerges as a butterfly, lays an egg, and the cycle repeats. Eric Carle's (1969) *The Very Hungry Caterpillar* is a good book to illustrate this for preschool or early elementary learners. Figure 6.6 (page 86) shows the cycle system knowledge map.

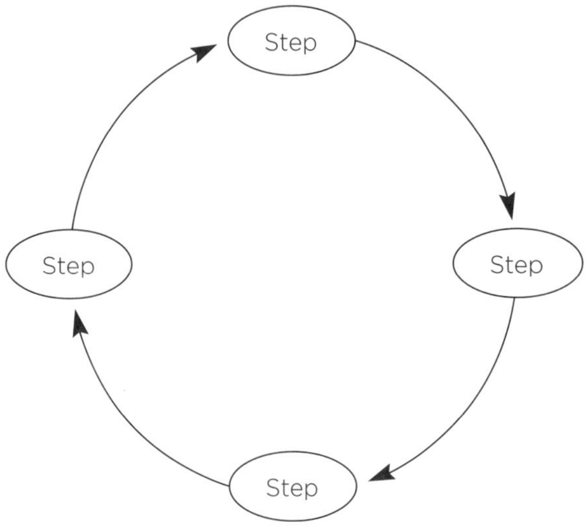

Figure 6.6: Cycle system knowledge map.

Visit ***go.SolutionTree.com/instruction*** *for a free reproducible version of this figure.*

Flowcharts keep track of a sequence of decisions that lead to other decisions. Figure 6.7 shows the flowchart system knowledge map.

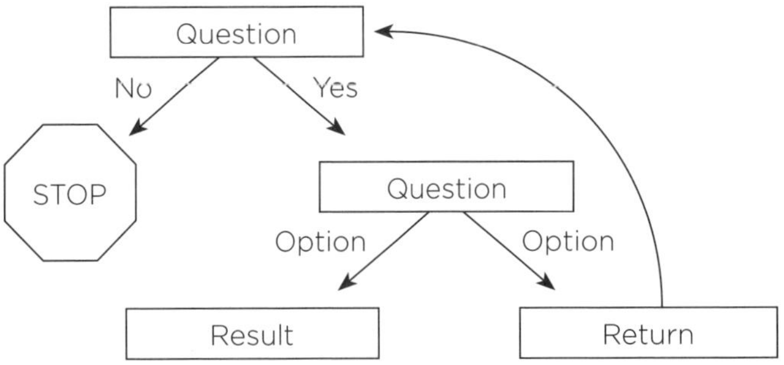

Figure 6.7: Flowchart system knowledge map.

Visit ***go.SolutionTree.com/instruction*** *for a free reproducible version of this figure.*

For example, students can use a flowchart to find errors in an argument. A student might begin by asking, "Is the information being presented important or trying to persuade me?"

If it is, the student could analyze it for errors. If it isn't, he or she might exit the analysis; if information is unimportant or not intended to persuade, analyzing it for errors might not be a smart use of time. Additional steps might include asking the following questions.

- "Does anything seem wrong about this information? If no, stop analysis."
- "If yes, what type of error might be present?"

Each type of error could have its own flowchart to help students isolate exactly where the faulty reasoning of an argument lies.

A *complex system* involves multiple parts that interact with and affect each other. Figure 6.8 shows the complex system knowledge map.

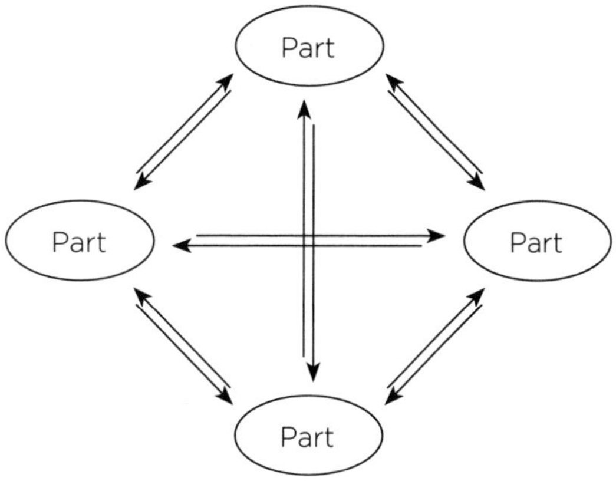

Figure 6.8: Complex system knowledge map.

Visit ***go.SolutionTree.com/instruction*** *for a free reproducible version of this figure.*

Complex systems appear in such places as:

- A nuclear reactor
- The Earth's climate
- The human brain
- Ecosystems
- Cells
- Cities
- Businesses
- Plot structures

Analyzing a system involves figuring out what will happen to other parts if one part is modified or eliminated. An entertaining example to illustrate a complex system is to think about the characters in the fairy tale *Cinderella*: stepmother, stepsisters, prince, and Cinderella herself. Students can use a system structure to diagram how they all feel toward each other.

Figure 6.9 contains the self-rating scale for element 12, engaging students in cognitively complex tasks.

Score	Description
4: Innovating	I adapt behaviors and create new strategies for unique student needs and situations.
3: Applying	I engage students in cognitively complex tasks, and I monitor the extent to which my actions affect students.
2: Developing	I engage students in cognitively complex tasks, but I do not monitor the effect on students.
1: Beginning	I use the strategies and behaviors associated with this element incorrectly or with parts missing.
0: Not Using	I am unaware of strategies and behaviors associated with this element.

Figure 6.9: Self-rating scale for element 12—Engaging students in cognitively complex tasks.

Element 13: Providing Resources and Guidance

Providing resources and guidance in the reading classroom involves the teacher coming alongside students as they work on cognitively complex tasks to provide the information and support students need. Relative to word recognition, if a student is having trouble reading a text, the teacher might be there to support the student's phonological recoding. Foorman and colleagues (2016) recommend directly teaching and then guiding students through the following three-step word-analysis strategy when students are stuck on a word.

1. Identify the word parts and vowels.
2. Say the different parts of the word.
3. Repeat the full sentence in which the word appears. (p. 27)

If the word-analysis strategy does not work because a word contains sound-spelling patterns the student does not yet know, or if the word is irregular, Foorman and colleagues (2016) recommend simply telling the student the word and asking him or her to repeat it and reread the sentence with the word in it to make sure it makes sense. Again, Foorman and colleagues caution teachers against encouraging students to use unproductive strategies, such as guessing, to figure out unknown words:

> The panel discourages teachers from allowing students to use guessing strategies to identify unfamiliar words, because these will not be effective with more-advanced texts. For example, discourage students from guessing unknown words using beginning letters or pictures. The panel also cautions against giving hints that encourage students to guess a word as if answering a riddle (e.g., "What do you call the place where you live?" if students cannot make sense of the letters *h-o-m-e*). (p. 34)

It is important to remember that the process of using phonological recoding to figure out a word facilitates students' implicit learning of orthographic knowledge. Therefore, teachers should always encourage students to use that strategy first, and to confirm their identification of the word using contextual, semantic, or syntactic clues.

Relative to fluency, students may need to read texts for their cognitively complex tasks that are simply too challenging for them to read fluently enough to support comprehension. In such cases, teachers can help students locate alternative media, such as sound recordings or videos, that will allow students to access the information they need even if they are unable to read the appropriate text. If using sound or video recordings of a text, students should follow along with the words of the text whenever possible.

Often, during cognitively complex tasks, students will encounter words (especially discipline-specific tier three terms) whose meanings they do not know. To prepare students for such situations, teachers can show students how to figure out word meanings from context. Michael F. Graves (2006) articulates a four-step strategy for such an endeavor that we describe in table 6.1.

Table 6.1: Four-Step Strategy for Inferring Word Meanings From Context

Step	Actions
1. Read and Question	Read carefully. Frequently ask yourself, "Does this make sense?"
2. Slow Advance	Notice when you don't know the meaning of a word and slow down. Read that sentence at least once more, looking for clues.
3. Stop and Rewind	If necessary, go back and reread the preceding sentence, looking for clues that help you figure out what the word might mean.
4. Read and Question	When you figure out what the word might mean, substitute your guess for the difficult word and see if it makes sense. If it does, keep on reading. If it doesn't, stop and rewind, and try again.

Source: Adapted from Graves, 2006.

Visit ***go.SolutionTree.com/instruction*** *for a free reproducible version of this table.*

Finally, some of the most powerful guidance a teacher can give students as they seek to comprehend texts related to their cognitively complex tasks is to ask them to determine the structure of the texts they are reading. We describe three of the most common text structures—(1) description, (2) sequence, and (3) causation—and their corresponding knowledge maps here.

Description structures list characteristics of an item. Items can include people, places, objects, animals, or processes. Figure 6.10 shows the description knowledge map.

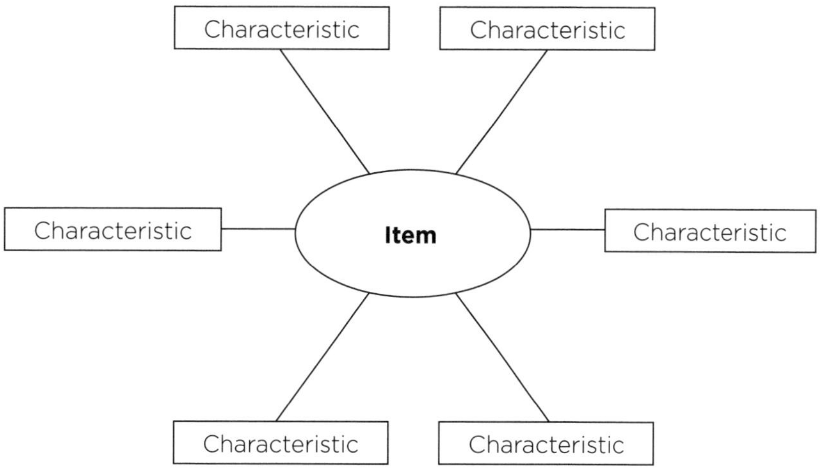

Figure 6.10: Description knowledge map.

Visit ***go.SolutionTree.com/instruction*** *for a free reproducible version of this figure.*

In narratives, description structures often feature sensory details that describe what something looks, sounds, smells, tastes, or feels like. In informational texts, description structures usually give facts about an item. For example, in Gail Gibbons's (1997) *The Moon Book*, she uses a description structure to share the following facts about the moon.

- It is the brightest and biggest light in the night sky.
- It is the only moon of Earth.
- It is about 238,900 miles away.
- It reflects the sun's light.
- It is about one quarter the size of Earth.
- It is made of rock and dust.
- It has no air or signs of life.
- In ancient times, people believed the moon was a god or goddess:
    - Romans—Diana
    - Greeks—Selene
    - Native American tribes—Sibling of the sun god

Students might use description structures to collect information related to the topic of their cognitively complex task.

A *simple sequence* structure lists events in order. Most narratives use an overall sequence structure. Figure 6.11 shows the simple sequence knowledge map.

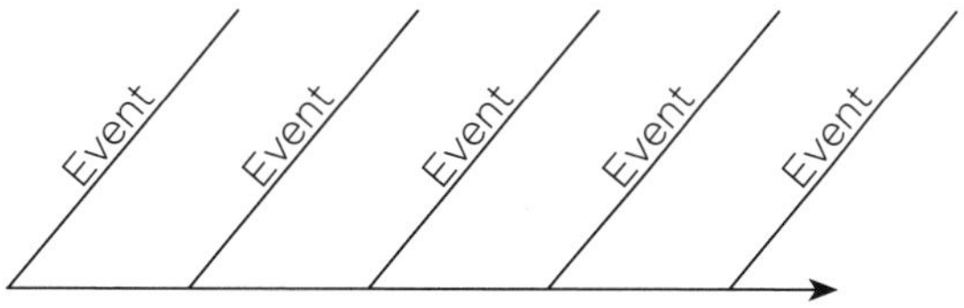

Figure 6.11: Simple sequence knowledge map.

Visit ***go.SolutionTree.com/instruction*** *for a free reproducible version of this figure.*

Maurice Sendak's (1963) *Where the Wild Things Are* features a simple sequence structure. The book recounts the following series of events.

- Max makes "mischief of one kind and another."
- Max's mother calls him "WILD THING."
- Max says, "I'LL EAT YOU UP."
- Max is sent to bed without supper.
- A forest grows in Max's room, and an ocean with a private boat appears.
- Max sails off "through night and day and in and out of weeks and almost over a year to where the wild things are."
- Max tames the wild things and becomes king.
- The wild rumpus happens.
- Max is lonely.
- He sails home.
- Supper is waiting, and it is still hot.

Sequence structures also show up in informational texts. Often, an informational text will tell about a later event in a sequence and then go back and fill in earlier events (which also relates to causation structures; see pages 92–94). For example, Tanya Lee Stone's (2015) *The House That Jane Built*, which describes how Jane Addams founded Hull House in Chicago in 1889, features the following sequence of events, the first of which is presented out of order.

- Jane, a wealthy young woman, moves into one of the poorest neighborhoods in Chicago.
- At six years old, Jane goes on a trip with her father and notices different social classes.
- She vows to find a way to help poor people.
- She demonstrates bravery (exploring caves, finding owl nests) as she grows up.
- She demonstrates intellect as she grows up.
- She goes to college.
- Her father dies, and Jane feels lost.
- Jane travels to London and sees poor people again.
- She visits Toynbee Hall, a settlement house in London (where rich and poor people live together in a house).
- She decides to build a settlement house in Chicago.
- She opens Hull House.

A *complex sequence* structure organizes a series of events occurring in different places or from different points of view. Figure 6.12 shows the complex sequence knowledge map.

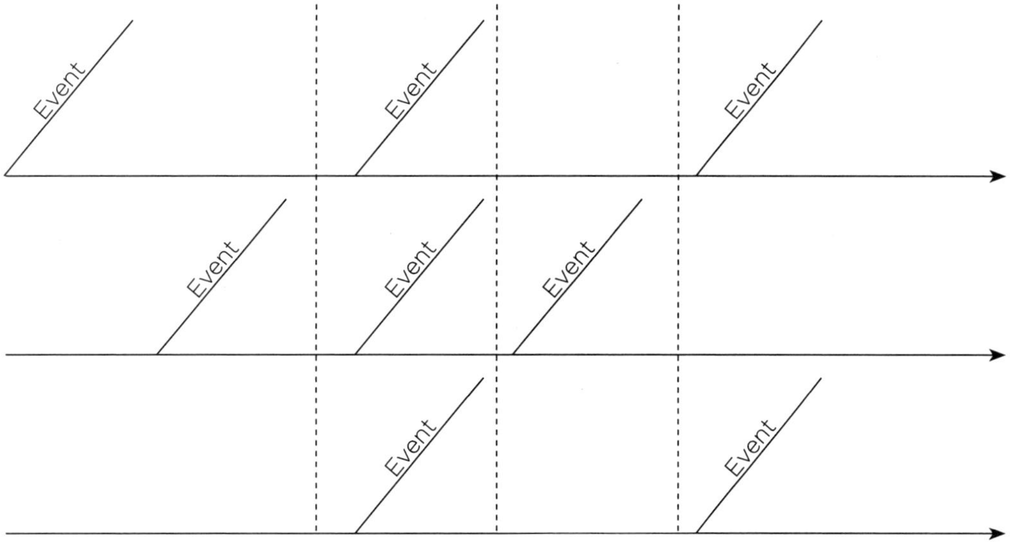

Figure 6.12: Complex sequence knowledge map.

*Visit **go.SolutionTree.com/instruction** for a free reproducible version of this figure.*

A fiction example is William Faulkner's (1929/1984) *The Sound and the Fury*. It tells the same story four times, from four characters' points of view.

1. Benjy
2. Quentin
3. Jason
4. Dilsey

An article about the events of World War II might describe what occurred in North America, Asia, Europe, and Africa during the war, as shown in figure 6.13.

	North America	Asia	Europe	Africa
September 1939			Germany invades Poland, starting World War II. Britain and France declare war on Germany.	
April 1940			Germany invades Norway and Denmark.	
May 1940			Germany invades Belgium and the Netherlands.	
July 1940			Germany begins bombing Britain.	
June 1941			Germany invades the Soviet Union.	
December 1941	Japan bombs Pearl Harbor. The U.S. declares war on Japan.			

Figure 6.13: Events of World War II.

continued →

	North America	Asia	Europe	Africa
February 1942		Japan captures Singapore.		
May 1942		Japan captures the Philippines and Burma.		
June 1942		The tide turns—the Allies defeat Japan in the Battle of Midway.		
February 1943			German troops surrender in Stalingrad, USSR.	
May 1943				Axis troops in northern Africa surrender.
September 1943			Italy surrenders.	
November 1943		U.S. forces invade Tarawa.		
June 1944			D-Day: Allied troops land in France and begin invasion.	
October 1944		Japan's navy is defeated near the Philippines.		
December 1944			Germans fight back in the Battle of the Bulge.	
March 1945		Allied troops capture Iwo Jima.		
May 1945			Germany surrenders, ending World War II in Europe.	
August 1945		U.S. drops atomic bombs on Hiroshima and Nagasaki.		
September 1945		Japan signs surrender agreement, ending war.		

A complex sequence organizer could reveal that most of the events of World War II happened in Asia and Europe.

Finally, causation structures show the causes and effects of events. A *simple causation* structure shows the causes and effects of a single event. Figure 6.14 shows the simple causation knowledge map.

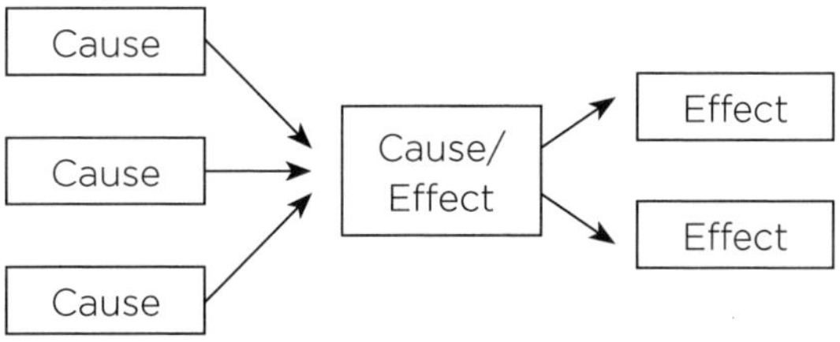

Figure 6.14: Simple causation knowledge map.

Visit ***go.SolutionTree.com/instruction*** *for a free reproducible version of this figure.*

As we mentioned previously, Tanya Lee Stone (2015) embeds a causation structure in the overall sequence structure of *The House That Jane Built*, as we show in figure 6.15.

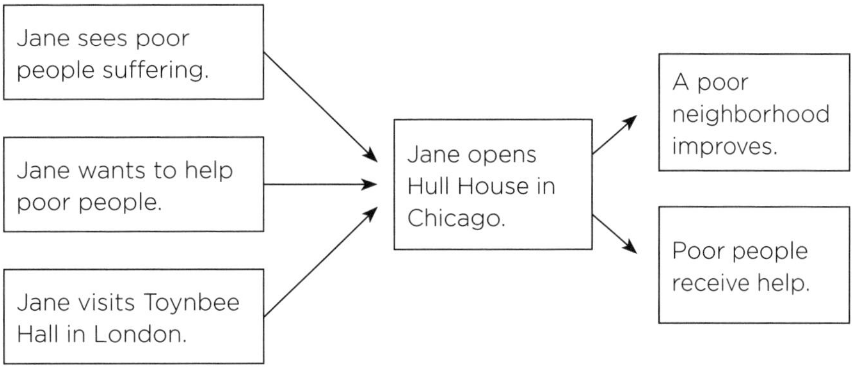

Figure 6.15: Causation structure in The House That Jane Built (Stone, 2015).

A *complex causation* structure involves extra causes and effects that aren't part of the main causal chain but branch off from it. Figure 6.16 shows the complex causation knowledge map.

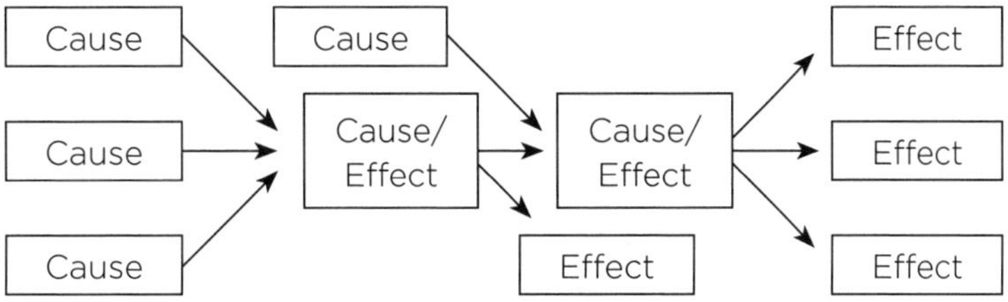

Figure 6.16: Complex causation knowledge map.

Visit ***go.SolutionTree.com/instruction*** *for a free reproducible version of this figure.*

For example, a text describing causes and effects of the stock market crash of 1929 might use a complex causation structure to organize the events, as we show in figure 6.17 (page 94).

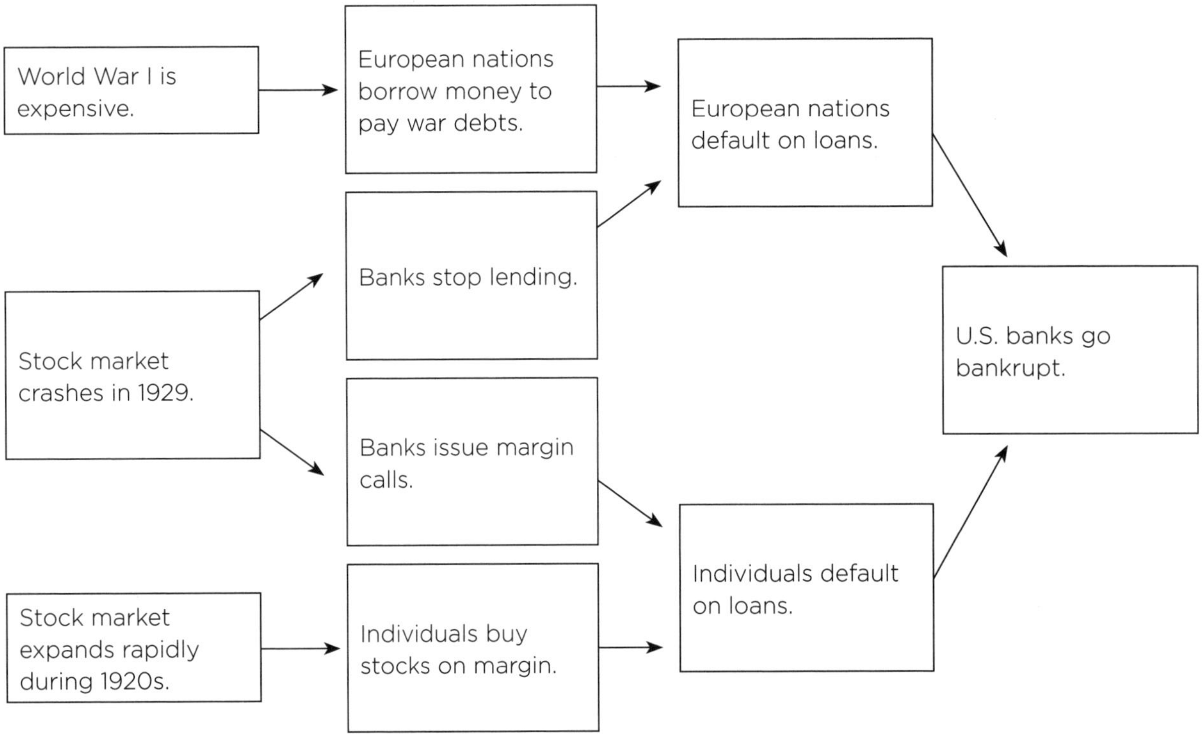

Figure 6.17: Causation structure of events surrounding the stock market crash of 1929.

*Visit **go.SolutionTree.com/instruction** for a free reproducible version of this figure.*

Students can use causation knowledge maps to keep track of causal information related to events during their cognitively complex tasks.

We depict the self-rating scale for element 13, providing resources and guidance, in figure 6.18.

Score	Description
4: Innovating	I adapt behaviors and create new strategies for unique student needs and situations.
3: Applying	I provide resources and guidance, and I monitor the extent to which my actions affect students' performance.
2: Developing	I provide resources and guidance, but I do not monitor the effect on students.
1: Beginning	I use the strategies and behaviors associated with this element incorrectly or with parts missing.
0: Not Using	I am unaware of strategies and behaviors associated with this element.

Figure 6.18: Self-rating scale for element 13—Providing resources and guidance.

Element 14: Generating and Defending Claims

Generating and defending claims is one of the most powerful elements of *The New Art and Science of Teaching* framework. For elementary students, generating and defending claims can be as simple as expressing an idea or opinion and explaining why they think that. For secondary students, argumentation can be extremely complex, involving claims, grounds, backing, qualifiers, rhetorical strategies, and the articulation of underlying lines of reasoning. Claims related to reading can take many forms: a student might make a claim about the morphology or etymology of a word, the quality of a dramatic performance, or the meaning of a text. Especially at upper grade levels, argumentation in the reading classroom will likely center around textual analysis—providing evidence to support one's interpretation of a text. There are two structures that are particularly salient to such work: (1) the episode structure (for analyzing narratives) and (2) the argumentation structure (for constructing arguments).

Students can use the *episode* structure to tell or analyze a narrative. Figure 6.19 shows the episode knowledge map.

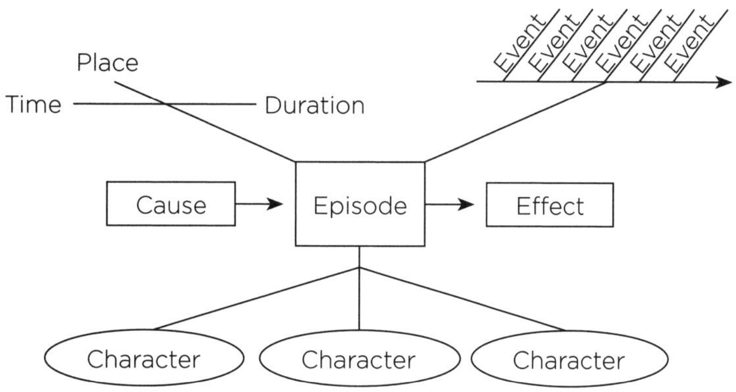

Figure 6.19: Episode knowledge map.

Visit ***go.SolutionTree.com/instruction*** *for a free reproducible version of this figure.*

Narratives might be fictional, historical, or personal. In the book *Baseball Saved Us*, author Ken Mochizuki (1993) uses an episode structure to relate his boyhood experiences in a Japanese internment camp during World War II. Figure 6.20 shows an episode knowledge map for that narrative.

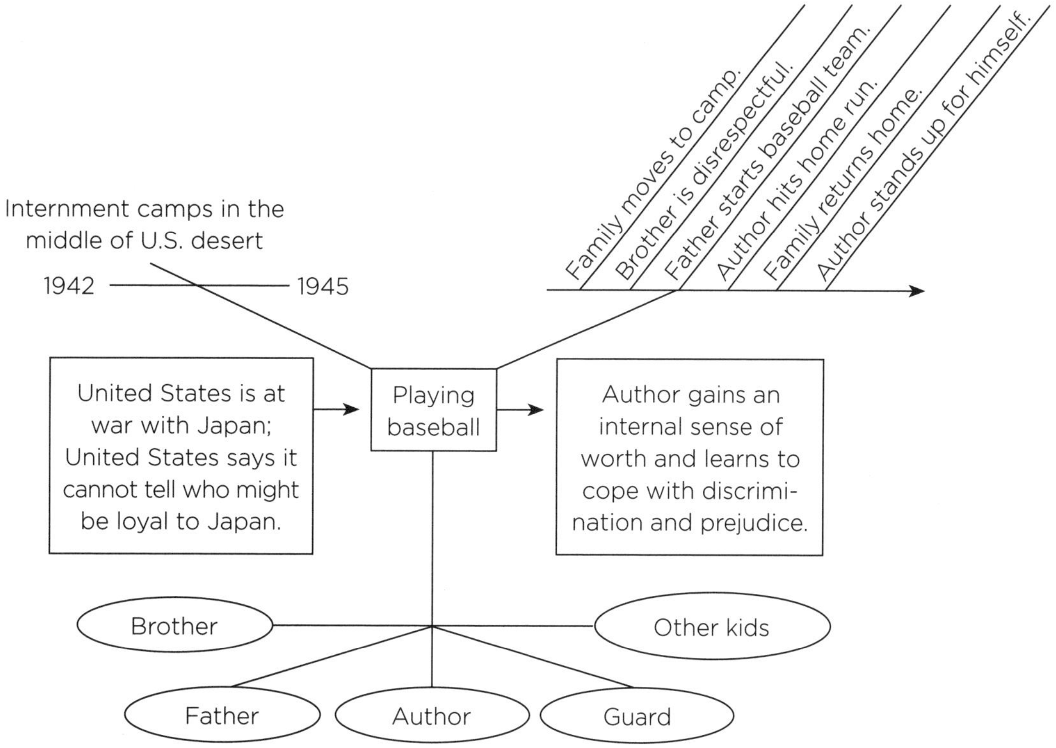

Figure 6.20: Episode knowledge map for *Baseball Saved Us* (Mochizuki, 1993).

Visit ***go.SolutionTree.com/instruction*** *for a free reproducible version of this figure.*

Argumentation structures are at the heart of many cognitively complex tasks, as they usually involve making and defending a claim about the best alternative for a decision, the solution to a problem, the best explanation for a line of inquiry, the best invention to meet an identified need, or the best way to clear up confusion or contradictions around a term or event. For elementary students, a *simple argumentation* structure involves articulating an idea and explaining why it is a good one. Figure 6.21 shows the simple argumentation knowledge map.

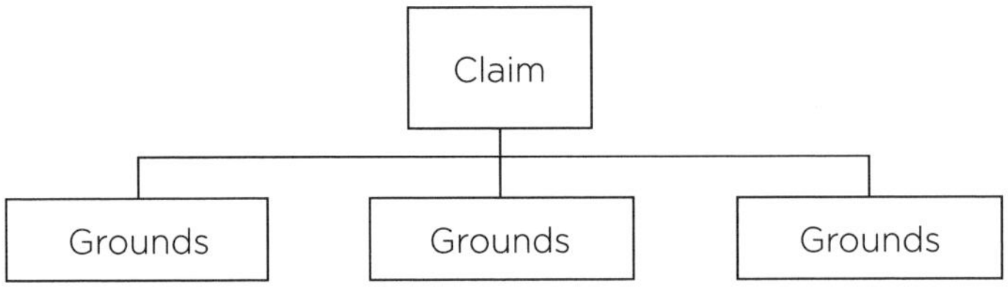

Figure 6.21: Simple argumentation knowledge map.

Visit ***go.SolutionTree.com/instruction*** *for a free reproducible version of this figure.*

For example, a student might claim that all students should play sports and give the following reasons (grounds).

- Playing sports helps you learn teamwork.
- Sports give you exercise, which is healthy.
- Sports are a lot of fun to play.

Or, as another example, a student might claim that all students should choose their own bedtimes and give the following reasons (grounds).

- Students will learn to take care of themselves better.
- Students will have more time for homework and reading.
- It will be easier for students to fall asleep if they go to bed when they feel tired.

A great book to illustrate this is Mo Willems's (2003) *Don't Let the Pigeon Drive the Bus!* The pigeon wants to drive the bus and gives many reasons why he should be allowed to do so.

For secondary students, a more *complex argumentation* structure, involving grounds, backing, and qualifiers to support a claim, is likely more appropriate. Figure 6.22 shows the complex argumentation knowledge map.

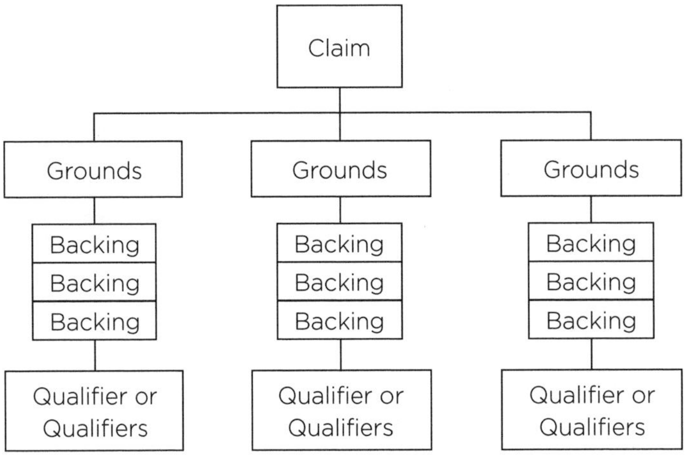

Figure 6.22: Complex argumentation knowledge map.

Visit ***go.SolutionTree.com/instruction*** *for a free reproducible version of this figure.*

For example, a student might use such a structure to analyze the argument in the Newsela article "Should Washington, D.C., Become a State? Its Mayor Says Yes" (Newsela, 2016). A claim is a new or controversial idea. For example, the claim of the article is that Washington, D.C., should become a state.

Grounds are the reasons for the claim, often signaled by the word *because*. For example, Washington, D.C., should become a state because its population is bigger than that of some states, and it pays more government taxes than many states.

Backing is evidence to support the grounds. For the grounds "its population is bigger than that of some states," backing could be a chart showing the population of various states and the population of D.C. arranged in ascending or descending order to show where D.C. falls. For the grounds "it pays more government taxes than many states," a similar chart could show how much various states and the District pay in taxes.

Qualifiers are additional information that may not support a claim. For example, it is interesting to note that the mayor of Washington, D.C., who wants the District to become the fifty-first state, is a Democrat. This is interesting because most of the people who live in D.C. are Democrats, so if it became a state with the ability to elect legislators, the Democratic Party would become stronger. So, while there may be good reasons for D.C. to become a state, the mayor may also be acting in the interests of her political party.

The ultimate goal of cognitively complex tasks is to give students the ability to generate and defend claims. Figure 6.23 contains the self-rating scale for element 14, generating and defending claims.

Score	Description
4: Innovating	I adapt behaviors and create new strategies for unique student needs and situations.
3: Applying	I engage students in activities that require them to generate and defend their own claims, and I monitor the extent to which students are applying their knowledge.
2: Developing	I engage students in activities that require them to generate and defend their own claims, but I do not monitor the effect on students.
1: Beginning	I use the strategies and behaviors associated with this element incorrectly or with parts missing.
0: Not Using	I am unaware of strategies and behaviors associated with this element.

Figure 6.23: Self-rating scale for element 14—Generating and defending claims.

GUIDING QUESTIONS FOR CURRICULUM DESIGN

To implement knowledge application lessons, this is the design question: *After presenting new content, how will I design and deliver lessons that help students generate and defend claims through knowledge application?* Consider the following questions aligned to the elements in this chapter to guide your planning.

- **Element 12:** How will I engage students in cognitively complex tasks?

- **Element 13:** How will I provide resources and guidance?

- **Element 14:** How will I help students generate and defend claims?

Summary

Conducting knowledge application lessons involves three elements: (1) engaging students in cognitively complex tasks, (2) providing resources and guidance, and (3) generating and defending claims. In the reading classroom, cognitively complex tasks usually require students to read a wide range of texts. Besides supporting word recognition and fluency development, this wide reading can expose students to texts that are potentially more complex than those with which they typically engage. Teachers can scaffold these encounters by providing a set of visual structures, or knowledge maps, that help students focus their analyses on salient features of each text. Finally, because cognitively complex tasks typically culminate in generating and defending claims, they give students valuable experience with critical argumentation skills.

CHAPTER 7

Using Strategies That Appear in All Types of Lessons

Elements in the sixth design area of *The New Art and Science of Teaching* framework help students go through content in a continual loop; this repeated review of content integrates new knowledge into a student's existing knowledge base. Such integration may require students to revise their present knowledge and perspectives, and teachers can facilitate that process by previewing content (element 15), highlighting critical information (element 16), reviewing content (element 17), revising knowledge (element 18), helping students to reflect on their learning (element 19), assigning purposeful homework (element 20), helping students elaborate on information (element 21), and organizing students to interact (both in small and large groups; element 22). Here we describe how each element of this design area might manifest in a reading classroom.

Element 15: Previewing Strategies

Previewing involves giving students a sneak peek at the content the teacher is about to address in order to activate their background knowledge relative to it. While previewing is an effective strategy with all reading content, here we highlight four specific types of content that a reading teacher could preview for students: (1) previewing irregular words, (2) previewing important or ambiguous passages, (3) previewing unknown or difficult words, and (4) previewing features of text.

Previewing Irregular Words

Relative to word recognition, the teacher might preview irregular words (such as *the* or *of*) in a passage or story students are about to read. Alternatively, the teacher could highlight words in a passage that follow a phonics pattern the student has just learned. For example, Foorman and colleagues (2016) suggest that teachers "preempt word-reading challenges presented in new texts by identifying and practicing challenging words with students before they read the full text" (pp. 36–37). The teacher could ask students to underline a specific type of word (for example, words they do not know, irregular words, or words that follow a specific phonics pattern) in a passage before reading it and then discuss the terms the student underlines and provide help if he or she needs it, potentially avoiding a situation in which the student becomes stuck on a word.

Previewing Important or Ambiguous Passages

Relative to fluency, a teacher might point out or highlight important or ambiguous passages before students read a text. The teacher could model several different ways to read each passage and discuss with students the nuances of each, particularly the effect of different intonations, pacing, and stress on the tone of a passage.

Previewing Unknown or Difficult Words

Relative to vocabulary, the teacher might identify words whose meanings may be unknown or difficult to determine in a passage that students are about to read. The teacher could either tell students the definition of the word before they read or model and discuss how to determine the word's meaning from context. For vague or ambiguous terms, the teacher could talk to students about different denotative and connotative meanings of the term. For polysemous terms (terms whose common meanings differ from their discipline-specific meanings; for example, the common meaning of *energy* differs from its scientific meaning), the teacher could talk about both meanings of the term and ask students to consider the genre and nature of the text to determine which meaning is most appropriate.

Previewing Features of Text

Relative to comprehension, the teacher could ask students to examine features of a text, such as illustrations, different fonts and print colors, headings, bold print, charts, graphs, tables, tables of contents, glossaries, indexes, and so forth, before reading the text. Research shows that when students use text features to try to determine the structure of a text before reading it, they understand and retain information from the text more effectively (Meyer et al., 1989). Additionally, teachers and students should both be aware that one type of text in particular requires an intentional approach to previewing: hypertext. Concerning the internet, Donald J. Leu and his colleagues (2008) write, "Never in the history of civilization have we seen a new technology adopted by so many, in so many different places, in such a short period of time" (p. 5). As teachers are well aware, reading on the internet differs from reading traditional text in several significant ways. While traditional print-based reading and internet reading both require students to use comprehension strategies and make comparisons among multiple texts, internet reading also requires constructing a coherent and meaningful reading path through myriad texts of widely varying credibility, relevance, and quality.

According to Byeong-Young Cho and Peter Afflerbach (2017), a *reading path* "traces how a reader determines, orders, and reads texts (Kress, 2003), or simply speaking, the route that one's eye (and attention) follows as he or she navigates within, between, and across texts (Hiippala, 2012)" (p. 115). A reading path is necessary for internet reading because of the internet's use of hypertext. George P. Landow (2006) defines *hypertext* as "blocks of words (or images) linked electronically by multiple paths, chains or trails in an open-ended, perpetually unfinished textuality described by the terms *link, node, network, web,* and *path*" (p. 2). Hypertext can lead to confusion and distraction in the online reading environment; however, a skilled reader leverages hypertext for his or her benefit:

> One of the fundamental characteristics of hypertext is that it is composed of bodies of linked texts that have no primary axis of organization. In other words, the metatext or document set—the entity that describes what in print technology is the book, work, or single text—has no center. Although this absence of a center can create problems for the reader and the writer, it also means that anyone who uses hypertext makes his or her own interests the de facto organizing principle (or center) for the investigation at the moment. One experiences hypertext as an infinitely decenterable and recenterable system, in part because hypertext transforms any document that has more than one link into a transient center, a partial sitemap that one can employ to orient oneself and to decide where to go next. (Landow, 2006, pp. 56–57)

Students who understand how hypertext works can make their interests and purposes the center of an online reading experience by constructing reading paths.

Constructing a reading path requires students to have a reading goal (for example, to learn about Jack London's life) before going online. Armed with an appropriate goal, students can use the following six-step protocol (based on the work of Cho & Afflerbach, 2017) to construct a reading path that will help them accomplish it.

1. **Search for relevant websites to create an information space** (for example, search for "Jack London" online and in a library database).
2. **Preview relevant websites to get an overview of the target content** (for example, look briefly at search results from Biography.com and Britannica to identify subtopics related to Jack London and find links to additional websites, such as Spartacus Educational, the American Society of Authors and Writers, and The Literature Network).
3. **Narrow search terms to reduce available information** (for example, search for "Jack London AND Klondike").
4. **Examine credibility and complexity to rate the usefulness of specific texts** (for example, select the article from Spartacus Educational as the best overview of his life and the article on Literary Traveler as the best source for his time in the Klondike).
5. **Sequence useful texts to create a reading path** (for example, [1] read Spartacus Educational article, and [2] read Literary Traveler article).
6. **Revise the reading path to account for new hyperlinks or information encountered while reading** (for example, click on links for "Klondike Gold Rush" and "Dawson City" while reading, see that they lead to Wikipedia articles, read a few paragraphs about each, and then return to the reading path; click on a link for "Jack London's Ranch," skim the article, and decide to return and read it more closely after finishing the Literary Traveler article).

A protocol such as this can structure students' internet searches and help them stay focused on their goals as they navigate hypertext and hypermedia environments.

Previewing helps students activate prior knowledge so that they might make connections with new knowledge. Figure 7.1 depicts the self-rating scale for previewing strategies.

Score	Description
4: Innovating	I adapt behaviors and create new strategies for unique student needs and situations.
3: Applying	I engage students in learning activities that require them to preview and link new knowledge to what we have already addressed, and I monitor the extent to which students are making linkages.
2: Developing	I engage students in learning activities that require them to preview and link new knowledge to what we have already addressed, but I do not monitor the effect on students.
1: Beginning	I use the strategies and behaviors associated with this element incorrectly or with parts missing.
0: Not Using	I am unaware of strategies and behaviors associated with this element.

Figure 7.1: Self-rating scale for element 15—Previewing strategies.

Element 16: Highlighting Critical Information

Due to the massive amount of information that students receive as they learn in school, teachers can help them categorize and prioritize it by highlighting the most important information. Here, we focus on three types of critical information related to reading: (1) high-frequency words, (2) directly instructed vocabulary terms, and (3) basic relationships between and among ideas.

Highlighting High-Frequency Words

High-frequency words are critical to both word recognition and fluency. *High-frequency words* are those that appear frequently in all kinds of texts. Foorman and colleagues (2016) suggest that teachers instruct students on high-frequency words with both irregular (*the, there, was, want, from, said, have, friend, of*) and regular (*in, did, and, then, had, with, that, down, him*) spellings. For regularly spelled high-frequency words, prompt students to decode them using their phonological recoding skills each time they encounter them in print. For irregular words:

> Teachers can use different strategies . . . such as teaching the words within the decoding sequence and correcting the pronunciation, labeling the words as rule-breakers and teaching them holistically, or having the student spell or write the words to draw attention to the middle sounds of the word. (Foorman et al., 2016, p. 28)

To help students practice high-frequency words, the teacher might show a student or small group of students each word on a flash card. If students can identify the word in three seconds, it goes in their score pile. If not, the teacher tells them the word and it goes in the teacher's score pile. The students try to beat the teacher by getting more cards in their score pile than the teachers. At the end of the game, the teacher can give the student or group additional practice with the words in the teacher's score pile. As students become better at recognizing the words, the teacher can decrease the allotted time to two seconds and eventually one second.

Highlighting Vocabulary Terms

As teachers select terms for direct instruction from tiers two and three, they could use the factors Nagy and Hiebert (2011) articulate to make decisions about the importance of various words. Table 7.1 lists those factors.

Table 7.1: Factors Impacting Choice of Words for Instruction

Role in the Language	**Frequency:** How often does this word occur in text? **Dispersion:** How does the frequency of this word differ for different genres, topics, or subject areas?
Role in the Lexicon	**Morphological relatedness:** How many words are part of this word's morphological family? **Semantic relatedness:** How is this word related to other words that the students know or need to know?
Role in Students' Existing Knowledge	**Familiarity:** Do students already know this word and, if so, to what degree? **Conceptual difficulty:** To what extent can teachers explain the meaning of this word to students in terms of words, concepts, and experiences with which they are already familiar?
Role in the Lesson	**Role in the particular text:** Does the student need to know this word in order to understand the text? **Role in the larger curriculum:** Will students encounter this word again in reading? Should students be able to use this word in their writing?

Source: Nagy & Hiebert, 2011, p. 389.

Highlighting Basic Relationships Between and Among Ideas

Relative to comprehension, highlighting basic relationships can raise students' awareness of how ideas relate to each other. Students store knowledge in networks in the brain (Anderson, 2010). When students pay attention to the types of connections between pieces of knowledge, it strengthens information in memory. Figure 7.2 shows the basic relationships knowledge map.

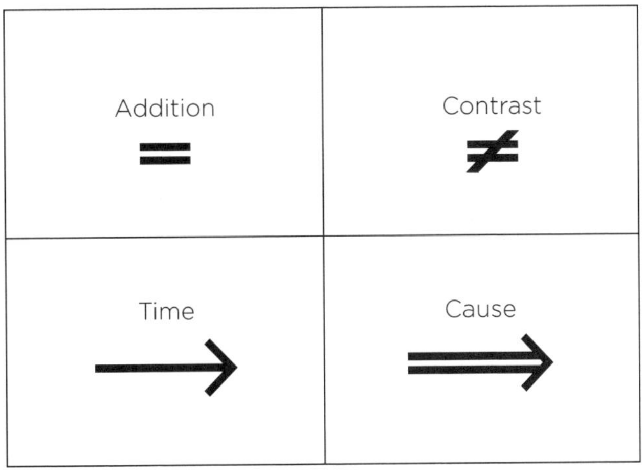

Figure 7.2: Basic relationships knowledge map.

Visit ***go.SolutionTree.com/instruction*** *for a free reproducible version of this figure.*

There are four types of basic relationships: (1) addition, (2) contrast, (3) time, and (4) cause.

Addition relationships indicate that things are alike or the same; words such as *and*, *additionally*, *as well as*, *likewise*, *that is*, *in fact*, *for example*, *in sum*, *overall*, and *together* signal these relationships. Addition relationships typically focus on connecting items that belong in the same category. For example, the following sentences identify a category and items that fit in that category.

- Jane has three pets: a cat, a dog, and a fish. (category: pets; members: cat, dog, fish)
- We read about famous baseball players, like Babe Ruth. (category: famous baseball players; member: Babe Ruth)
- Sam exercised a lot today! He did push-ups, lifted weights, and ran four miles. (category: exercise; members: push-ups, weights, running)

Addition relationships are also in evidence when one presents the same idea twice, in slightly different ways. For example, in the sentences, "I love to read. In fact, reading is my favorite activity," the idea the author is communicating is a preference for reading; he or she is simply expressing such an idea in multiple ways. That is, both of the statements belong in the category of "statements that express a preference for reading."

Contrast relationships indicate that things are opposite or different: words such as *but*, *on the other hand*, *rather*, *alternatively*, *in contrast*, *in comparison*, *however*, *in spite of*, and *nevertheless* signal these relationships. Contrast relationships focus on distinguishing items that belong in different categories. For example, the following sentences identify a category and items that do not fit in that category.

- I like pizza but I don't like salad. (category: food I like; nonmember: salad)
- Tony must either vacuum the floor or put the dishes away. (category: chores Tony must do; potential nonmember one: vacuum; potential nonmember two: put dishes away)
- Anna has red hair but mine is brown. (category: Anna's hair color; nonmember: brown)

Contrast relationships can also pair two ideas that don't go together. For example, in the sentence, "My brother is really annoying, but I love him anyway," the author is saying that her brother is annoying (which makes us think she doesn't like him) but that, in spite of his annoying behavior, she loves him anyway.

Time relationships talk about when things happened; words such as *before, after, while, later, earlier, until, in the meantime,* and *meanwhile* signal these relationships. For example, the following sentences express things happening at the same time, before other events, or after other events.

- It is summer in the northern hemisphere while it is winter in the southern hemisphere.
- We waited for fifteen minutes before my friend showed up.
- I didn't understand until after the teacher explained the math problem.

Cause relationships talk about why things happened; words such as *because, as a result, consequently, thus, so,* and *hence* signal these relationships. For example, the following sentences express a cause and an effect.

- The flying rock made a hole in the window. (cause: flying rock; effect: hole in window)
- I got sunburned because I didn't wear sunscreen at the pool. (cause: no sunscreen; effect: sunburn)
- If we go to the mall, I will buy a pair of shoes! (cause: going to the mall; effect: buying shoes)

These types of basic relationships are critical because recognizing them is the foundational skill that students will use to identify the presence of more complex structures in texts.

Highlighting critical information helps students attend to the most important content out of all the content they encounter each day. Figure 7.3 depicts the self-rating scale for highlighting critical information.

Score	Description
4: Innovating	I adapt behaviors and create new strategies for unique student needs and situations.
3: Applying	I signal to students which content is critical versus noncritical, and I monitor the extent to which students are attending to critical information.
2: Developing	I signal to students which content is critical versus noncritical, but I do not monitor the effect on students.
1: Beginning	I use the strategies and behaviors associated with this element incorrectly or with parts missing.
0: Not Using	I am unaware of strategies and behaviors associated with this element.

Figure 7.3: Self-rating scale for element 16—Highlighting critical information.

Element 17: Reviewing Content

Reviewing content simply means helping or prompting students to revisit content they have already learned. Reviewing vocabulary terms is an essential part of steps 4, 5, and 6 of the six-step process (pages 27–28). To support such review, teachers might implement word walls in their classrooms and use collection and classification structures.

Using Word Walls

According to Edna G. Brabham and Susan K. Villaume (2001), word walls are displays of words students are studying. They can include only words, or words accompanied by definitions, pictures, symbols, or other reminders about meaning or pronunciation. By definition, word walls are not static; teachers should add to them (and in some cases, remove words) according to the instructional needs of students and the content students are studying. Many teachers use interactive word walls, wherein they invite students to add terms to the word wall or augment the information accompanying a term already on the wall. Teachers can organize word walls alphabetically or semantically. Research shows that grouping words semantically (by meaning) mirrors how the human brain stores words (Marzano, 2004). Finally, although many elementary teachers use word walls already, research by Jean P. Vintinner, Janis Harmon, Karen Wood, and Katie Stover (2015) finds that they are effective instructional tools at the high school level as well.

Using Collection and Classification Structures

Relative to comprehension, students might review what they have learned from a text or passage of text by expressing it using a different structure from the one in the passage. Depending on the information the passage presents, students might review it by translating it into either a collection structure or a classification structure.

Collection structures are lists. There are four different kinds of lists.

1. Simple list
2. Combined list
3. Intersecting list
4. Nested list

A *simple list* is a collection of items that fit in a category. Figure 7.4 shows the simple list knowledge map.

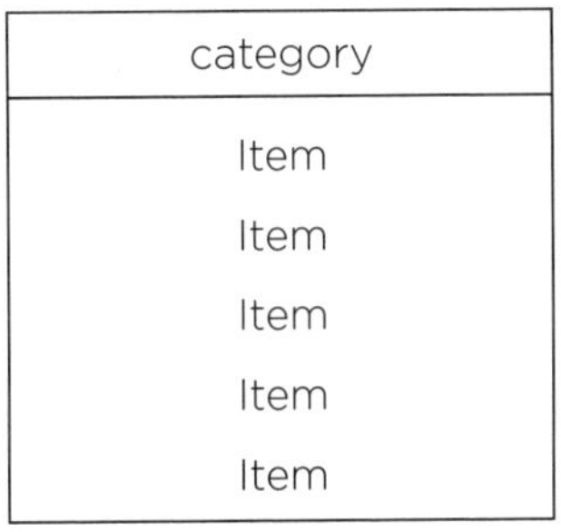

Figure 7.4: Simple list knowledge map.

Visit ***go.SolutionTree.com/instruction*** *for a free reproducible version of this figure.*

As an example of a simple list structure, *Zin! Zin! Zin! A Violin* by Lloyd Moss (1995) lists the following musical instruments.

- Trombone
- Trumpet
- French horn
- Cello
- Violin
- Flute
- Clarinet
- Oboe
- Bassoon
- Harp

Each of these instruments is an item in the category of musical instruments.

A *combined list* pairs a collection of items with data for each item. Figure 7.5 (page 106) shows the combined list knowledge map.

Item Category	Data Category	Data Category
Item	Data	Data
Item	Data	Data
Item	Data	Data
Item	Data	Data
Item	Data	Data

Figure 7.5: Combined list knowledge map.

Visit ***go.SolutionTree.com/instruction*** *for a free reproducible version of this figure.*

At the end of *Zin! Zin! Zin! A Violin* (Moss, 1995), the text provides categories into which one can organize the instruments: strings, reeds, and brasses.

A reader could also pair the instruments with data about their typical pitch range: high-, medium-, or low-pitched. Therefore, a combined list for the instruments, their category, and their range would likely look like that shown in figure 7.6.

Musical Instrument	Type of Instrument	Typical Pitch Range
Trombone	Brass	Medium
Trumpet	Brass	High
French horn	Brass	High
Cello	String	Low
Violin	String	High
Clarinet	Reed	Medium
Oboe	Reed	High
Bassoon	Reed	Low
Harp	String	Low, medium, and high

Figure 7.6: Combined list of instruments, categories, and pitches.

An *intersecting list* eliminates redundancy in a combined list. Figure 7.7 shows the intersecting list knowledge map.

Data Category B Data Category A	Data	Data
Data		Item
Data	Item Item	
Data	Item	Item
Data		Item Item
Data	Item	

Figure 7.7: Intersecting list knowledge map.

Visit ***go.SolutionTree.com/instruction*** *for a free reproducible version of this figure.*

With the previous musical instrument example, an intersecting list might show types of instruments as row headers and pitch ranges as column headers, as we show in figure 7.8.

	Low	Medium	High
String	Cello Harp	Harp	Violin Harp
Reed	Bassoon	Clarinet	Oboe
Brass		Trombone	Trumpet French horn

Figure 7.8: Intersecting list of instruments, categories, and pitches.

A *nested list* allows students to create an intersecting list that contains more than three sets of information. Figure 7.9 shows the nested list knowledge map.

		Data A1			Data A2		
		Data B1	**Data B2**	**Data B3**	**Data B1**	**Data B2**	**Data B3**
Data C1	Data D1	Item	Item	Item	Item	Item	Item
	Data D2	Item	Item	Item	Item	Item	Item
Data C2	Data D3	Item	Item	Item	Item	Item	Item
	Data D4	Item	Item	Item	Item	Item	Item
Data C3	Data D5	Item	Item	Item	Item	Item	Item

Figure 7.9: Nested list knowledge map.

Visit ***go.SolutionTree.com/instruction*** *for a free reproducible version of this figure.*

A student might want to add data pertaining to how to play the various instruments (bowing, plucking, blowing, or striking). He or she might also want to indicate which type of group (symphony orchestra or marching band) the instrument appears in. And the student might want to add instruments that *Zin! Zin! Zin! A Violin* (Moss, 1995) does not feature. Such an endeavor might result in a nested list like the one in figure 7.10.

		Symphony			Marching Band		
		High	**Medium**	**Low**	**High**	**Medium**	**Low**
Play by bowing or plucking	Strings	Violin	Viola Harp	Cello Bass			
Play by blowing through mouthpiece	Reeds	Oboe	Clarinet Saxophone	Bassoon	Oboe	Clarinet Saxophone	Bassoon
	Brasses	Trumpet French horn	Trombone	Tuba	Trumpet Mellophone	Trombone	Tuba
	Woodwinds	Piccolo Flute			Piccolo Flute		
Play by striking a surface	Percussion	Triangle	Piano	Bass drum	Triangle		Bass drum

Figure 7.10: Nested list of instruments, categories, pitches, playing methods, and group types.

Students can also use classification structures to review content. A *simple classification* structure sorts items into categories. Figure 7.11 shows the simple classification knowledge map.

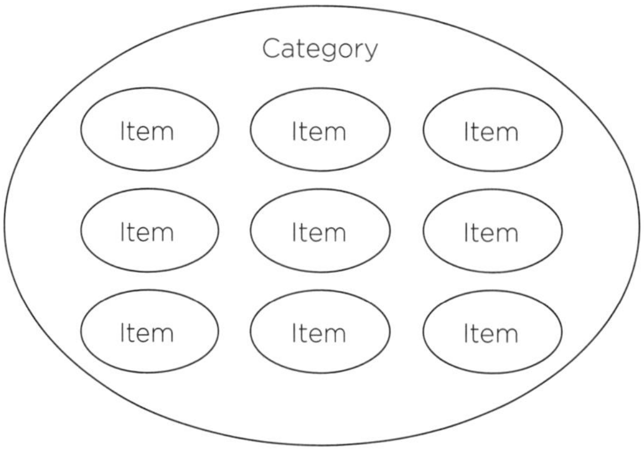

Figure 7.11: Simple classification knowledge map.

Visit ***go.SolutionTree.com/instruction*** *for a free reproducible version of this figure.*

A large circle represents the category, and the smaller circles represent the items that meet the requirements for membership in the category. A student could use a *complex classification* structure if more than one category is necessary for classification. Figure 7.12 shows the complex classification knowledge map.

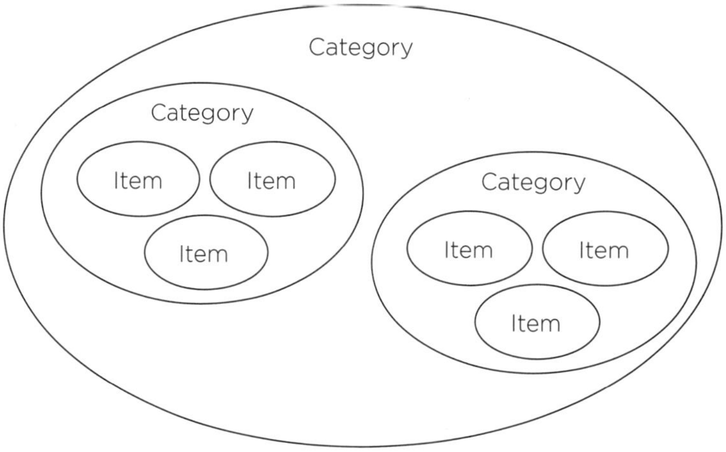

Figure 7.12: Complex classification knowledge map.

Visit ***go.SolutionTree.com/instruction*** *for a free reproducible version of this figure.*

Multiple large circles represent categories. Categories can then nest within other categories. Rochelle Strauss's (2004) *Tree of Life: The Incredible Biodiversity of Life on Earth* uses a classification structure to present information about various organisms. To diagram information from the book, a student might use five large circles to represent the five kingdoms (Monera, Fungi, Protoctista, Plants, and Animals). Within those five circles, the student would then use smaller circles to represent the different species or subcategories that Strauss presents. For example, smaller circles within the Animals category would be labeled *invertebrates* and *vertebrates*. In turn, the vertebrates category would include circles for fish, birds, reptiles, amphibians, and mammals.

Reviewing content provides students with the opportunity to recall material that they have learned. Figure 7.13 depicts the self-rating scale for reviewing content.

Score	Description
4: Innovating	I adapt behaviors and create new strategies for unique student needs and situations.
3: Applying	I engage students in a brief review of content that highlights the critical information, and I monitor the extent to which students can recall and describe previous content.
2: Developing	I engage students in a brief review of content that highlights the critical information, but I do not monitor the effect on students.
1: Beginning	I use the strategies and behaviors associated with this element incorrectly or with parts missing.
0: Not Using	I am unaware of strategies and behaviors associated with this element.

Figure 7.13: Self-rating scale for element 17—Reviewing content.

Element 18: Revising Knowledge

The difference between reviewing and revising knowledge is that revising knowledge involves changing, adding to, or deleting what students have previously learned. Relative to word recognition, once students have learned the letters of the alphabet and the sounds they represent, the teacher might give students additional information about both the spellings and pronunciation of different phonemes. For example, the teacher might describe how people pronounce different phonemes in different parts of the mouth using different oral structures (such as the lips, teeth, tongue, nose, throat, and vocal cords). Once students have learned the most common spelling or spellings for each phoneme, the teacher might expose them to less common spellings (see appendix E, available at **go.SolutionTree.com/instruction**, for a detailed guide to English phonemes and their spellings).

One way to prompt students to add, delete, or change what they have previously learned about a vocabulary term is to engage them in academic games that require them to operationalize their understanding of various terms. We describe these games in detail in chapter 7, page 99. Here, the important point is that after students have played games with vocabulary terms, they should return to the entries for the terms in their academic or vocabulary notebooks and make changes based on what they learned during the game.

Relative to both fluency and comprehension, analyzing a text from a different point of view can help students revise their initial understanding and interpretations of the text. For example, depending on a student's level, he or she might engage in one of the analysis activities we describe in table 7.2.

Table 7.2: Analyzing Point of View

Level	Activity	Example
Primary	Identify who is speaking at different places in a text.	For a narrative text, the student identifies passages where the narrator speaks and passages where specific characters speak. For an informational text, the student identifies passages where the author gives information and passages where the author quotes experts or other authors. For a persuasive text, the student identifies passages where the author expresses his or her opinion, passages that quote people with alternative opinions, and passages that quote people in support of the author's opinion.

continued →

Level	Activity	Example
Intermediate	Articulate the point of view that a speaker in the text expresses.	For a narrative text, the student describes the point of view the narrator or a character articulates. For an informational or persuasive text, the student describes the point of view the author or people quoted in the text articulate.
Middle School	Compare a point of view a text expresses with one's own point of view.	The student describes how the point of view of the author, a character, or a quoted person is similar to or different from his or her personal point of view.
High School	Evaluate how effectively an author presents his or her point of view in a text.	The student connects the author's purpose with the point of view he or she expresses in a text and explains why the author did or did not achieve his or her purpose through expressing his or her point of view.

Figure 7.14 depicts the self-rating scale for element 18, revising knowledge.

Score	Description
4: Innovating	I adapt behaviors and create new strategies for unique student needs and situations.
3: Applying	I engage students in revision of previous content, and I monitor the extent to which these revisions deepen students' understanding.
2: Developing	I engage students in revision of previous content, but I do not monitor the effect on students.
1: Beginning	I use the strategies and behaviors associated with this element incorrectly or with parts missing.
0: Not Using	I am unaware of strategies and behaviors associated with this element.

Figure 7.14: Self-rating scale for element 18—Revising knowledge.

Element 19: Reflecting on Learning

Reflecting on learning in the reading classroom involves stepping back from the actual learning tasks and asking questions about the learning process itself. Teachers might use questions such as the following to prompt students to think about their learning while reading a text.

- What did I do when I encountered words I didn't know? How did that response affect my learning?
- How did figuring out this text's structure help me understand it better?
- How did I respond to special features of this text (callout boxes, glosses, and headings)? Did they help or hinder my reading?
- Was it easy or difficult for me to figure out the main idea and themes in this text? Why?
- What did I do when I disagreed with something in this text?
- What elements of this text affected my emotions? How did my emotional response influence my learning?
- Did I associate myself with the point of view the text expresses, or did I set myself in opposition to it? How did that affect my learning?
- How would I describe the tone of this text? How did that tone affect my learning?
- What words in this text were especially powerful? How did those words affect my learning?

Students might answer questions such as these in an academic notebook or on an exit slip.

Figure 7.15 depicts the self-rating scale for element 19, reflecting on learning.

Score	Description
4: Innovating	I adapt behaviors and create new strategies for unique student needs and situations.
3: Applying	I engage students in reflecting on their own learning and the learning process, and I monitor the extent to which students self-assess their understanding and effort.
2: Developing	I engage students in reflecting on their own learning and the learning process, but I do not monitor the effect on students.
1: Beginning	I use the strategies and behaviors associated with this element incorrectly or with parts missing.
0: Not Using	I am unaware of strategies and behaviors associated with this element.

Figure 7.15: Self-rating scale for element 19—Reflecting on learning.

Element 20: Assigning Purposeful Homework

Homework, rather than being a matter of routine, should be purposeful. If parents are to be involved, they should receive clear instructions as well as possess the resources and skills required to perform the roles teachers request of them.

Research indicates that shared book-reading activities at home have numerous benefits. For instance, Laura M. Justice and Paige C. Pullen (2003) find that shared book reading supports students' emotional development in addition to their cognitive and linguistic development. For students who cannot yet read independently, teachers can ask parents to read aloud to their children. For students who can read independently, teachers can ask parents to engage in shared or paired reading with their children. Figure 7.16 gives guidelines for parents as they engage in these activities.

Type of Reading	Guidelines
General Reading	• Create a happy and relaxed atmosphere in a quiet environment. • Try not to make your child read when he or she really wants to do something else. • Ask the child to select a book that appeals to him or her and is at a suitable level (especially for shared and paired reading). • Make sure that both you and your child can see the book. • Always keep in mind that the goal of reading at home is to reinforce the idea that reading is pleasurable and meaningful.
Reading Aloud	**Making Meaning** • Discuss the title of the book (for example, "This book is called *Jumanji*. That's a strange word. What do you think it means? There are monkeys on the cover, but they are in somebody's kitchen. Why are they in the kitchen?"). • Ask questions that begin with *what*, *where*, *when*, and *who* (for example, "What do you see on this page? Where are these people going? Who is happy?"). • When a child answers a question, sometimes repeat what the child said and add to it (for example, "Yes, you see that the octopus is in the water. I see the mouse in the boat"). • When a child answers a question, sometimes follow up with a question that prompts him or her to add detail to the answer (for example, "Yes, the fox is in the dark. Who is in the light?").

Figure 7.16: Guidelines for parent read-alouds, shared reading, and paired reading. continued →

Type of Reading	Guidelines
Reading Aloud	**Noticing Print** • Make comments about the words and letters on the page (for example, "Look, here's an S. That's the first letter in your name!" or "Which of these words starts with a W?"). • Track the words when reading the story (for example, run your finger under the line you are reading, or point to specific words as you say them). • Point out rhyming words or words with interesting relationships (for example, "This says *chitter, chatter*. Those words sound the same except for one letter. Which letter is different?" or "There are rhyming words in this book. Which word rhymes with *cat*?").
Shared Reading	• Read aloud together with your child. Pace your reading to his or her reading speed. • If it is helpful, the child may track the print with his or her finger during reading. However, if the child does not need this support, do not force him or her to do it. • If the child gets a word wrong, simply tell him or her what the word is, ask the child to repeat it after you, then read the sentence with the word in it together again and continue reading. Do not make the child sound out the incorrect or unknown word. • At appropriate intervals (such as at the end of a page), praise your child for all of the words he or she read correctly. Do not worry about the words your child gets wrong. • At appropriate junctures (such as at the end of a page), talk about the pictures in the book and ask your child what he or she thinks will happen next.
Paired Reading	• As the child develops confidence, shared reading should transition to paired reading, wherein the child reads aloud and the parent listens. • The child can signal to the parent (with words or gestures) when he or she is ready to read by himself or herself. Or, the parent can simply notice when the child seems to be reading smoothly and with confidence and fade out his or her voice to let the child continue alone. • If the child gets a word wrong, tell him or her what the word is, ask the child to repeat it after you, then read the sentence with the word in it together again. Continue reading together for a few sentences before fading your voice out again. Do not make the child sound out the incorrect or unknown word. • At appropriate intervals (such as at the end of a page), praise your child for all of the words he or she read correctly. In particular, praise your child when he or she corrects himself or herself on a misread word before you do. • At appropriate junctures (such as at the end of a page), talk about the pictures in the book and ask your child what he or she thinks will happen next.

Source: Adapted from National Educational Psychological Service, 2016; Sim & Berthelsen, 2014.
Visit ***go.SolutionTree.com/instruction*** *for a free reproducible version of this figure.*

Relative to fluency, students should be able to independently read a passage before the teacher asks him or her to practice reading it at home for homework. Ideally, such a passage would be funny, entertaining, or otherwise engaging so that students are motivated to share it with family members and friends. Similarly, students might take vocabulary games (which they have played in class and are familiar with) home to play with family members and friends. Such games should include all the materials necessary and clear instructions for how to play so that the student is successful in explaining how to play the game.

Relative to comprehension, asking students to read a passage of text at home before discussing it in class the next day can be very effective. However, we recommend that teachers give students strategies to remember what they have read and access the important ideas from it the next day in class. One of the best strategies for this purpose is annotation. Mortimer J. Adler and Charles Van Doren (1972), in their classic work, *How to Read a Book*, give the following reasons for annotation (although they talk specifically about annotating a book, their ideas apply equally well to articles, passages, and shorter texts):

> Why is marking a book indispensable to reading it? First, it keeps you awake—not merely conscious, but wide awake. Second, reading, if it is active, is thinking, and thinking tends to express itself in words, spoken or written. The person who says he knows what he thinks but cannot express it usually does not know what he thinks. Third, writing your reactions down helps you to remember the thoughts of the author. (p. 49)

They offer the following list of annotations that readers might use:

> 1. **Underlining**—of major points; of important or forceful statements.
> 2. **Vertical lines at the margin**—to emphasize a statement already underlined or to point to a passage too long to be underlined.
> 3. **Star, asterisk, or other doodad at the margin**—to be used sparingly, to emphasize the ten or dozen most important statements or passages in the book. You may want to fold a corner of each page on which you make such marks or place a slip of paper between the pages. In either case, you will be able to take the book off the shelf at any time and, by opening it to the indicated pages, refresh your recollection.
> 4. **Numbers in the margin**—to indicate a sequence of points made by the author in developing an argument.
> 5. **Numbers of other pages in the margin**—to indicate where else in the book the author makes the same points, or points relevant to or in contradiction of those marked; to tie up the ideas in a book, which, though they may be separated by many pages, belong together. Many readers use the symbol "Cf" to indicate the other page numbers; it means "compare" or "refer to."
> 6. **Circling of key words or phrases**—This serves much the same function as underlining.
> 7. **Writing in the margin, or at the top or bottom of the page**—to record questions (and perhaps answers) which a passage raises in your mind; to reduce a complicated discussion to a simple statement; to record the sequence of major points right through the book. The endpapers at the back of the book can be used to make a personal index of the author's points in the order of their appearance. (pp. 49–50)

We should note that the type of annotation Adler and Van Doren (1972) describe is most appropriate for close reading. When students are skimming, overviewing, or otherwise quickly previewing a text (to see if it is relevant and worth reading closely, for instance), they may want to use a more constrained set of annotation techniques, such as circling, underlining, and asterisks.

Teachers frequently use homework, but not always in ways that enhance student learning. Figure 7.17 represents the self-rating scale for this element.

Score	Description
4: Innovating	I adapt behaviors and create new strategies for unique student needs and situations.
3: Applying	When appropriate (as opposed to routinely), I assign homework that is designed to deepen knowledge of information or provide practice with a skill, strategy, or process, and I monitor the extent to which students understand the homework.
2: Developing	When appropriate (as opposed to routinely), I assign homework that is designed to deepen knowledge of information or provide practice with a skill, strategy, or process, but I do not monitor the effect on students.
1: Beginning	I use the strategies and behaviors associated with this element incorrectly or with parts missing.
0: Not Using	I am unaware of strategies and behaviors associated with this element.

Figure 7.17: Self-rating scale for element 20—Assigning purposeful homework.

Element 21: Elaborating on Information

Elaborating on information in the reading classroom typically involves teachers asking students questions that will prompt them to deepen and enhance their understanding of content and material. When discussing texts with students, we recommend an approach to questioning called questioning sequences (Marzano & Simms, 2014). *Questioning sequences* are series of questions designed to lead students through an inductive reasoning process (details to categories to elaborations to evidence). *Detail questions* help students notice and describe specific details in a particular text. For example, if students are reading a narrative text, the teacher might begin by asking them detail questions about the antagonist and protagonist in the text. Detail questions that focus students' attention on different types of details appear in table 7.3.

Table 7.3: Detail Questions

Type of Detail	Questions
People	When did this person live? Where did this person live? What happened to this person? What did this person do?
Organizations or Groups	What beliefs or commonalities define this group? When and where did this group exist? What did this group do?
Intellectual or Artistic Products	Who made this product? Where and when was this product made? Why was this product made? What happened because of this product?
Objects and Animals	What does this object or animal look like? What system is this object or animal a part of? Why is this object or animal worth noticing?
Places	Where is this place? What happened in this place?
Events	What happened during this event? Where did this event happen? What caused this event? What happened because of this event?
Mental and Physical Actions	What process is associated with this action? Why is this action performed?
Feelings	What causes this feeling? What benefits or consequences are associated with this feeling?
Structures	What sorts of things does this structure keep organized? Why do people use this structure?

*Visit **go.SolutionTree.com/instruction** for a free reproducible version of this table.*

Not all texts will feature all of these types of details; teachers should use the list to select the most important details in a text and ask questions about those.

Once students have noticed the most important details and familiarized themselves with them, teachers should ask students to start thinking about categories that the details fit into. Question stems for *category questions* include the following.

- What larger category do these details fit into?

- What are general characteristics of things in this category? (for a specific category)
- How are the things within this category similar or different? (for a specific category)
- How are things in these categories similar or different? (for two specific categories)

For example, to help students think about the larger categories of "antagonists" and "protagonists," the teacher might ask students to compare the specific antagonist and protagonist from a text with antagonists and protagonists in other narratives to draw conclusions about those groups in general.

After students have articulated the general characteristics of a category, the teacher can ask them to make claims about that category using elaboration questions. *Elaboration questions* ask students to explain reasons for characteristics of a category, describe the effects of specific characteristics of a category, and predict how members of a category might behave under certain conditions. For example, the teacher could ask students to make claims about antagonists and protagonists. Students might claim things such as "Protagonists don't always make good choices" or "Antagonists keep the protagonist from achieving his or her goal." Once students have made claims like these, the teacher uses evidence questions to help students articulate support for their claims. *Evidence questions* include the following.

- Why do you think that?
- Can you think of any situations in which that might not be true?
- What other sources agree with you? What sources disagree with you?
- Why might someone think differently than you?

Leading students through a questioning sequence helps them gradually layer new information onto their existing knowledge and scaffolds the articulation of more substantive claims than if a teacher simply asked students to make and defend a claim about a text.

Elaboration is an inferential act that fosters new awareness when students engage in it effectively. Figure 7.18 depicts the self-rating scale for this element.

Score	Description
4: Innovating	I adapt behaviors and create new strategies for unique student needs and situations.
3: Applying	I ask students to elaborate on information, and I monitor the extent to which my actions affect students' responses.
2: Developing	I ask students to elaborate on information, but I do not monitor the effect on students.
1: Beginning	I use the strategies and behaviors associated with this element incorrectly or with parts missing.
0: Not Using	I am unaware of strategies and behaviors associated with this element.

Figure 7.18: Self-rating scale for element 21—Elaborating on information.

Element 22: Organizing Students to Interact

As teachers think about organizing students to interact in the reading classroom, it is important to keep in mind a strand of research known as *child-by-instruction interactions*. Carol M. Connor and her colleagues (Connor et al., 2004, 2009; Connor, Morrison, & Katch, 2004; Connor, Morrison, & Petrella, 2004; Connor, Morrison, & Slominski, 2006; Connor, Morrison, & Underwood, 2007) have found:

> The effects of particular literacy instructional strategies may depend on the language and literacy skills children bring to the learning opportunity. Generally, children with weaker skills in a particular area (e.g., word reading) appear to show greater progress

> when they receive more time in explicit instruction on that target outcome, whereas the same instructional strategy may be negatively associated with or have little effect on growth for children with stronger skills. At the same time, children with stronger skills tend to demonstrate greater progress when provided more opportunities in higher-order meaning-focused instructional activities (e.g., comprehension strategies or opportunities to read books independently) or more advanced code-focused skills (e.g., morphological awareness) when compared with students with weaker skills. Overall, children with stronger vocabulary skills learn from a wider range of learning opportunities than do children with weaker vocabulary skills, who, by contrast, tend to show greater progress when instruction is more explicit and targeted toward ameliorating their assessed weaknesses. (Foorman & Connor, 2011, p. 146)

This research provides guidance for teachers who have to decide how to allocate limited reading block time among groups of students at different levels. While it may seem intuitive to try to give students of all levels the same amount of time in a small group with the teacher, Connor and colleagues' research shows that this is not necessarily the best solution. While acknowledging that the relationships involved in child-by-instruction interactions are complex, Connor and Morrison (2016) give the following example of how one group of students might benefit most from working on phonics in a small group with the teacher, while another group of students might benefit most from engaging in independent silent reading:

> [Students with] weaker decoding scores made greater gains when their teachers taught them phonics and related code-focused skills, whereas students with strong vocabulary scores made greater gains when they spent more time in meaning-focused activities, such as sustained independent silent reading. (p. 56)

These findings are consistent with the research on phonological recoding ability and the self-teaching hypothesis we describe in chapter 1 (see page 23). Specifically, it supports the idea that the most efficient way for students who have already acquired phonological recoding skill to improve their reading is to read independently (or to engage in other independent or partner activities that require independent reading). This gives them the greatest number of opportunities to acquire the extensive and implicit knowledge of English orthography and vocabulary that skilled reading requires. Spending time in small groups with the teacher and working on word recognition skills is a waste of these students' time.

Conversely, for students who have not acquired phonological recoding abilities, attempting to engage in independent reading (or reading center activities that require independent reading) simply wastes time that they need to spend in phonics-focused teacher-directed small-group instruction. Ruth Wharton-McDonald and Joy Erickson (2017) elaborate:

> When students lack fluency and automaticity, they tend to read less and avoid difficult material (see Chall, 1983, 1996; Stanovich, 1986). Thus, not only is their comprehension affected directly by their lack of fluency, but an avenue to improvement (extensive reading) is also restricted (Allington, 2006; Lewis & Dahbany, 2008; Rasinski & Hoffman, 2003). (pp. 355–356)

Therefore, it is imperative for students to enter the full and consolidated alphabetic phases (via phonological recoding) as soon as possible so that they reap the benefits of independent reading for as long as possible.

Therefore, as teachers plan their reading groups and the centers and seatwork activities that students will engage with during the reading block in their classrooms, we recommend that they create rotations and student schedules that prioritize students' individual needs (for example, students with strong word recognition and vocabulary skills spend most of their time reading independently) over more intuitive notions of what is most fair (for example, every student spends twenty minutes in a small group with the teacher twice a week). Child-by-instruction interaction research shows that what is most "fair" (that is, most beneficial) for each student depends critically on the "constellation of skills" (Connor & Morrison, 2016, p. 55) he or she brings to the reading task.

Figure 7.19 depicts the self-rating scale for element 22, organizing students to interact.

Score	Description
4: Innovating	I adapt behaviors and create new strategies for unique student needs and situations.
3: Applying	I organize students to interact in a thoughtful way that facilitates collaboration, and I monitor the extent to which students collaborate.
2: Developing	I organize students to interact in a thoughtful way that facilitates collaboration, but I do not monitor the effect on students.
1: Beginning	I use the strategies and behaviors associated with this element incorrectly or with parts missing.
0: Not Using	I am unaware of strategies and behaviors associated with this element.

Figure 7.19: Self-rating scale for element 22—Organizing students to interact.

GUIDING QUESTIONS FOR CURRICULUM DESIGN

For using strategies that appear in all types of lessons—direct instruction, practicing and deepening, and knowledge application lessons—this is the design question: *Throughout all types of lessons, what strategies will I use to help students continually integrate new knowledge with old knowledge and revise their understanding accordingly?* The following specific questions align to each of the eight elements in this chapter and serve to guide teachers in planning instruction. Although theoretically teachers could incorporate all elements in every kind of lesson, this would not necessarily be wise practice. Rather, teachers should use their professional judgment to judiciously balance the use of these elements.

- **Element 15:** How will I help students preview strategies?

- **Element 16:** How will I highlight critical information?

- **Element 17:** How will I help students review content?

- **Element 18:** How will I help students revise knowledge?

- **Element 19:** How will I help students reflect on their learning?

- **Element 20:** How will I use purposeful homework?

- **Element 21:** How will I help students elaborate on information?

- **Element 22:** How will I organize students to interact?

Summary

Using strategies that appear in all types of lessons involves eight elements: (1) previewing, (2) highlighting critical information, (3) reviewing content, (4) revising knowledge, (5) reflecting on learning, (6) assigning purposeful homework, (7) elaborating on information, and (8) organizing students to interact. In the reading classroom, these elements operationalize in a variety of ways. Students might learn to construct reading paths when using online texts, identify basic relationships in texts, list and classify words and ideas, and reflect on their own and alternate perspectives. Teachers can use questioning sequences, shared reading experiences, and thoughtful grouping strategies to facilitate and scaffold students' experiences as they revisit and revise their understanding of content.

PART III

Context

CHAPTER 8

Using Engagement Strategies

In addition to feedback and the presentation of content, *The New Art and Science of Teaching* framework also takes into account a student's mental readiness to learn. Engagement, the focus of the seventh design area, is the gateway to such readiness. To help students pay attention, the teacher must notice and react when students are not engaged (element 23). The teacher might employ various strategies for increasing response rates (element 24), use physical movement (element 25), and maintain a lively lesson pace (element 26), intervening when he or she notices that engagement is low. Demonstrating a personal sense of intensity and enthusiasm about the content (element 27), presenting unusual information (element 28), instigating friendly controversy (element 29), and employing academic games (element 30) can add energy and excitement to the classroom. Giving students opportunities to connect content to their personal interests and talk about themselves (element 31) can motivate and inspire students (element 32) and extend learning beyond the classroom. Here we describe how these elements of engagement might manifest in a reading classroom.

Element 23: Noticing and Reacting When Students Are Not Engaged

One area of research relevant to both reading and this element of *The New Art and Science of Teaching* is mind wandering. Jonathan Smallwood and Jonathan W. Schooler (2006) describe *mind wandering* as "a situation in which executive control shifts away from a primary task to the processing of personal goals" (p. 946). Most people have experienced mind wandering while reading; the experience of reading a page (or several pages) and then realizing that one has no idea of what was just read is fairly ubiquitous for skilled readers. In fact, researchers estimate that people spend 30 to 50 percent of daily life in off-task thought (Giambra, 1995; Killingsworth & Gilbert, 2010).

Amy A. Pachai, Anita Acai, Andrew B. LoGiudice, and Joseph A. Kim (2016) explain that mind wandering often has negative effects:

> Mind wandering during reading can come at a significant cost to comprehension. . . . The brain only superficially encodes what is being read during episodes of mind wandering; in other words, incoming information is only partially retained. . . . This affects not only immediate understanding, such as the recall of factual information, but also more complex forms of understanding, such as the ability to make inferences from the text. (p. 138)

However, Benjamin Baird, Jonathan Smallwood, and Jonathan W. Schooler (2011) find that mind wandering can also have positive effects. In particular, many thoughts during mind wandering are future oriented. Smallwood and Schooler (2006) note that "in mind wandering, it seems that the automatic activation of a pertinent personal goal temporarily overshadows the more immediate goal of task completion. . . . Mind wandering may share important similarities with incubation processes related to creativity" (p. 956). That is, mind wandering may give us the opportunity to think about and solve problems that are of personal interest to us. Additionally, mind wandering gives our brains a break when they are tired and can help to relieve boredom. Pachai and colleagues (2016) explain that mind wandering can:

> give a student's mind a temporary "break" from the primary task, allowing their attention to be refreshed and eventually redirected back to the task once again. Similarly, mind wandering may also serve as a way of relieving boredom while performing monotonous tasks (Mooneyham & Schooler, 2013). (p. 140)

Fascinatingly for teachers of reading, certain types of reading are more conducive to mind wandering than others. Trish L. Varao Sousa, Jonathan S. A. Carriere, and Daniel Smilek (2013) find that mind wandering occurs most often during read-alouds and less often during silent reading or when students read aloud to themselves.

So what can teachers do to help students reap the positive benefits of mind wandering and avoid the negative consequences? Pachai and colleagues (2016) offer the following suggestions.

- **Integrate "checkpoint" questions throughout lessons and reading assignments:** The positive learning effects of stopping every so often to check one's understanding have a strong research base (Roediger & Karpicke, 2006; see Dunlosky, Rawson, Marsh, Nathan, & Willingham, 2013, for a review). Therefore, teachers can help students chunk a text into smaller passages and give them prompts or questions to ask themselves each time they finish a section. This allows them to check their comprehension and reset their attention.
- **Incorporate mindfulness training to help students become more aware:** Mindfulness training involves learning to focus awareness on one's current emotions, thoughts, and sensations. Research by Michael D. Mrazek, Michael S. Franklin, Dawa Tarchin Phillips, Benjamin Baird, and Jonathan W. Schooler (2013) shows that mindfulness training can reduce mind wandering and improve reading comprehension. Strategies related to mindfulness include focusing on breathing and posture, reframing distracting thoughts, and mental relaxation. For more information about teaching mindfulness, see *Cultivating Mindfulness in the Classroom* (Iberlin, 2017).
- **Teach students how to let their minds wander appropriately:** Since it is unlikely that teachers will ever be able to entirely eliminate students' mind wandering in the classroom, giving students short breaks (or teaching them to take short breaks every so often when reading) can help them properly rest and reset their minds between tasks or before returning to a task.

These strategies can help students and teachers notice when minds are wandering and help them recenter in productive and positive ways.

Figure 8.1 depicts the self-rating scale for this element about noticing and reacting when students are disengaged.

Score	Description
4: Innovating	I adapt behaviors and create new strategies for unique student needs and situations.
3: Applying	I notice and react when students are not engaged, and I monitor the extent to which my actions affect students' engagement.
2: Developing	I notice and react when students are not engaged, but I do not monitor the effect on students.
1: Beginning	I use the strategies and behaviors associated with this element incorrectly or with parts missing.
0: Not Using	I am unaware of strategies and behaviors associated with this element.

Figure 8.1: Self-rating scale for element 23—Noticing and reacting when students are not engaged.

Element 24: Increasing Response Rates

Using student-generated questions as a way to improve students' reading comprehension has been the subject of much research over many years (Chin, Brown, & Bruce, 2002; Davey & McBride, 1986; King & Rosenshine, 1993; Nolte & Singer, 1985; Rosenshine, Meister, & Chapman, 1996; Taboada & Guthrie, 2006; Taylor, Alber, & Walker, 2002; Therrien & Hughes, 2008; Wong & Jones, 1982). Most children are naturally curious: Brandy N. Frazier, Susan A. Gelman, & Henry M. Wellman (2009) find that children ages two to ten years ask their mothers an average of 288 questions per day. Michelle M. Chouinard, P. L. Harris, and Michael P. Maratsos (2007) estimate that children ask four hundred to twelve hundred questions every week! And research shows that generating questions does indeed support reading comprehension. William J. Therrien and Charles Hughes (2008) performed a meta-analysis of thirteen studies, and their findings indicate that question generation results in significant gains in reading comprehension scores. Ana Taboada and John T. Guthrie (2006) find that "questioning contributed to reading comprehension for students with low prior knowledge, as well as for students with high prior knowledge" (p. 24). Discipline-specific research shows that generating questions improves students' retention of mathematics content (Di Teodoro, Donders, Kemp-Davidson, Robertson, & Schuyler, 2011), explanations of their own thinking processes (Gillies, Nicols, Burgh, & Haynes, 2013), engagement in science topics (Hung et al., 2014), and responses to literature (Peterson & Taylor, 2012). Nancy Boyles (2012) finds that asking and answering questions builds students' ability to uncover layers of meaning in a text (also known as *close reading*).

Molly Ness (2016) describes a simple six-step strategy, called Book Bits, that teachers can use with students of all ages to help them generate questions about a text.

1. Select short phrases from a text. Write them on index cards or slips of paper.
2. Without telling students the title of the book or showing them the cover, distribute one card or piece of paper to each student.
3. Ask, "What does your Book Bit tell you about the text we're going to read?" and "What might we be reading about?" Have students jot answers down or share them orally.
4. Ask students to walk around and talk to at least three other people, sharing their Book Bit and reading the other students'. Then ask them to revise their answers to the questions from step 3.
5. Show the class the full list of Book Bit phrases. Model how to generate a question using the list and questions that start with *who*, *what*, *where*, *when*, *why*, and *how*. Record students' questions.

6. If students will read the text aloud, ask them to signal with a thumbs up or other quiet sign every time they hear an answer to one of the questions. If they will read the text silently, ask students to annotate answers to their questions that they find in the text.

Such activities scaffold the process of answering questions to help students generate substantive questions that will facilitate meaning-making processes with texts.

Figure 8.2 depicts the self-rating scale for element 24, increasing response rates.

Score	Description
4: Innovating	I adapt behaviors and create new strategies for unique student needs and situations.
3: Applying	I use response-rate techniques to maintain student engagement, and I monitor the extent to which the techniques keep students engaged.
2: Developing	I use response-rate techniques to maintain student engagement in questions, but I do not monitor the effect on students.
1: Beginning	I use the strategies and behaviors associated with this element incorrectly or with parts missing.
0: Not Using	I am unaware of strategies and behaviors associated with this element.

Figure 8.2: Self-rating scale for element 24—Increasing response rates.

Element 25: Using Physical Movement

Research on embodied cognition is particularly relevant to using physical movement in the reading classroom. *Embodied cognition* is the idea that "sensorimotor processes facilitate cognitive processes" (Berenhaus, Oakhill, & Rusted, 2015, p. 331). Robb Lindgren and Mina Johnson-Glenberg (2013) explain that "human cognition is deeply rooted in the body's interactions with its physical environment" (p. 446) and G. Patricia Wilson (2003) states that "gesture does more than express thought, it is thought" (p. 378). Several fascinating experiments illustrate the brain-body connection. When comparing people who heard a list of action phrases with people who acted out the action phrases, those who acted them out remembered the list better (Engelkamp & Zimmer, 2001). Olaf Hauk, Ingrid Johnsrude, and Friedemann Pulvermüller (2004) used MRI technology to study the sensorimotor areas of the brain activated when participants listened to action words (such as *lick* or *kick*); when someone heard a word such as *kick*, the areas of the brain associated with actual foot and leg movement were activated (even though the participant wasn't moving). Véronique Boulenger, Olaf Hauk, and Friedemann Pulvermüller (2009) took this one step further. They found that even when one uses an action word in an abstract sense (such as *grasp* in *She grasped the idea*), the same effect occurred; parts of the brain associated with physically grasping an object were activated. Table 8.1 describes additional research studies of note.

Table 8.1: Research on Embodied Cognition

Study	Findings
Noice and Noice (2001)	Students in an acting class remembered more of their lines when they read their part aloud using emotional expression and body movements (as opposed to only using emotion expression while sitting still).
Glenberg, Gutierrez, Levin, Japuntich, and Kaschak (2004)	Students who acted out a story about farm animals using toy farm animals remembered more of the story than those who only read the story.
Noice and Noice (2006)	Students who acted out a text using emotional expression and gestures recalled the text better than those who simply read the text.

Study	Findings
Cook, Mitchell, and Goldin-Meadow (2008)	Students who gestured while learning a new mathematics concept understood the concept better than students who only discussed the concept with the teacher.
Cutica, Ianì, and Bucciarelli (2014)	Students who gestured while reading science texts remembered concepts and ideas better than students who only read the text (without gesturing).
Berenhaus et al. (2015)	Students who acted out a story remembered details and ideas from the story better than students who simply read the story.

Source: Adapted from Berenhaus et al., 2015.

Lindgren and Johnson-Glenberg (2013) emphasize that physical movement activities:

> must be *designed* such that they engineer the desired instances of understanding. Simply giving in to a physically active student's urge to move around the classroom is not likely to, by itself, engender new conceptual knowledge. On the other hand, such outcomes can be expected by having children move in prescribed ways so as to experience critical phenomena that highlight congruencies between those movements and abstract formalisms. (p. 448)

Here, we present two strategies that teachers might use to incorporate embodied cognition in the reading classroom: (1) enacted reading comprehension and (2) tableaux.

Enacted Reading Comprehension

The *enacted reading comprehension* strategy (Kaschak, Connor, & Dombek, 2017) helps students use gestures to represent increasingly abstract concepts in texts. In a study designed to help students understand opposing forces in various contexts and disciplines, students first used gestures to represent the opposing forces present in earthquakes; they used their hands to model movement and friction between tectonic plates. Then, they used similar gestures to model the movement of air masses that create tornadoes and hurricanes (slightly more abstract content). Next, they gestured in similar ways to model the opposing forces between two people who disagree about an issue (more abstract still). And finally, while reading Linda Sue Park's (2001) *A Single Shard*, they used gestures to model the opposing forces that occur within the character Tree-ear from the story (most abstract). Beginning with concrete examples of a relationship allows students to identify that relationship (and use gestures to represent it) in increasingly abstract contexts.

Tableaux

A strategy called *tableaux* (Branscombe, 2015) helps students connect their brains and bodies while reading. A *tableau* "is a silent, human sculpture that is created by a group of participants to 'represent an interpretation of an event, action, location, or scene from a book'" (Tortello, 2004, p. 207, as cited in Branscombe, 2015, p. 321). In addition to the support that tableaux provide for students in visualizing and acting out a text, the collaborative nature of this strategy can also be beneficial. Rebecca Tortello (2004) notes that students "may feel less anxious about taking part in a silent group activity than about interpreting the book orally on their own in front of the class" (p. 207). Additionally, it gives students an opportunity to incorporate their life experiences with a text. Wilson (2003) points out that "each performer drew on his or her understandings from life experiences and negotiated an overall interpretation for the tableau with others" (p. 380). To introduce tableaux to students, a teacher might explain that "tableau" is French for "painting" and have them look at a few paintings that feature characters frozen in time; ask them to talk about what is happening, what the characters might be thinking or feeling, and so on. Then, have students practice creating their own tableau based on a scene from a text; Margaret Branscombe (2015) recommends teaching tableaux by playing a charades-like game with students where one group acts out a scene while the other group tries to guess what it is (locations are particularly good for early tableaux, such as "grocery store" or "park"). When creating tableaux, students should think about:

- Facial expressions
- Use of their hands
- Body posture
- Space between participants in the tableau

Students can strike poses one at a time, building on each other's decisions, or work to negotiate how the group will depict the concept or scene. Once a group has created a tableau, the audience can offer thoughts and feedback to the group.

Energy is essential to engagement; physical movement is a straightforward approach to raising energy. Figure 8.3 depicts the self-rating scale for this element about incorporating physical movement into the classroom.

Score	Description
4: Innovating	I adapt behaviors and create new strategies for unique student needs and situations.
3: Applying	I use physical movement to maintain student engagement, and I monitor the extent to which these activities enhance student engagement.
2: Developing	I use physical movement to maintain student engagement, but I do not monitor the effect on students.
1: Beginning	I use the strategies and behaviors associated with this element incorrectly or with parts missing.
0: Not Using	I am unaware of strategies and behaviors associated with this element.

Figure 8.3: Self-rating scale for element 25—Using physical movement.

Element 26: Maintaining a Lively Pace

One way to maintain a lively pace in the reading classroom is to occasionally engage in storytelling. Brian W. Sturm (1999) studied what happens to listeners during storytelling sessions. His findings show that listeners often enter a trancelike state while listening to stories: time slows down or speeds up, listeners cease to be aware of their actual surroundings and perceive that they have entered the environment of the story, characters in the story become "real" to listeners, and listeners' visual, auditory, kinesthetic, and emotional responses fully align with the story. There are many resources available (books and online) that teachers might use to sharpen their storytelling skills.

- TED.com offers a playlist called "How to Tell a Story" (www.ted.com/playlists/62/how_to_tell_a_story).
- Khan Academy has partnered with Pixar to provide a course called "The Art of Storytelling" (www.khanacademy.org/partner-content/pixar/storytelling).
- WHEEL Council has compiled a succinct list of pointers and tips for how to learn and tell stories (www.wheelcouncil.org/storytellers).

We adapted the following list of guidelines for storytelling from Julie DeNeen's (2012) "30 Storytelling Tips for Educators: How to Capture Your Student's Attention."

- **Every part of a story must be essential:** Every character, event, or setting should relate to the ending of the story. Remove anything that does not affect the outcome of the story.
- **Have a hook in the opening:** Articulating a problem is the classic opening storytelling move. For example, if a character will discover something at the end of the story, describe the problems not knowing it causes in the beginning.
- **Know your theme:** Everything in the story should relate back to this theme. For example, if the theme is finding beauty, the details should showcase examples and nonexamples of beauty.
- **Keep it simple:** Simpler is better, and not just for young students. For example, try explaining an electrical circuit by telling the story of a train that could only travel along connected tracks.
- **Maintain eye contact:** Eye contact equals credibility and trust. When you look at students, it conveys the importance of the information you're communicating and brings them into the world you're creating.
- **Pick a few interesting words to use over and over again throughout the story:** If you've ever read Rudyard Kipling's (1902/2008) *Just So Stories*, you understand the power of this, oh Best Beloved. Repeated words and phrases can also be a great way to introduce or reinforce specific vocabulary terms.
- **Move around and make some noise:** Stand up and use gestures, whole-body movements, facial expressions, and voices to help students visualize the story.
- **Pause at critical junctures:** Silence increases dramatic tension and gives students a chance to guess what will happen next or try to solve a character's problem themselves. Some of the best storytellers point out that listeners actually *want* to do some cognitive work as a part of the storytelling experience.

Start by finding (or writing) a story that you personally enjoy and then cultivate your ability to tell it well. Then, acquire another story. Over time, you can develop a repertoire of engaging tales to enliven the pace of your reading classroom.

When teachers maintain a lively pace, they generate heightened energy levels in students. Figure 8.4 depicts the self-rating scale for maintaining a lively pace.

Score	Description
4: Innovating	I adapt behaviors and create new strategies for unique student needs and situations.
3: Applying	I use pacing techniques to maintain students' engagement, and I monitor the extent to which these techniques keep students engaged.
2: Developing	I use pacing techniques to maintain students' engagement, but I do not monitor the effect on students.
1: Beginning	I use the strategies and behaviors associated with this element incorrectly or with parts missing.
0: Not Using	I am unaware of strategies and behaviors associated with this element.

Figure 8.4: Self-rating scale for element 26—Maintaining a lively pace.

Element 27: Demonstrating Intensity and Enthusiasm

Talk to students about the books and texts you read yourself and explain why you read. Letting students into your reading world allows them to consider different future possible selves that relate to reading (Markus & Nurius, 1986). Ulrich Schiefele, Ellen Schaffner, Jens Möller, and Allan Wigfield (2012) list the following reasons that students tend to read: "curiosity, involvement, competition, recognition, grades, compliance, and work avoidance" (p. 458). Using data from the 2015 International Study of Avid Book Readers, Margaret K. Merga (2017) synthesized reasons that adults read, as we show in table 8.2.

Table 8.2: Reasons Adults Read

Reason	Description
Perspective Taking	Reading books allows the reader to think about topics and ideas from another person's point of view. Reading can make a person more open minded.
Knowledge	Adult readers seek two types of knowledge in particular: (1) general knowledge and (2) sociological knowledge (knowledge about how people think and act). Knowing more is linked to a sense of satisfaction with oneself.
Personal Development	Adult readers read to better understand the world and learn how to better deal with situations. Self-help books are designed to meet this desire among readers, although autobiographies and books on spirituality also fit in this category.
Mental Stimulation	Adults read to make themselves better thinkers. They want to be able to think critically and analyze information; reading gives them practice with those skills.
Habit, Entertainment, and Pleasure	Some adults simply read because they have always read. Many adults prefer reading books to watching movies, viewing them as better entertainment.
Escapism and Mental Health	Adults read to escape into another world. Sometimes this is for the thrill of experiencing a different reality; sometimes it is to avoid experiencing their own reality.
Books as Friends	Adults have favorite books that they see as friends. They read them over and over again, enjoying the familiar parts and noticing new things on subsequent encounters.
Imagination and Creative Inspiration	Adults draw imaginative fodder from books. They use what they read to inspire their artistic and creative endeavors.
Writing, Language, and Vocabulary	Adults read because they love language. They enjoy seeing how authors communicate concepts in fresh or particularly engaging ways, and they enjoy adding terms to their vocabularies.

Source: Adapted from Merga, 2017.

A teacher might identify the reasons from table 8.2 that he or she reads as an adult, and then ask students to select some reasons why they currently read and why they might continue to read as they grow up (from either Schiefele et al.'s [2012] or Merga's [2017] lists).

Teacher intensity and enthusiasm about content can be contagious. Figure 8.5 depicts the self-rating scale for this element.

Score	Description
4: Innovating	I adapt behaviors and create new strategies for unique student needs and situations.
3: Applying	I demonstrate intensity and enthusiasm, and I monitor the extent to which students' engagement increases.
2: Developing	I demonstrate intensity and enthusiasm, but I do not monitor the effect on students.
1: Beginning	I use the strategies and behaviors associated with this element incorrectly or with parts missing.
0: Not Using	I am unaware of strategies and behaviors associated with this element.

Figure 8.5: Self-rating scale for element 27—Demonstrating intensity and enthusiasm.

Element 28: Presenting Unusual Information

There are a number of different types of unusual information a teacher might present to students in the reading classroom. The lives of famous authors can yield many unusual facts—for example, did you know that Ernest Hemingway's mother dressed him as a girl for the first four years of his life? In addition to this type of unusual information, teachers might also share unusual information related to the process of reading. One of the most interesting lines of research related to reading concerns eye movements that occur during reading and what they tell us about how the brain processes print. Students may find it fascinating to think about their visual perception system and how it facilitates (and can get in the way of) effective reading. As Keith Rayner (1998) explains:

> When we read, look at a scene, or search for an object, we continually make eye movements called *saccades*. Between the saccades, our eyes remain relatively still during *fixations* for about 200–300 ms. . . . We do not obtain new information during a saccade, because the eyes are moving so quickly . . . that only a blur would be perceived. (p. 373)

While a full understanding of the eye movement research is likely to be too in-depth for the reading classroom, there are a number of interesting facts related to eye movement during reading that teachers might relate to students. For example, Rayner (1998) provides the following interesting facts.

- The eye has three zones: (1) the foveal, (2) the parafoveal, and (3) the peripheral. The only zone that can detect details is the fovea, which is about the size of your thumb held at arm's length from your eye. When we focus or *fixate* on something, we are aiming our fovea at it. The parafoveal and peripheral zones detect general information, including movement. If we detect something in those zones that seems interesting, we move our fovea to look at it.
- Eye movements are slightly different when reading silently than when reading aloud (or listening to someone read aloud while following along). When reading aloud or listening to another read text aloud, the eyes run ahead of the voice. Consequently, the eyes often have to pause so as not to get too far ahead of the voice.
- When reading silently, the average eye fixation lasts 200–250 milliseconds, half the time it takes you to blink. The average distance of a saccade is seven characters (including spaces). That distance doesn't change whether the text is close to your eyes or far away from your eyes.
- Sometimes the eyes skip words! Readers fixate on words related to the content of a text about 85 percent of the time; they fixate on function words (*the*, *is*, *of*) only about 35 percent of the time. This means you don't actually look at all of the words when you read! Your brain fills some of them in based on context and what you know about how writers typically form sentences (called *syntax*).
- The eyes choose which words to fixate on based on how long the word is. Readers look at words that are two or three letters long only 25 percent of the time. In contrast, they almost always look at words that are eight letters or longer.
- Your eyes do not always move forward during reading! About 10–15 percent of saccades are backwards (called *regressions*). Regressions usually happen when a reader realizes that he or she didn't understand what he or she just read. So the eyes go back to figure out what they missed.

Not only are these facts interesting, but they can make students more aware of what their eyes are doing during reading. This can be useful as students think about the techniques that they use to read a passage. Under-standing a bit about eye movements makes it easier to explain what happens while skimming a passage—fewer fixations and longer saccades. Also, for students who are still engaging in phonological recoding to build up their knowledge of orthography, it is actually critical that they intentionally fixate on the individual letters of an unknown word (since linking those letters to sounds is key to being able to sound out the word). If a student is having trouble with phonological recoding, it may be because he or she is not looking at each letter in an unknown word.

Unusual information generally stimulates students' interest and intrigue and is an excellent way to provoke engagement. Figure 8.6 depicts the self-rating scale for element 28.

Score	Description
4: Innovating	I adapt behaviors and create new strategies for unique student needs and situations.
3: Applying	I use unusual or intriguing information to capture students' attention, and I monitor the extent to which this information enhances engagement.
2: Developing	I use unusual or intriguing information to capture students' attention, but I do not monitor the effect on students.
1: Beginning	I use the strategies and behaviors associated with this element incorrectly or with parts missing.
0: Not Using	I am unaware of strategies and behaviors associated with this element.

Figure 8.6: Self-rating scale for element 28—Presenting unusual information.

Element 29: Using Friendly Controversy

In the reading classroom, literary criticism provides an excellent instructional opportunity for engaging students in friendly controversy, where students engage in civil dialogue regarding topics about which they have different opinions. According to Deborah Appleman (2009), *literary criticism* is an attempt to evaluate and understand the work of an author in an attempt to expose hidden ideologies that may be present in a text. Literary criticism involves viewing texts through various critical lenses. Table 8.3 describes some of the major critical lenses teachers might use.

Table 8.3: Critical Lenses

Critical Lens	Description	Questions
Reader Response	Examines the effect of a text on the reader	• How did the text make you feel? • What do you think the text means? • What parts of the text did you identify with? • What experiences did the text remind you of?
Formalist or New Criticism	Examines the various components of a text to draw conclusions about its meaning	• What literary elements, literary devices, symbolism, and themes are in the text? • What are the strengths and weaknesses of the text? • What is the purpose of the text, and does it accomplish that purpose?
Historical or Biographical Criticism	Examines a text within its historical context (social, political, economic, cultural, or intellectual climate)	• How did historical context influence the events and themes in the text? • What does this text tell us about its author? Why did he or she write it?
Feminist or Gender Criticism	Examines gender roles in a text	• What gender roles or identities are present in the text? • Does the text portray characters positively or negatively depending on their gender? • How does the text affirm or reject sexist ideas?

Critical Lens	Description	Questions
Marxist and Social Power Criticism	Examines social class in a text	• How does the text portray social classes? • Does the text portray characters positively or negatively depending on their social class? • How does the text relate power to money and social class?
Psychological Criticism	Examines a text as an expression of the mind, feelings, and desires of its author	• What psychological conflicts drive the characters or the plot? • What psychological concepts can help us understand the way the author sees the world?
Archetypal Criticism	Examines patterns and models of storytelling across many texts	• What universal themes, situations, symbols, and characters are present in the text? • How is the hero or villain similar to heroes or villains in other stories?

Note: This is a partial list. For a complete list and descriptions of critical lenses to use for literary criticism, visit "Literary Theory and Schools of Criticism" at http://owl.english.purdue.edu (Purdue University's Online Writing Lab).

Source: Adapted from Appleman, 2009.

The reason that literary criticism is such a good match for friendly controversy is because when critiquing a text, there is no one correct interpretation, nor even one correct critical lens through which to view a text. The factor that determines the validity of an interpretation or a decision to use a specific lens is the quality of support a reader provides for it. Therefore, two students might disagree about the interpretation of a specific text and take turns providing evidence to support their perspectives.

When executed well, friendly controversy helps students analyze content with a critical eye. Figure 8.7 depicts the self-rating scale for this element.

Score	Description
4: Innovating	I adapt behaviors and create new strategies for unique student needs and situations.
3: Applying	I use friendly controversy techniques to maintain student engagement, and I monitor the effect on students.
2: Developing	I use friendly controversy techniques to maintain student engagement, but I do not monitor the effect on students.
1: Beginning	I use the strategies and behaviors associated with this element incorrectly or with parts missing.
0: Not Using	I am unaware of strategies and behaviors associated with this element.

Figure 8.7: Self-rating scale for element 29—Using friendly controversy.

Element 30: Using Academic Games

Although teachers can use academic games with all types of reading content, one of the best places to incorporate academic games is vocabulary instruction. Camille L. Z. Blachowicz and Peter Fisher (2012) explain:

- Word play is a motivating and important component of the word-rich classroom.
- Word play calls on students to reflect metacognitively on words, word parts, and context.
- Word play requires students to be active learners and capitalizes on possibilities for the social construction of meaning.
- Word play develops domains of word meaning and relatedness as it engages students in the practice and rehearsal of words. (p. 190)

They point out that word play can be as simple as sharing puns or jokes, such as the following science-related quips, with students:

- Never trust an atom; they make up everything.
- The other day I made a chemistry joke, but I got no reaction.
- I bet Earth makes fun of all the other planets for having no life.
- Two atoms were walking down the sidewalk and suddenly one slipped off the curb and said, "Oh no, I've lost my electron!" The other atom said, "Are you sure?" and the first atom replied, "Yes, I'm positive!"
- I would make a science joke, but all the good ones argon. (Marzano et al., 2015, p. 42)

Blachowicz and Fisher (2012) explain that beyond being funny, puns and jokes naturally engage students' cognitive and metacognitive systems:

> Anyone who understands [a] pun has performed a metacognitive act. . . . The groan or laugh that results is our metacognitive check. We get the joke and we exhibit cognitive flexibility, the ability to look at the same thing in different ways. . . . Creating and sharing jokes, riddles, and puns can help develop this flexibility. (p. 192)

Other vocabulary-related games are more structured, with rules and turn-taking. Marzano and Simms (2013) present a list of such vocabulary games; we describe twenty-eight of these games in appendix F. (Visit **go.SolutionTree.com/instruction** to access appendices E, F, and G.)

Academic games are quick remedies for disengagement and provide students with a fresh look at content. When using academic games, it is important to preserve inconsequential competition. Such competition is done in the spirit of fun; teams should be changed periodically so that all students have the opportunity to be on a winning team, and any rewards associated with winning should be minimal. Figure 8.8 depicts the self-rating scale for this element.

Score	Description
4: Innovating	I adapt behaviors and create new strategies for unique student needs and situations.
3: Applying	I use academic games and inconsequential competition to maintain student engagement, and I monitor the extent to which students focus on the academic content of the game.
2: Developing	I use academic games and inconsequential competition to maintain student engagement, but I do not monitor the effect on students.
1: Beginning	I use the strategies and behaviors associated with this element incorrectly or with parts missing.
0: Not Using	I am unaware of strategies and behaviors associated with this element.

Figure 8.8: Self-rating scale for element 30—Using academic games.

Element 31: Providing Opportunities for Students to Talk About Themselves

Marzano (2017) explains that the purpose of giving students opportunities to talk about themselves is that doing so allows them to articulate their interests. Connecting content to students' interests can make class more interesting and relevant for them. In contrast to a more generalized motivation to read, students' *interests* are typically related to a specific activity or topic. For example, a student who has a general preference for reading might experience an aversion to a text on a topic of low interest to him or her. Conversely, a student with an aversion to reading in general might experience a high level of interest when reading a text about a topic in which he or she is intensely interested. Sara M. Fulmer and Jan C. Frijters (2011) find that students reported high interest and high enjoyment while reading a text they rated as personally interesting, even though the text was written at their frustration level. And, compared to students reading personally uninteresting texts, students reading difficult but interesting texts were almost twice as likely to persist in reading their texts when given a chance to stop. Connecting reading to students' interests is especially important for adolescents "since they have so many activities to fill their time, and what activity gets chosen depends in large part on what they value" (Springer, Dole, & Hacker, 2017, p. 520). To the extent that teachers can help students connect their interests to the texts they read in the classroom, teachers can likely enhance student learning.

Given the benefits of being interested in the content of a text, a teacher might also teach students how to cultivate interest in texts that they must read. The RAND Reading Study Group (2002) points out that "the proficient adult reader can read a variety of materials with ease and interest, can read for varying purposes, and can read with comprehension even when the material is neither easy to understand nor intrinsically interesting" (p. xiii). Carol Sansone and colleagues (Sansone & Thoman, 2005; Sansone, Thoman, & Smith, 2000) suggest that students can best regulate their interest by being aware of the process they use to determine whether a task or text is interesting. They propose that students use the following four questions when deciding whether or not they are interested in completing a task (such as reading a text).

1. Is this interesting to me? If yes, engage in the task. If no, go to question 2.
2. Is there enough extrinsic motivation (personal belief, reward, punishment, getting a grade) to continue despite my lack of interest? If no, stop. If yes, go to question 3.
3. Will I just grit my teeth and perform the task, or will I try to enhance my interest in it? If I will try to enhance my interest, go to question 4.
4. What strategies can I use to enhance my interest in this task?

Interest-enhancing strategies, according to Sansone and colleagues (2000), include increasing the level of challenge associated with the task, altering the context of the task, changing the procedure the task requires, and making the task more artistic or creative. For example, a student who dislikes poetry but needs to read and compare several poems for class might use the aforementioned strategies as follows.

- **Increase the level of challenge associated with the task:** A student might incorporate elements of literary criticism (something she is very interested in and likes doing) into her comparison of the poems, even though the teacher has not explicitly asked her to read the poems through specific critical lenses.
- **Alter the context of the task:** If the student is reading the poetry as part of a unit on Romantic literature, the student might imagine, instead, that the teacher has asked her to read the poems and select one to give to her significant other on the occasion of their anniversary.
- **Change the procedure required for the task:** If the teacher has asked the student to do a close reading and explication of each poem, using her analysis to draw general conclusions about a specific era of poetic work (an inductive approach, from specific to general), she might, instead, use a deductive approach, first researching generalizations about the era of poetic work, and then looking for specific instances of each generalization in the poems.
- **Make the task more artistic or creative:** In order to compare the poems, the student might first draw a picture to represent the critical elements of each poem, and then compare her pictures to make conclusions about similarities and differences between them.

Thus, students can learn to seek out tasks that pique their intrinsic interests and modify tasks that don't to make them more engaging.

When students have opportunities to talk about themselves in relation to academic content, it creates connections for them that are inherently engaging. Figure 8.9 depicts the self-rating scale for this element.

Score	Description
4: Innovating	I adapt behaviors and create new strategies for unique student needs and situations.
3: Applying	I provide opportunities for students to talk about themselves, and I monitor the extent to which my actions affect students' engagement.
2: Developing	I provide opportunities for students to talk about themselves, but I do not monitor the effect on students.
1: Beginning	I use the strategies and behaviors associated with this element incorrectly or with parts missing.
0: Not Using	I am unaware of strategies and behaviors associated with this element.

Figure 8.9: Self-rating scale for element 31—Providing opportunities for students to talk about themselves.

Element 32: Motivating and Inspiring Students

One of the unique benefits of the reading classroom is that a colorful array of personalities populates it—authors and the characters in their works. As individuals who have made a career of expressing themselves in words, authors' quotes (and their characters' dialogue) can be a rich source of inspiration and motivation for students. Here we list some of our favorite reading-related inspirational quotes.

"The more that you read, the more things you will know. The more that you learn, the more places you'll go" (p. 27).

—Dr. Seuss (1978), *I Can Read With My Eyes Shut!*

"Until I feared I would lose it, I never loved to read. One does not love breathing." (p. 23)

—Harper Lee (1960), *To Kill a Mockingbird*

Reader's Bill of Rights

1. The right to not read
2. The right to skip pages
3. The right to not finish
4. The right to reread
5. The right to read anything
6. The right to escapism
7. The right to read anywhere
8. The right to browse
9. The right to read out loud
10. The right to not defend your tastes

—Daniel Pennac (2006), *The Rights of the Reader*

"A classic is a book that has never finished saying what it has to say." (p. 128)

—Italo Calvino (1986), *The Uses of Literature*

Students might compile lists of their favorite reading-related quotes. Additionally, they might complete reading-related personal projects. For example, one student might set as a goal to read all of the works by a particular author. Although accomplishing such a goal might take several years (or several decades), he or she could make a plan and begin working on it right away. At a simpler level, a student might set as a goal to read a particular book that is longer, more challenging, or of a different genre than those he or she typically reads.

Ultimately, the highest form of engagement occurs when students are intrinsically motivated and inspired. Figure 8.10 depicts the self-rating scale for this element.

Score	Description
4: Innovating	I adapt behaviors and create new strategies for unique student needs and situations.
3: Applying	I use activities designed to motivate and inspire students, and I monitor the extent to which my actions affect students.
2: Developing	I use activities designed to motivate and inspire students, but I do not monitor the effect on students.
1: Beginning	I use the strategies and behaviors associated with this element incorrectly or with parts missing.
0: Not Using	I am unaware of strategies and behaviors associated with this element.

Figure 8.10: Self-rating scale for element 32—Motivating and inspiring students.

GUIDING QUESTIONS FOR CURRICULUM DESIGN

This design question focuses on engagement: *What engagement strategies will I use to help students pay attention, as well as be energized, intrigued, and inspired?* The following questions, which align to each of the elements in this chapter, guide teachers to plan instruction. Teachers would clearly not use all elements in a single unit of instruction but would frequently—if not daily—notice when students are disengaged or unresponsive and respond with appropriate strategies.

- **Element 23:** What will I do to notice when students are not engaged and react?

- **Element 24:** What will I do to increase students' response rates?

- **Element 25:** What will I do to increase students' physical movement?

- **Element 26:** What will I do to maintain a lively pace?

- **Element 27:** What will I do to demonstrate intensity and enthusiasm?

- **Element 28:** What will I do to present unusual information?

- **Element 29:** What will I do to engage students in friendly controversy?

- **Element 30:** What will I do to engage students in academic games?

- **Element 31:** What will I do to provide opportunities for students to talk about themselves?

- **Element 32:** What will I do to motivate and inspire students?

Summary

Using engagement strategies involves ten elements: (1) noticing when students are not engaged and reacting, (2) increasing response rates, (3) using physical movement, (4) maintaining a lively pace, (5) demonstrating intensity and enthusiasm, (6) presenting unusual information, (7) using friendly controversy, (8) using academic games, (9) providing opportunities for students to talk about themselves, and (10) motivating and inspiring students. In the reading classroom, teachers have a vast array of options to implement each element. Techniques such as Book Bits and storytelling grab students' attention. Tableaux and academic games keep students energized, and research findings about mind wandering and eye movement during reading are likely to intrigue students. Textual criticism (and the friendly controversies that may arise from it) gives students a window into their own interests and perspectives, and inspirational quotes offer excellent vehicles for students to cultivate motivation and inspiration.

CHAPTER 9

Implementing Rules and Procedures

CONTEXT

The eighth design area of *The New Art and Science of Teaching* framework involves creating predictable and dependable modes of interaction between and among the people in a classroom. To effectively implement such a system, teachers must use strategies for establishing rules and procedures (element 33) and clearly articulate and communicate them. They must organize the physical layout of the classroom (element 34) to create spaces that facilitate learning; they must also demonstrate withitness (element 35). Finally, teachers must use strategies for acknowledging adherence, and lack of adherence, to rules and procedures (elements 36 and 37) by monitoring students' behavior and providing both positive reinforcement and consequences as appropriate. Together, these elements create a classroom environment that is orderly and safe. Here we describe how each element might manifest in a reading classroom.

Element 33: Establishing Rules and Procedures

Rules and procedures play a critical role in the reading classroom. Most obviously, a poorly managed classroom without clear rules and procedures inhibits the learning of any type of content. It also fails to provide structure for students with low social skills. Jeanne R. Paratore and colleagues (2011) explain:

> Children who enter kindergarten with antisocial behavior, especially aggressiveness, develop fewer friendships and less positive relationships with teachers than do children who have positive social skills. Peer rejection and conflict with the teacher mediate classroom participation, which, in turn, has a direct effect on achievement. Ladd et al. (1999) found that initial antisocial behavior and subsequent classroom participation accounted for close to 60% of the indirect effects on achievement. (pp. 113–114)

Clear rules and procedures, along with the other elements in this category, are also critical to developing a reading classroom that includes productive discussion, dialogue, and discourse.

P. Karen Murphy, Ian A. G. Wilkinson, Anna O. Soter, Maeghan N. Hennessey, and John F. Alexander (2009) explain that using discussion to enhance reading comprehension positions talk as "a *means* and not an *end*" (p. 761, original emphasis). Joshua F. Lawrence and Catherine E. Snow (2011) list the following features of classroom discourse that tend to promote students' comprehension skills:

- Establishing a purpose for reading
- Activating relevant background knowledge

- Posing open-ended questions that require deep processing
- Responding to student initiatives
- Promoting peer interaction (p. 324)

Within the elements in this chapter, we focus specifically on three ideas related to cultivating classroom discussions: (1) arranging the classroom for student interaction, (2) monitoring and facilitating student interactions, and (3) scaffolding student interactions (encouraging productive talk and preventing unproductive talk).

Establishing rules and procedures plays a key role in promoting order or the lack of it in the classroom. Figure 9.1 depicts the self-rating scale for this element.

Score	Description
4: Innovating	I adapt behaviors and create new strategies for unique student needs and situations.
3: Applying	I establish rules and procedures, and I monitor the extent to which my actions affect students' behavior.
2: Developing	I establish rules and procedures, but I do not monitor the effect on students.
1: Beginning	I use the strategies and behaviors associated with this element incorrectly or with parts missing.
0: Not Using	I am unaware of strategies and behaviors associated with this element.

Figure 9.1: Self-rating scale for element 33—Establishing rules and procedures.

Element 34: Organizing the Physical Layout of the Classroom

Obviously, the physical layout of the classroom helps or hinders student learning. According to Sapna Cheryan, Sianna A. Ziegler, Victoria C. Plaut, and Andrew N. Meltzoff (2014), basic environmental elements such as natural light, low levels of external noise, appropriate temperatures, good air quality, and adequate accessibility for students with disabilities have a significant relationship with student learning. However, symbolic elements of a classroom also influence student learning and performance. For example, Ioana M. Latu, Marianne Schmid Mast, Joris Lammers, and Dario Bombari (2013) conducted a study in which they asked male and female students to give a persuasive speech to an audience in rooms where there was either a photograph of Bill Clinton, Hillary Clinton, German Chancellor Angela Merkel, or no photograph on the back wall of the room. When the photograph of Bill Clinton or no photograph was present, men gave longer, higher-rated speeches than women. However, when Hillary Clinton's or Angela Merkel's photograph was displayed, the differences between men's and women's speeches disappeared. In their studies, Cheryan and colleagues (2014) comment:

> Objects in the environment signaled who "belonged" in the space. . . . To feel like they belong, students must be able to relate to the other people who commonly seem to inhabit a space or pursue a type of career. Objects shape this sense of belonging. (p. 7)

Therefore, as teachers design classrooms to promote discussion, they may want to include a diverse set of pictures of orators and rhetorical role models.

Finally, teachers should take the arrangement of furniture into account when considering how to best promote student discussion and interaction. Teachers might consider the seven classroom layouts Darrell Scott and Robert J. Marzano (2014) describe, as we depict in figure 9.2.

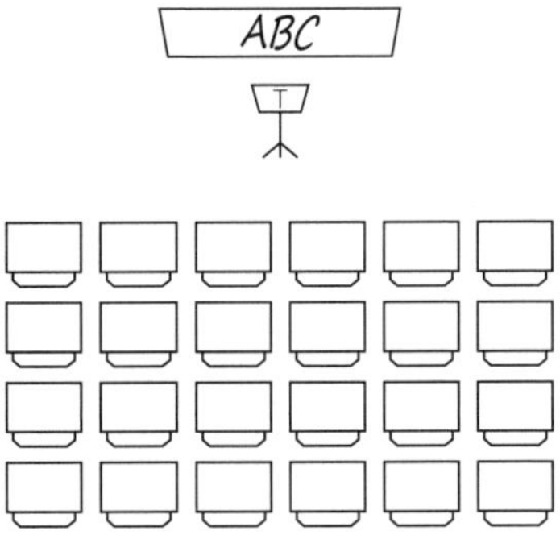

Traditional Seating

Desks are in rows, all facing the front of the room. This type of setup establishes a climate in which lecturing from the teacher is the norm. However, it can stifle interaction and collaboration between students.

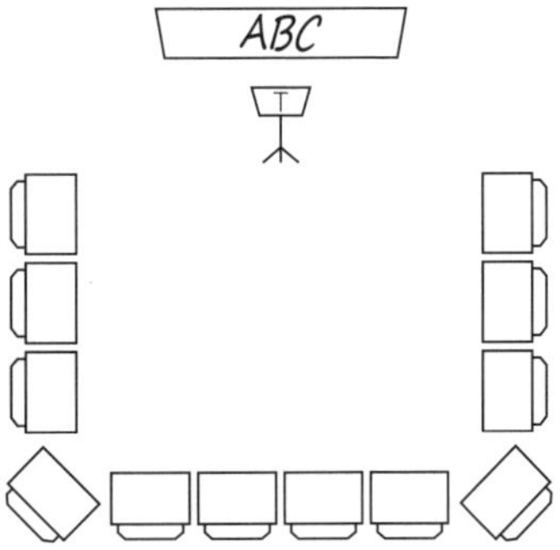

U-Shaped Seating

This setup creates an open, warm atmosphere and provides good visibility for all students. Teachers can use it for lecturing but also to encourage discussion among students. Keep in mind, however, that it may not be ideal for collaborative work.

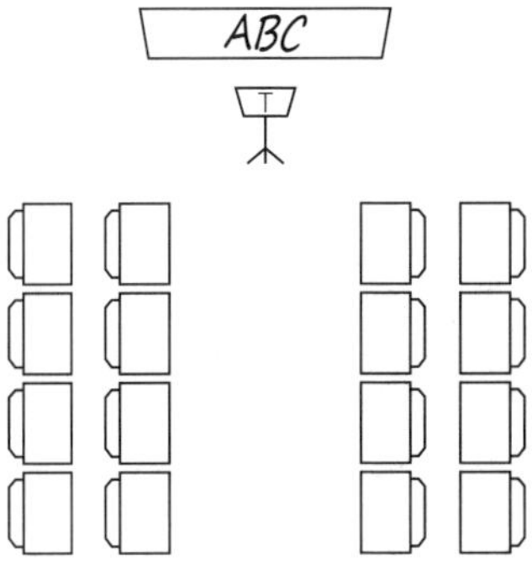

Debate-Style Seating

This arrangement lines desks up in rows facing each other. Teachers might choose to use two rows on either side (as shown) or a single row on each side.

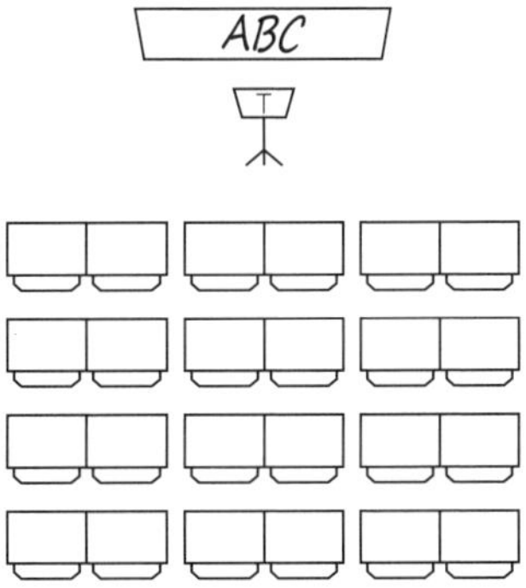

Paired Seating

This type of seating works well when resources (such as computers, lab equipment, or print materials) need to be shared. It can also facilitate partner discussions and collaborative work.

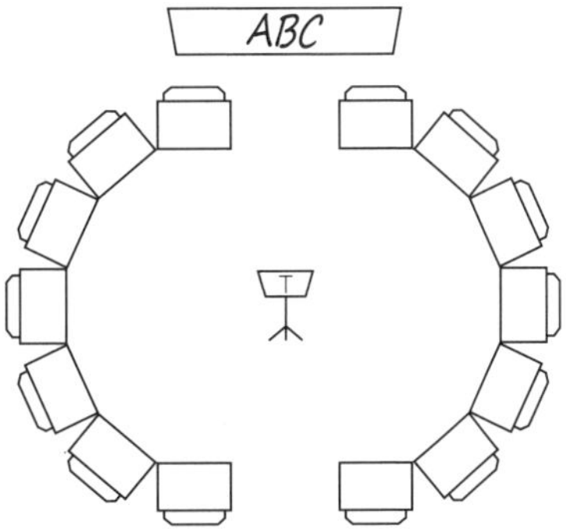

Circular Seating

This arrangement encourages student involvement and discussion by allowing all members of the class to make eye contact with each other. However, it may not work well for group work or lecturing.

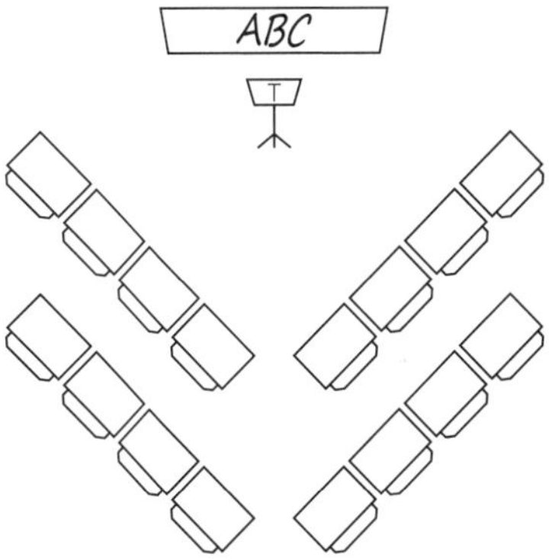

V-Shaped Seating

This arrangement is a bit less casual than U-shaped seating. However, it still results in excellent interaction between students and the teacher.

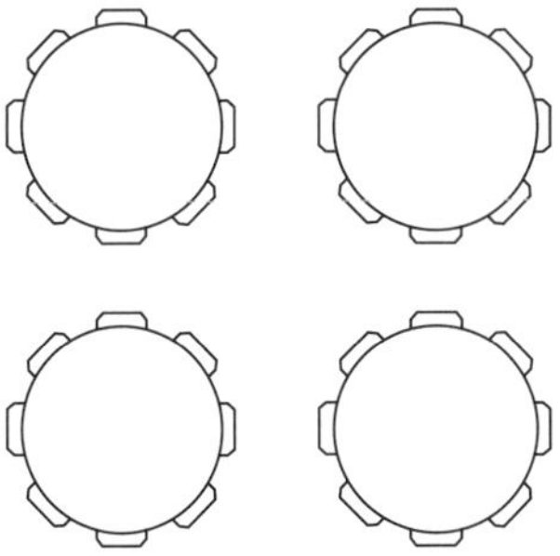

Small-Group Seating

This seating is perfect for collaboration and cooperative learning.

Source: Scott & Marzano, 2014, pp. 69–71.

Figure 9.2: Various classroom seating arrangements.

Depending on the type of discussion the teacher will use, different seating arrangements might be more appropriate than others.

The physical environment of the classroom can help stimulate a sense of order or lack of it in the classroom. Figure 9.3 depicts the self-rating scale for this element.

Score	Description
4: Innovating	I adapt behaviors and create new strategies for unique student needs and situations.
3: Applying	I organize the physical layout of the classroom, and I monitor the extent to which my actions affect students' behavior.
2: Developing	I organize the physical layout of the classroom, but I do not monitor the effect on students.
1: Beginning	I use the strategies and behaviors associated with this element incorrectly or with parts missing.
0: Not Using	I am unaware of strategies and behaviors associated with this element.

Figure 9.3: Self-rating scale for element 34—Organizing the physical layout of the classroom.

Element 35: Demonstrating Withitness

Withitness in the reading classroom, among other things, involves the teacher effectively monitoring and facilitating student interactions during discussions. Lawrence and Snow (2011) state that "by attending to their talk moves and how they set up student discussion routines, teachers can provide the scaffolding for students to have rich discussions using a range of reading strategies and techniques" (p. 331). Table 9.1 lists four talk moves that teachers might use to facilitate student discussions.

Table 9.1: Teacher Talk Moves

Talk Move	Description	Example
Modeling	The teacher models how he or she would handle a reading or discussion challenge by thinking aloud for students.	The teacher models how he or she would respond to a peer who has just articulated an idea or thought that she disagrees with.
Direct Explanation	The teacher names specific strategies and talks about when to use them.	The teacher describes the strategy of perspective taking, listing its four steps, and explains that it is a good strategy to use when you disagree with a perspective that another has voiced.
Marking	The teacher responds to a question or comment in a way that highlights specific information or content.	The teacher responds to a student's question during a discussion about who is right or wrong by asking, "What evidence or thinking supports each position?"
Verifying and Clarifying Student Understandings	The teacher paraphrases a student's comment (using different words than the student used) and asks the student to confirm or revise the paraphrase.	In response to a student saying, "That's a stupid way to think about this issue," the teacher says, "Are you saying that you disagree with a specific perspective on this issue?"

Source: Adapted from Lawrence & Snow, 2011.

The talk moves in table 9.1 allow the teacher to monitor and guide student interactions while still permitting students to take a lead role in the discussion.

Figure 9.4 depicts the self-rating scale for element 35, demonstrating withitness.

Score	Description
4: Innovating	I adapt behaviors and create new strategies for unique student needs and situations.
3: Applying	I demonstrate withitness, and I monitor the extent to which my actions affect students' behavior.
2: Developing	I demonstrate withitness, but I do not monitor the effect on students.
1: Beginning	I use the strategies and behaviors associated with this element incorrectly or with parts missing.
0: Not Using	I am unaware of strategies and behaviors associated with this element.

Figure 9.4: Self-rating scale for element 35—Demonstrating withitness.

Element 36: Acknowledging Adherence to Rules and Procedures

Productive talk in the reading classroom is synonymous with responsible communication. Katie Rogers and Julia A. Simms (2015) describe *responsible communication* as:

- Speaking with a calm demeanor, including reasonable volume and tone of voice
- Listening actively (sitting up, making eye contact, nodding, and asking questions) while others are speaking
- Using disciplined and respectful word choice
- Critiquing ideas instead of individuals (pp. 42–43)

Sarah Michaels and colleagues (Michaels, O'Connor, & Resnick, 2008; Michaels, O'Connor, & Hall, 2013; Wolf, Crosson, & Resnick, 2005) at the University of Pittsburgh have designed a set of concrete practices called Accountable Talk that a teacher might use to establish rules and procedures for responsible communication. Michaels and colleagues (2013) explain:

> Accountable Talk® classrooms are filled with talk that seriously responds to and further develops what others in the group have said. It puts forth and demands knowledge that is accurate and relevant to the issue under discussion. This academically productive talk uses evidence appropriate to the discipline (e.g., proofs in mathematics, data from investigations in science, textual references in literature, documentary sources in history) and follows established norms of good reasoning. This discourse sharpens students' thinking by reinforcing their ability to use and create knowledge. (p. 1)

Michaels and colleagues (2013) suggest that the teacher focus on two overarching rules to facilitate such talk: "(1) all students must have access to the learning conversation, and (2) the content of the talk must consistently further academic learning" (p. 16). Teachers and students could work together to articulate procedures that operationalize each of these rules.

Additionally, the teacher could work with students to articulate examples of sentence stems that illustrate what responsible communication looks like for various student talk moves. Figure 9.5 (page 142) shows an example of what this might look like.

Student Talk Move	Sentence Stem
Clarifying	How is this relevant to your point? Can you explain what you mean? So what you're saying is _________.
Connecting	I want to say more about what _________ said about _________. I'd like to add _________. I noticed that _________. What _________ said reminded me of _________.
Agreeing	I agree with _________ because _________. I think _________ made a great point about _________. Yes, and furthermore _________. Although we still disagree on the claim overall, it seems to me that we *can* agree on _________.
Disagreeing	I disagree with _________ because _________. Couldn't it also be that _________? I see why _________ might say that, but _________. While I think _________ had a point that _________, I disagree with the part where he or she said _________. It seems to me that _________ committed an error in reasoning when he or she said _________.
Changing the Subject	It seems to me that we're spending a lot of time discussing _________, when maybe we should be discussing _________. I'd like to change the subject to _________. Something I think the other side has not addressed is _________.
Taking Responsibility	I must have miscommunicated my point earlier; I apologize. What I intended to say was _________. Earlier, I neglected to point out _________. I'm sorry, I misunderstood you. I thought you meant _________. You're right. Those words were hurtful and uncalled for. I shouldn't have said that.

Source: Adapted from Michaels et al., 2013.

Figure 9.5: Student talk moves and sentence stems.

Visit ***go.SolutionTree.com/instruction*** *for a free reproducible version of this figure.*

Figure 9.6 depicts the self-rating scale for element 36, acknowledging adherence to rules and procedures.

Score	Description
4: Innovating	I adapt behaviors and create new strategies for unique student needs and situations.
3: Applying	I acknowledge adherence to rules and procedures consistently and fairly, and I monitor the extent to which my actions affect students' behavior.
2: Developing	I acknowledge adherence to rules and procedures consistently and fairly, but I do not monitor the effect on students.
1: Beginning	I use the strategies and behaviors associated with this element incorrectly or with parts missing.
0: Not Using	I am unaware of strategies and behaviors associated with this element.

Figure 9.6: Self-rating scale for element 36—Acknowledging adherence to rules and procedures.

Element 37: Acknowledging Lack of Adherence to Rules and Procedures

In their discussion of Accountable Talk, Michaels and colleagues (2013) discuss three ways that students might fail to be accountable and questions that teachers can use to redirect them and keep them accountable. First, students might fail to be *accountable to the learning community* by not listening to one another, not listening carefully enough to be able to build on others' ideas, disagreeing disrespectfully, or challenging the person who made a claim, rather than the claim itself. To acknowledge and correct such a lack of responsible communication, the teacher might use the following questions.

- **"Did everyone hear that?"** This question communicates to students that they are required to listen to what others say. It also provides an opportunity for the teacher to encourage a student to speak louder, if necessary.
- **"Can you repeat what he said in your own words?"** This question helps keep the class together, following the thread of a discussion. Also, once a student paraphrases, the teacher can follow up by asking the original speaker if the paraphrasing captures what he or she said.

Second, students might fail to be *accountable to accurate knowledge* by speaking generally instead of specifically, failing to offer sufficient evidence to support their point, offering evidence that does not meet the established standards for credibility or accuracy, or not making evidence explicit. The following questions help the teacher address these issues.

- **"Where can we find that?"** This question prompts students to be explicit, detailed, and specific when offering evidence for their statements. It also provides an opportunity for the student to correct inaccurate evidence before the discussion continues.
- **"How does this connect?"** This question reminds students that they cannot assume that others will see the link between their thoughts and a previous topic. Asking them to make the connection explicit prompts students to explain the line of reasoning they are using to build on ideas they previously articulated.

Finally, students may fail to be *accountable to rigorous thinking* by making invalid arguments, offering irrelevant evidence for their claims, committing errors in reasoning, or assuming that implicit conclusions will be obvious to all. Teachers can draw attention to these areas using the following questions.

- **"Why do you think that?"** This question communicates to students that simply making a statement (without a *because* clause following it) is unacceptable. Students should develop the habit of labeling their statements using the parts of an argument (that is, claim, grounds, backing, qualifier, reasoning; see page 97 for details).
- **"Will you please say more about that?"** This question gives a student additional time to think through his or her ideas and defuses the pressure that can accompany thinking out loud in front of a group. The teacher should follow up this question with plenty of wait time to allow a student to think deeply about his or her statement.

The teacher can use these six questions to maintain a classroom environment that preserves and cultivates trust, risk taking, and respect.

Figure 9.7 (page 144) depicts the self-rating scale for element 37, acknowledging lack of adherence to rules and procedures.

Score	Description
4: Innovating	I adapt behaviors and create new strategies for unique student needs and situations.
3: Applying	I apply consequences for not following rules and procedures consistently and fairly, and I monitor the extent to which students follow rules and procedures.
2: Developing	I apply consequences for not following rules and procedures consistently and fairly, but I do not monitor the effect on students.
1: Beginning	I use the strategies and behaviors associated with this element incorrectly or with parts missing.
0: Not Using	I am unaware of strategies and behaviors associated with this element.

Figure 9.7: Self-rating scale for element 37—Acknowledging lack of adherence to rules and procedures.

GUIDING QUESTIONS FOR CURRICULUM DESIGN

The design questions in this chapter focus on implementing rules and procedures: *What strategies will I use to help students understand and follow rules and procedures?* The following questions, which align to each of the elements in this chapter, guide teachers as they plan for this design area.

- **Element 33:** What will I do to establish rules and procedures in the classroom?
- **Element 34:** What will I do to make the physical layout of the classroom most conducive to learning?
- **Element 35:** What will I do to demonstrate withitness?
- **Element 36:** What will I do to acknowledge adherence to rules and procedures?
- **Element 37:** What will I do to acknowledge lack of adherence to rules and procedures?

Summary

Implementing rules and procedures involves five elements: (1) establishing rules and procedures, (2) organizing the physical layout of the classroom, (3) demonstrating withitness, (4) acknowledging adherence to rules and procedures, and (5) acknowledging lack of adherence to rules and procedures. In the reading classroom, rules and procedures are critical to establishing an environment in which productive discussions, discourse, and disagreements about texts can occur.

CHAPTER 10

Building Relationships

The ninth design area of *The New Art and Science of Teaching* framework involves creating a classroom context in which students feel welcome, accepted, and valued. In a community with high levels of relational trust, students can relax their defenses and focus their attention on the content at hand. Relationships are not always easy to build, but teachers can create a conducive atmosphere by appropriately using verbal and nonverbal behaviors that indicate affection for students (element 38), understanding students' backgrounds and interests (element 39), and adhering to personal standards of behavior that communicate and display objectivity and control (element 40). Here we describe how each of these elements might manifest in a reading classroom.

Element 38: Using Verbal and Nonverbal Behaviors That Indicate Affection for Students

When considering how verbal and nonverbal behaviors impact relationships in the reading classroom, it is important to consider culture. Robert Rueda (2011) defines *culture* as "the daily patterns of living . . . that allow individuals to relate to the surrounding social order. . . . Culture helps determine what is customary and 'normal'" (p. 85). He adds, "Culture is often treated as a function of students primarily, rather than as a feature that permeates social contexts and learning processes in classrooms and schools" (p. 97). Guofang Li (2011) explains that "literacy . . . is part of a culture. . . . Literacy is seen as a means by which individuals conduct and construct their lives in the community and the society" (p. 516). Whenever a student's heritage culture (what they have grown up with and experienced at home) conflicts with their mainstream culture (what they experience at school and other public places), it creates tension for the student. Research finds that three reading-related areas can be particularly ripe for these heritage-mainstream culture conflicts (Compton-Lilly, 2003; Delgado-Gaitan, 1990; Heath, 1983; Li, 2002, 2009; Ogbu, 1982; Taylor & Dorsey-Gaines, 1988; Valdés, 1996).

1. What it means to be literate
2. The acquisition of literacy
3. The role of schooling in achieving literacy

Teachers can use verbal and nonverbal behaviors to help defuse the cultural tension that students may feel related to reading in these three areas.

For example, the teacher could survey or informally question students about their families' approach to reading. Questions might include the following.

- How often do you read at home? What about the rest of your family?
- Do you ever read with your parents? Do you ever read with other members of your family?
- Where do you like to read?
- Do you prefer to read aloud or silently?
- What kinds of things (like books, magazines, blogs, and news articles) do you usually read? How about your family?
- What are some of the reasons that you read at home? How about the rest of your family?
- How did you learn to read?
- What was the first thing you read?

These sorts of questions communicate to students that there are no right or wrong ways to read; different cultures approach reading differently. Such acceptance can communicate affection for students and their heritage cultures. It also opens the door for a discussion about what reading typically looks like at school, which is a culture all its own.

Figure 10.1 depicts the self-rating scale for element 38, using verbal and nonverbal behaviors that indicate affection for students, so teachers can gauge their performance.

Score	Description
4: Innovating	I adapt behaviors and create new strategies for unique student needs and situations.
3: Applying	I use verbal and nonverbal behaviors that indicate affection for students, and I monitor the extent to which my actions affect students.
2: Developing	I use verbal and nonverbal behaviors that indicate affection for students, but I do not monitor the effect on students.
1: Beginning	I use the strategies and behaviors associated with this element incorrectly or with parts missing.
0: Not Using	I am unaware of strategies and behaviors associated with this element.

Figure 10.1: Self-rating scale for element 38—Using verbal and nonverbal behaviors that indicate affection for students.

Element 39: Understanding Students' Backgrounds and Interests

When seeking to understand students' backgrounds and interests in the reading classroom, it is useful to consider cognitive load theory. Similar to LaBerge and Samuels's (1974) theory of automatic information processing in reading (see chapter 1, page 19), *cognitive load theory* stipulates that human limitations on working memory capacity mediate learning, and any demands on working memory for storage or processing that are not directly related to the learning task at hand make learning less efficient (Paas, Renkl, & Sweller, 2003). *Schemata*—familiar patterns of information, activity, or interaction—reduce demands on working memory because they help people sort incoming information into categories; those categories allow people to easily make decisions about what to do with or about such information, freeing working memory to keep learning.

Think of culture as a schema. As Rueda (2011) explains, "Being in a culturally familiar setting is relatively effortless compared with being in a strange cultural setting" (p. 94). The learning implications of this for students with heritage-mainstream cultural differences are significant. A student who is trying to figure out and resolve conflicts between the culture he or she is accustomed to and the culture of the classroom has fewer working memory resources available to dedicate to learning. Rueda (2011) further points out:

> Cultural unfamiliarity with specific tasks, texts, discourse and interactional processes, and other important classroom features may therefore lead to . . . negative outcomes. . . . The reverse situation is likewise possible, whereby the cultural schemas some students bring to classroom learning activities advantage them in ways that reduce cognitive load and thus make learning more efficient. (p. 94)

Therefore, creating a culturally facilitative classroom has benefits for students beyond simply making them feel more comfortable. The fewer working memory resources that students have to devote to figuring out the classroom's culture, the more resources they will have available for learning.

One way that teachers can create a culturally facilitative classroom is through text selection. Texts that contain culturally familiar characters, structures, concepts, ideas, and dialogue will be easier to comprehend than those that do not. While part of schooling is learning about academic culture (including formal patterns of discourse, vocabulary, and interaction), texts that contain familiar cultural elements can make such learning easier for students. Appendix G lists a number of books for various ages that may be helpful in this endeavor. Visit **go.SolutionTree.com/instruction** to access appendices E, F, and G.

Understanding students' backgrounds and interests goes a long way in developing positive relationships between the teacher and students. Figure 10.2 depicts the self-rating scale for this element so teachers can gauge their performance.

Score	Description
4: Innovating	I adapt behaviors and create new strategies for unique student needs and situations.
3: Applying	I understand students' backgrounds and interests, and I monitor the extent to which my actions affect students.
2: Developing	I understand students' backgrounds and interests, but I do not monitor the effect on students.
1: Beginning	I use the strategies and behaviors associated with this element incorrectly or with parts missing.
0: Not Using	I am unaware of strategies and behaviors associated with this element.

Figure 10.2: Self-rating scale for element 39—Understanding students' backgrounds and interests.

Element 40: Displaying Objectivity and Control

As teachers strive to display objectivity and control in the reading classroom, they may benefit from familiarizing themselves with some of the cultural values and norms of their students. Understanding the cultural norms and values that underlie students' decisions to act in certain ways can help the teacher maintain an objective perspective and explain, if necessary, how classroom culture compares to their heritage culture. Kenneth M. Tyler and colleagues (2008) study the cultural values of ethnic minority groups. Table 10.1 (page 148) summarizes their findings.

Table 10.1: Cultural Values of Ethnic Minority Groups

Group	Cultural Values
African American	• **Communalism** is the idea that a person considers duty to his or her social group as more important than individual rights and privileges. Therefore, social identity is intricately tied to group membership, not to individual status and possessions. The community promotes sharing because it affirms the importance of social interconnectedness, whereas self-centeredness and individual greed are discouraged. • **Movement** indicates a premium placed on the amalgamation of movement, polyrhythm, dance, percussiveness, and syncopation embodied in musical beats. A person with a movement orientation prefers or is oriented toward physical movement, music, and rhythm, particularly in speech, thought, and behavioral patterns. Coupled with a movement orientation is the preference for rhythmic activity, particularly with syncopated music in the background. • **Verve** is the propensity for high levels of physical stimulation. Qualities such as intensity (or liveliness) and variability are associated with this value. Intensity means the amount of stimulation and excitement associated with a task. Variability involves changing or alternating between activities (often induced by the individual).
Asian American	• **Collectivism** is the belief (influenced by Confucianism) that benevolence, respect for authority, cooperation, harmony, and a duty toward the group should always take precedence over individual needs and desires. • **Conformity to norms** provides order in the community and maintains in-group harmony. • **Emotional self-control**, or holding emotions inside, is preferable to expressing emotions so as not to burden others in the group with disharmonious ideas. • **Humility**, or refraining from expressing pride, is important because the community views accomplishments as contributions to communal welfare. • **Achievement** is a way to show appreciation to one's family and reflects on the family's reputation. While humility is important, the academic achievement of their children is a source of pride for parents and families. • **Deference to authority figures** is appropriate as the community sees teachers, parents, and the elderly as sources of wisdom; such deference also brings a sense of obligation to care for parents and elders as they age or become ill.
Latino	• **Collectivism**, a sense of interconnectedness, is important both within a household and also between family members from different households. Each individual strives to make personal contributions that benefit the family. Social responsibility centers on the good of the whole group or family; a person's responsibilities are geared toward advancing or maintaining the group. • **Simultaneity** is the occurrence of multiple activities at the same time, along with active engagement in such activities simultaneously.
Native American	• **Sharing and cooperation** mean that whatever the individual possesses also belongs to the group. Individual survival is synonymous with the survival of the family and larger community. Important questions upon meeting a person are "Where do you come from?" or "Who is your family?" • **Noninterference** is the belief that everything was created to fulfill a specific purpose. Thus, the community discourages personal interference in fulfillment of that purpose. This means that it is not unusual for a member of the group to withdraw from the group to deal with an emotional or academic disturbance. The community welcomes back the individual into the larger group afterward with no explanation required. • **Harmony** is the belief that people should allow situations to occur uninterrupted. This promotes a sense of harmony between a troubled individual and an intervening individual, and also within the troubled individual. The community sees situations as something the individual is supposed to experience and should therefore be allowed to occur free from outside intervention. • **Present-time orientation** is a value that focuses on the here and now. Activities begin when everyone arrives and end when they are socially completed (that is, when everyone agrees that the end has arrived). • **Reverence for elders** is a strong value, as the community believes elders possess wisdom acquired throughout their lives. Elders fill important roles such as parents, teachers, and spiritual leaders. This reverence for elders often manifests as avoidance of eye contact by a younger individual with the elder and by an absence of critical analysis or refutation of an elder's knowledge.

Source: Adapted from Tyler et al., 2008.

While it is important to avoid using the information in table 10.1 to stereotype students based on their ethnic backgrounds, staying aware of such information can help a teacher relate to students from a more informed perspective. Understanding the values that they may have learned from their heritage culture can help the teacher maintain objectivity and control when interacting with students.

Displaying objectivity and control involves the teacher staying calm in potentially agitating situations. Figure 10.3 depicts the self-rating scale for this element so teachers can gauge their performance.

Score	Description
4: Innovating	I adapt behaviors and create new strategies for unique student needs and situations.
3: Applying	I display objectivity and control, and I monitor the extent to which my actions affect students.
2: Developing	I display objectivity and control, but I do not monitor the effect on students.
1: Beginning	I use the strategies and behaviors associated with this element incorrectly or with parts missing.
0: Not Using	I am unaware of strategies and behaviors associated with this element.

Figure 10.3: Self-rating scale for element 40—Displaying objectivity and control.

GUIDING QUESTIONS FOR CURRICULUM DESIGN

The design question in this chapter focuses on building relationships: *How will I help students feel welcome, accepted, and valued?* The following questions, which align to each of the elements in this chapter, guide teachers as they build relationships.

- **Element 38:** What verbal and nonverbal behaviors will I use to indicate affection for students?

- **Element 39:** What strategies will I use to demonstrate that I understand students' backgrounds and interests?

- **Element 40:** What strategies will I use to display objectivity and control?

Summary

Building relationships involves three elements: (1) using verbal and nonverbal behaviors that indicate affection for students, (2) understanding students' backgrounds and interests, and (3) displaying objectivity and control. In the reading classroom, cultural characteristics have enormous potential to impact relationships both positively and negatively. Reading teachers who acknowledge, appreciate, and leverage cultural knowledge can smooth the path toward safe, trusting relationships with their students.

CHAPTER 11

Communicating High Expectations

The tenth and final design area of *The New Art and Science of Teaching* framework addresses the critical need for teachers to cultivate and maintain high expectations for all students. While teachers may struggle internally to expect high levels of achievement from all students, there are specific outward actions teachers can take to ensure that they communicate positive beliefs about all students' abilities. Specific patterns of interaction, questioning, and responding (highlighted in the elements of this design area) can make typically reluctant leaners feel valued and eager to interact with both the teacher and their peers. Teachers must use strategies for demonstrating value and respect for reluctant learners (element 41), asking in-depth questions of reluctant learners (element 42), and probing incorrect answers with reluctant learners (element 43). Here we describe how each element might manifest in a reading classroom.

Element 41: Demonstrating Value and Respect for Reluctant Learners

In the reading classroom, reluctant learners typically fall into two categories: struggling readers and English learners. For both groups, the type of high-quality instruction we describe in previous chapters of this book is most appropriate. For example, many struggling readers have "well-documented difficulties discriminating among sound, letter-sound patterns, and different orthographic representations of the same sounds" (Klingner et al., 2016, p. 646). That is, many struggling readers are still in the prealphabetic or partial alphabetic phase relative to word recognition. Providing them with instruction in alphabet and phonics knowledge and phonological and phonemic awareness will address these difficulties and help them move to the full and consolidated alphabetic phases. Similarly, relative to English learners, Claude Goldenberg (2011) points out that "what we know about effective reading curriculum and instruction for students in general tends to be true for ELLs [English language learners] as well" (p. 694). Goldenberg (2011) does stipulate that English learners will require additional oral language and vocabulary instruction; we address this in the sections on tier one vocabulary instruction (see pages 17–18). In sum, the type of instruction we describe throughout this book is effective for all readers, including reluctant ones. Richard L. Allington and Anne McGill-Franzen (2017) state that "good instruction of any sort emerges from a teacher's knowledge of the problem and of his or her students" (p. 288). That is, the teacher's role is to determine what a student currently knows and can do, and to use his or her knowledge of how reading develops (as we describe in chapter 1) to determine what instruction that student needs next, relative to foundational skills, word recognition, fluency, vocabulary, and comprehension.

Such observations notwithstanding, there are specific concerns that reading teachers should consider when interacting with either struggling readers or English learners. For instance, struggling readers and English learners may have difficulty with their reading-related identity. Linda Kucan and Annemarie S. Palincsar (2011) explain that "students who identify themselves as struggling readers may participate in classes in particular ways to hide that identity. They may act out to divert attention from their lack of understanding, or remain silent to avoid notice" (p. 352). Building strong and supportive relationships with students, regardless of their academic achievement, can help them retool their identities. Christopher Murray and Mark T. Greenberg (2001, 2006) find that students with disabilities who reported having supportive and warm relationships with their teachers experienced lower levels of anxiety, depression, delinquent acts, and conduct problems compared to students with disabilities who frequently experienced conflict with their teachers.

Figure 11.1 depicts the self-rating scale for element 41, demonstrating value and respect for reluctant learners, so teachers can gauge their performance.

Score	Description
4: Innovating	I adapt behaviors and create new strategies for unique student needs and situations.
3: Applying	I exhibit behaviors that demonstrate value and respect for reluctant learners, and I monitor the impact on reluctant learners.
2: Developing	I exhibit behaviors that demonstrate value and respect for reluctant learners, but I do not monitor the effect on students.
1: Beginning	I use the strategies and behaviors associated with this element incorrectly or with parts missing.
0: Not Using	I am unaware of strategies and behaviors associated with this element.

Figure 11.1: Self-rating scale for element 41—Demonstrating value and respect for reluctant learners.

Element 42: Asking In-Depth Questions of Reluctant Learners

As Marzano (2017) explains, it is important to ask in-depth questions of all students, regardless of their level of academic achievement. Relative to reading, and as we discuss in chapter 1, it is critical to teach comprehension skills to students who may struggle with word recognition and fluency. Educators can teach comprehension orally (as listening comprehension) until students acquire the necessary knowledge and skills to read independently (at which juncture students can apply listening comprehension skills during independent reading). As teachers encourage struggling students or English learners to answer in-depth questions, they should remain aware of strategies that such students may need to use in order to answer such questions. Jeffrey J. Walczyk and Diana A. Griffith-Ross (2007) review the literature on how struggling readers compensate for and overcome various difficulties they encounter as they read. They summarize their findings by articulating seven strategies that struggling readers use to compensate for reading difficulties. Table 11.1 lists these strategies from the least to the most disruptive for students; in general, students tend to use less disruptive strategies first, only moving to more disruptive ones if the initial strategies are ineffective.

Table 11.1: Compensatory Strategies Struggling Readers Use

Strategy	Description
Slowing Reading Rate	Slowing reading helps prevent confusion by allowing inefficient readers to read text at a pace that their skills can handle, whereas faster reading might overwhelm their skills.
Pausing	A pause is compensatory if it is an uncommonly long delay during reading that allows an inefficient reading subcomponent (such as reading a word by sight) sufficient time to succeed. When slowing reading does not allow enough time, pausing may be its backup. Furthermore, when the source of confusion is unclear, pausing can occur as readers try to understand its nature and select other compensations for resolving it.
Looking Back	Looking back occurs when readers briefly glance to text they have read previously; it is the reprocessing of three words or less, which is slightly more disruptive of word reading than slowing reading rate or pausing. Looking back is compensatory when it resolves confusion by restoring information the student has forgotten from working memory or by providing information he or she overlooked on the first pass through text (such as what *it* refers to).
Reading Aloud	Reading aloud helps focus attention when readers are tired or bored. It can also help drown out distractions and provides the reader with auditory feedback on the accuracy of word reading attempts.
Sounding Out, Analogizing to Known Sight Words, or Contextual Guessing	Sounding out involves using the rules of phonics to match a letter string to a spoken word in memory (also called phonological recoding). Analogizing to known sight words occurs when readers look at a word's spelling and bring to mind similarly spelled words to cue its meaning. Contextual guessing is using surrounding text to infer an unknown word's meaning.
Jumping Over	If readers conclude that an unfamiliar word or other confusion involves a minor detail, or that resolving it will take too much time, they can jump over it. For example, if the meaning of an unfamiliar word seems tangential to understanding the overall text, choosing to overlook it makes sense. More experienced readers know that spending too much time resolving such confusion can cause them to forget important information they have read previously, making it harder to form connections. Of course, jumping over too often will lower comprehension.
Rereading Text	Rereading (the reprocessing of four or more words) is compensatory when it resolves confusion from an earlier pass through text but is more disruptive of reading than the preceding compensations. As a consequence, skilled readers will employ it only after other compensations have not prevented or resolved their confusion.

Source: Adapted from Walczyk & Griffith-Ross, 2007.

After asking a student an in-depth question about a reading passage, the teacher might observe to see if the student is using any of the strategies in table 11.1. If so, the teacher can create time for the students to use the strategy (by providing wait time, or by moving on and coming back to the student at a later time). If the student is not using any compensatory strategies, the teacher might overtly or covertly cue the student to engage in such strategies to help him or her articulate an answer to the question the teacher has asked.

Figure 11.2 (page 154) depicts the self-rating scale for element 42, asking in-depth questions of reluctant learners, so teachers can gauge their performance.

Score	Description
4: Innovating	I adapt behaviors and create new strategies for unique student needs and situations.
3: Applying	I ask questions of reluctant learners with the same frequency and depth as with high-expectancy students, and I monitor the quality of participation of reluctant learners.
2: Developing	I ask questions of reluctant learners with the same frequency and depth as with high-expectancy students, but I do not monitor the effect on students.
1: Beginning	I use the strategies and behaviors associated with this element incorrectly or with parts missing.
0: Not Using	I am unaware of strategies and behaviors associated with this element.

Figure 11.2: Self-rating scale for element 42—Asking in-depth questions of reluctant learners.

Element 43: Probing Incorrect Answers With Reluctant Learners

When a student responds incorrectly to a question, the teacher can probe the student's answer to guide him or her in revising it until it is correct. Relative to reading, a simple way that teachers can do this is to prompt students to use specific comprehension strategies. For example, if a teacher asks a student to interpret a character's response to an event in a narrative, and the student's answer indicates that the student did not fully understand what the character's response was, the teacher might prompt that student to engage in summarizing or retelling to clear up confusion about what happened in the text. Alternatively, if the teacher asks a student to compare an author's perspective (as articulated in a persuasive text) to his or her own, and the student's answer reveals that he or she does not have a perspective on the issue, the teacher could prompt the student to activate his or her relevant prior knowledge or to make a prediction about how he or she would respond in a relevant situation. Timothy Shanahan and colleagues (2010) provide examples of effective, research-based comprehension strategies that teachers might use in such cases. Table 11.2 describes each of these strategies.

Table 11.2: Effective Reading Comprehension Strategies

Strategy	Description
Activating Prior Knowledge and Predicting	Students think about what they already know and use that knowledge in conjunction with other clues to construct meaning from what they read or to hypothesize what will happen next in the text. The teacher assumes that students will continue to read to see if their predictions are correct.
Questioning	Students develop and attempt to answer questions about the important ideas in the text while reading, using words such as *where* or *why* to develop their questions.
Visualizing	Students develop a mental image of what the text describes.
Monitoring, Clarifying, and Fix-Up	Students pay attention to whether they understand what they are reading, and when they do not, they reread or use strategies that will help them understand what they have read.
Drawing Inferences	Students generate information that is important to constructing meaning but that is missing from, or not explicitly stated in, the text.
Summarizing and Retelling	Students briefly describe, orally or in writing, the main points of what they read.

Source: Shanahan et al., 2010, pp. 12–13.

Figure 11.3 depicts the self-rating scale for element 43, probing incorrect answers with reluctant learners, so teachers can gauge their performance.

Score	Description
4: Innovating	I adapt behaviors and create new strategies for unique student needs and situations.
3: Applying	I probe incorrect answers with reluctant learners in the same manner as with high-expectancy students, and I monitor the level and quality of responses of reluctant learners.
2: Developing	I probe incorrect answers with reluctant learners in the same manner as with high-expectancy students, but I do not monitor the effect on students.
1: Beginning	I use the strategies and behaviors associated with this element incorrectly or with parts missing.
0: Not Using	I am unaware of strategies and behaviors associated with this element.

Figure 11.3: Self-rating scale for element 43—Probing incorrect answers with reluctant learners.

GUIDING QUESTIONS FOR CURRICULUM DESIGN

The design question in this chapter focuses on communicating high expectations to all students, especially reluctant learners: *What strategies will I use to help typically reluctant students feel valued and comfortable interacting with their peers or me?* The following questions, which align to each of the elements in this chapter, guide teachers as they plan to communicate high expectations.

- **Element 41:** What will I do to demonstrate value and respect for reluctant learners?

- **Element 42:** What strategies will I use to ask in-depth questions of reluctant learners?

- **Element 43:** How will I probe incorrect answers with reluctant learners?

Summary

Communicating high expectations involves three elements: (1) demonstrating value and respect for reluctant learners, (2) asking in-depth questions of reluctant learners, and (3) probing incorrect answers with reluctant learners. In the reading classroom, the expectations a teacher expresses toward a student can have a significant impact on their reading-related identities. Asking and expecting all students to use effective comprehension strategies, while also providing word recognition and fluency instruction to those students who need it, communicates that teachers expect all students to achieve high levels of reading success.

CHAPTER 12

Developing Expertise

One of the most powerful aspects of *The New Art and Science of Teaching* framework is its granularity. Simply put, this means that the framework describes effective teaching in such detail that educators can pinpoint areas of strength and weakness, set goals to improve in specific areas, select strategies to implement as they seek to improve, track progress as they go, and make subsequent plans for future growth. In this book, we have specifically applied the forty-three elements of *The New Art and Science of Teaching* framework to the reading classroom. Thus, a reading teacher can use the guidance from chapters 1 through 11, along with a reflective process, to enhance their professional practice.

For example, a reading teacher might identify engagement (the seventh design area) as an area of potential improvement for his or her practice. On closer inspection, this teacher might decide to start working on the third element of engagement, using physical movement. Chapter 8 details two reading-specific strategies that this teacher could implement: enacted reading comprehension and tableaux. This particular teacher might decide to try tableaux. His first attempt does not go well, but upon reflection, the teacher realizes that he made some errors in his implementation of the strategy. He failed to teach his students the important things to think about in a tableau—facial expressions, use of hands, body posture, and space between participants—and did not give them opportunities to practice with easy scenes before asking them to create a tableau for a scene from a text. He corrects these errors on subsequent attempts and tracks his progress until he is able to clearly explain and give examples of how the tableaux strategy is resulting in increased attention and energy among his students. He decides to focus on strategies related to using friendly controversy (particularly textual criticism) next.

This reflective process involves four steps.

1. Conduct a self-audit.
2. Select goal elements and specific strategies.
3. Engage in deliberate practice and track progress.
4. Seek continuous improvement by planning for future growth.

Here we provide details and resources for each step.

Step 1: Conduct a Self-Audit

The reflective process commences with a *self-audit*. Using a developmental scale such as the one we show in figure 12.1 (and found throughout this book as a part of each element), teachers rate themselves on the forty-three elements of *The New Art and Science of Teaching* framework.

Score	Description
4: Innovating	I adapt behaviors and create new strategies for unique student needs and situations.
3: Applying	I use the strategies and behaviors associated with this element, and I monitor the extent to which my actions affect students' performance.
2: Developing	I use the strategies and behaviors associated with this element, but I do not monitor the effect on students.
1: Beginning	I use the strategies and behaviors associated with this element incorrectly or with parts missing.
0: Not Using	I am unaware of strategies and behaviors associated with this element.

Source: Marzano, 2017, p. 104.

Figure 12.1: Developmental scale for elements.

Teachers can use the self-audit form in figure 12.2 to record the results of the self-audit.

Element	4	3	2	1	0
1. Providing scales and rubrics					
2. Tracking student progress					
3. Celebrating success					
4. Using informal assessments of the whole class					
5. Using formal assessments of individual students					
6. Chunking content					
7. Processing content					
8. Recording and representing content					
9. Using structured practice sessions					
10. Examining similarities and differences					
11. Examining errors in reasoning					
12. Engaging students in cognitively complex tasks					
13. Providing resources and guidance					
14. Generating and defending claims					
15. Previewing					
16. Highlighting critical information					
17. Reviewing content					
18. Revising knowledge					
19. Reflecting on learning					
20. Assigning purposeful homework					
21. Elaborating on information					
22. Organizing students to interact					

Element	4	3	2	1	0
23. Noticing and reacting when students are not engaged					
24. Increasing response rates					
25. Using physical movement					
26. Maintaining a lively pace					
27. Demonstrating intensity and enthusiasm					
28. Presenting unusual information					
29. Using friendly controversy					
30. Using academic games					
31. Providing opportunities for students to talk about themselves					
32. Motivating and inspiring students					
33. Establishing rules and procedures					
34. Organizing the physical layout of the classroom					
35. Demonstrating withitness					
36. Acknowledging adherence to rules and procedures					
37. Acknowledging lack of adherence to rules and procedures					
38. Using verbal and nonverbal behaviors that indicate affection for students					
39. Understanding students' backgrounds and interests					
40. Displaying objectivity and control					
41. Demonstrating value and respect for reluctant learners					
42. Asking in-depth questions of reluctant learners					
43. Probing incorrect answers with reluctant learners					

Figure 12.2: Self-audit for *The New Art and Science of Teaching* framework.

Visit ***go.SolutionTree.com/instruction*** *to download a free reproducible version of this figure.*

Once a teacher has completed the self-audit form in figure 12.2, he or she examines the elements in which he or she assigned the lowest ratings. These are candidates to become growth goals.

Step 2: Select Goal Elements and Specific Strategies

We recommend that teachers identify no more than three growth goals to work on during one school year. For example, a teacher might identify one goal area (such as displaying objectivity and control) to work on from August until November, a different goal area (such as motivating and inspiring students) to work on from December until March, and a final goal area (such as reviewing content) to work on during April and May. Once the teacher identifies a goal area, he or she should decide how long to work on that area and what score on the developmental scale he or she would like to achieve by the end of that time period. For example, a teacher might decide to increase her score on displaying objectivity and control from a 1 (beginning) to a 3 (applying) between August and November.

A reading teacher who has decided to work on displaying objectivity and control could examine the appropriate section of chapter 10 in this book and determine that she would like to try two strategies: (1) familiarizing herself with the cultural norms and values of her students and (2) identifying similarities and differences between students' heritage cultures and the culture of her classroom. She decides that to familiarize herself with the cultural norms and values of her students she will read the information in table 10.1 (page 148) and ask students to write down answers to a few questions about their cultural values and norms. For identifying similarities and differences, she decides to create a Venn diagram for each distinct culture she identifies in her classroom that compares it to her classroom culture.

Step 3: Engage in Deliberate Practice and Track Progress

The process of developing expertise in a particular area follows a predictable progression (as figure 12.1, page 158, and the rating scales throughout this book suggest). At the Not Using (0) level, the teacher is simply not using a strategy or behavior. By choosing to try out a strategy, he or she moves to the Beginning (1) level.

It is normal, when beginning to use a strategy, to execute the strategy or behavior incorrectly or with parts missing. In the case of the teacher working on displaying objectivity and control (element 40), she might begin by incorrectly identifying the cultural backgrounds present in her classroom (she might leave out some cultures that are present or misidentify a student's cultural background).

The next level, Developing (2), involves correcting errors or filling in missing pieces. The teacher working on displaying objectivity and control, at this stage, might have correctly identified each student's cultural background and drafted a few questions that she would like students to answer about their cultural backgrounds. At the Developing (2) level, a teacher does not yet monitor the effect of the strategy or behavior on students.

Monitoring how one's actions are affecting student performance is the hallmark of the Applying (3) level. The teacher in our example might achieve this level by administering her questionnaire, compiling student answers, and adjusting her interactions with students (and the way she scaffolds their interactions with each other) based on her findings. She notices that students seem more relaxed and comfortable in her classroom and that students who were previously reluctant to engage in discussions are sharing more frequently.

Finally, a teacher who has progressed to the Innovating (4) level is monitoring students so closely that he or she adapts strategies (or creates new ones if necessary) to ensure that all students are performing at high levels, regardless of their unique needs and situations. A tracking chart like the one in figure 12.3 can help a teacher track his or her progress through each level of the scale.

Teacher Progress Chart

Name: Heidi McDonald

Element: 40—Displaying Objectivity and Control

Instructional strategy: Understanding cultural backgrounds

My initial score: 1 My goal is to be at 3 by November 15.

Specific things I am going to do to improve: learn about cultural norms and values, try to identify my students' cultural norms and values, and survey students about their cultural norms and values.

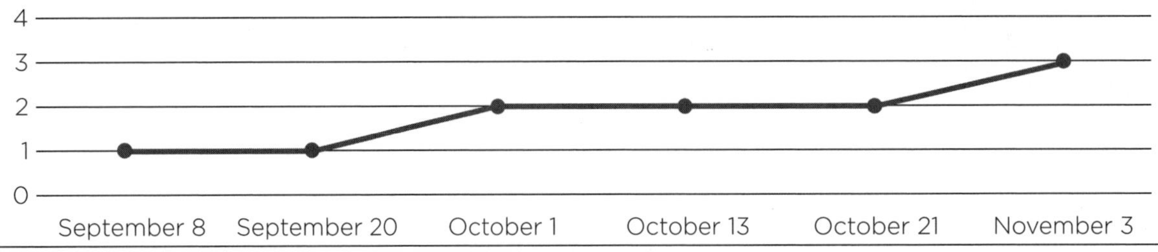

Figure 12.3: Teacher progress for the strategy of understanding cultural backgrounds.

Step 4: Seek Continuous Improvement by Planning for Future Growth

Once a teacher has achieved his or her goal, or the time period he or she set for the completion of the goal has expired, the teacher evaluates his or her current situation and makes plans for the future. For example, the reading teacher in the previous example, having achieved her goal for displaying objectivity and control, would move on to her next goal of motivating and inspiring students (element 32).

Summary

The focus of this book is effective instruction in the reading classroom. By combining the general model of effective instruction that *The New Art and Science of Teaching* articulates with our reading-specific developmental model, we present a comprehensive approach to effective reading instruction. Reading teachers can use the research and strategies we offer in this book to apply effective instructional strategies in the classroom. The goal of using such instructional strategies is for students to achieve the mental states and processes that decades of research have shown lead to enhanced student learning.

Afterword

The New Art and Science of Teaching (Marzano, 2017) presents a comprehensive model of teaching that organizes all or most of the instructional strategies available to teachers. The science reference is predicated on the fact that these strategies are founded on decades of research and theory and contribute to effective teaching. The art component indicates that factors other than research are attributed to student learning, such as which strategies are used together and how teachers use them for express purposes. This analogy can help elucidate this point:

> Instructional strategies are best likened to techniques an artist might develop and refine over years of practice. The artist then uses these techniques to create works that are not only unique and complex but elegantly focused. The more skill the artist exhibits with available techniques, the better his or her creations. Likewise, the more skill the classroom teacher has with the instructional strategies that research and theory have uncovered over the decades, the better the teacher will be able to create lessons that optimize student learning. (Marzano, 2017 p.2)

It is the duty, the call to action, and the mission of educators everywhere to meet students where they are and elevate them to the next level of learning. This is an awesome task indeed and extremely rewarding when students move from not knowing to awareness. As teachers endeavor to undertake this responsibility, they need tools, resources, and support to help guide them so they can be the best possible conduit of learning for their charges. *The New Art and Science of Teaching Reading* presents myriad strategies to assist teachers in this work. We invite all teachers to raise their own bar of professional capacity so they can, in turn, open the door for the students they are so fortunate to lead.

Appendix A
Framework Overview

As explained in the introduction, *The New Art and Science of Teaching* framework involves three overarching categories—(1) feedback, (2) content, and (3) context. These categories contain the ten design areas, each of which is associated with a specific teacher action, desired student mental states and processes, and a design question to help teachers plan units and lessons within those units. The forty-three individual elements of the model reside within the design areas. Figure A.1 (page 166) presents a comprehensive list of the overarching categories, design areas, teacher actions, desired student mental states and processes, design questions, and elements.

***The New Art and Science of Teaching* Framework Overview**

Category	Design Areas—Teacher Actions	Desired Student Mental States and Processes	Design Questions	Elements
Feedback	**1. Providing and Communicating Clear Learning Goals**	Students understand the progression of knowledge they are expected to master and where they are along that progression.	How will I communicate clear learning goals that help students understand the progression of knowledge I expect them to master and where they are along that progression?	**1. Providing scales and rubrics** How will I design scales or rubrics? **2. Tracking student progress** How will I track progress? **3. Celebrating success** How will I celebrate success?
	2. Using Assessments	Students understand how test scores and grades relate to their status on the progression of knowledge they are expected to master.	How will I design and administer assessments that help students understand how their test scores and grades relate to their status on the progression of knowledge I expect them to master?	**4. Using informal assessments of the whole class** How will I informally assess the whole class? **5. Using formal assessments of individual students** How will I formally assess individual students?
Content	**3. Conducting Direct Instruction Lessons**	When content is new, students understand which parts are important and how the parts fit together.	When content is new, how will I design and deliver direct instruction lessons that help students understand which parts are important and how the parts fit together?	**6. Chunking content** How will I chunk the new content into short, digestible bites? **7. Processing content** How will I help students process the individual chunks and the content as a whole? **8. Recording and representing content** How will I help students record and represent their knowledge?
	4. Conducting Practicing and Deepening Lessons	After teachers present new content, students deepen their understanding and develop fluency in skills and processes.	After presenting content, how will I design and deliver lessons that help students deepen their understanding and develop fluency in skills and processes?	**9. Using structured practice sessions** How will I use structured practice? **10. Examining similarities and differences** How will I help students examine similarities and differences? **11. Examining errors in reasoning** How will I help students examine errors in reasoning?

The New Art and Science of Teaching Framework Overview				
Category	**Design Areas—Teacher Actions**	**Desired Student Mental States and Processes**	**Design Questions**	**Elements**
Content	**5. Conducting Knowledge Application Lessons**	After teachers present new content, students generate and defend claims through knowledge application tasks.	After presenting content, how will I design and deliver lessons that help students generate and defend claims through knowledge application?	**12. Engaging students in cognitively complex tasks** How will I engage students in cognitively complex tasks? **13. Providing resources and guidance** How will I provide resources and guidance? **14. Generating and defending claims** How will I help students generate and defend claims?
	6. Using Strategies That Appear in All Types of Lessons	Students continually integrate new knowledge with old knowledge and revise their understanding accordingly.	Throughout all types of lessons, what strategies will I use to help students continually integrate new knowledge with old knowledge and revise their understanding accordingly?	**15. Previewing strategies** How will I help students preview content? **16. Highlighting critical information** How will I highlight critical information? **17. Reviewing content** How will I help students review content? **18. Revising knowledge** How will I help students revise knowledge? **19. Reflecting on learning** How will I help students reflect on their learning? **20. Assigning purposeful homework** How will I use purposeful homework? **21. Elaborating on information** How will I help students elaborate on information? **22. Organizing students to interact** How will I organize students to interact?
Context	**7. Using Engagement Strategies**	Students are paying attention, energized, intrigued, and inspired.	What engagement strategies will I use to help students pay attention, be energized, be intrigued, and be inspired?	**23. Noticing and reacting when students are not engaged** What will I do to notice and react when students are not engaged? **24. Increasing response rates** What will I do to increase students' response rates? **25. Using physical movement** What will I do to increase students' physical movements? **26. Maintaining a lively pace** What will I do to maintain a lively pace? **27. Demonstrating intensity and enthusiasm** What will I do to demonstrate intensity and enthusiasm? **28. Presenting unusual information** What will I do to present unusual information?

Figure A.1: *The New Art and Science of Teaching* framework overview.

continued ↓

The New Art and Science of Teaching Framework Overview

Category	Design Areas—Teacher Actions	Desired Student Mental States and Processes	Design Questions	Elements
Context	**7. Using Engagement Strategies**	Students are paying attention, energized, intrigued, and inspired.	What engagement strategies will I use to help students pay attention, be energized, be intrigued, and be inspired?	**29. Using friendly controversy** What will I do to engage students in friendly controversy? **30. Using academic games** What will I do to engage students in academic games? **31. Providing opportunities for students to talk about themselves** What will I do to provide opportunities for students to talk about themselves? **32. Motivating and inspiring students** What will I do to motivate and inspire students?
	8. Implementing Rules and Procedures	Students understand and follow rules and procedures.	What strategies will I use to help students understand and follow rules and procedures?	**33. Establishing rules and procedures** What will I do to establish rules and procedures? **34. Organizing the physical layout of the classroom** What will I do to make the physical layout of the classroom most conducive to learning? **35. Demonstrating withitness** What will I do to demonstrate withitness? **36. Acknowledging adherence to rules and procedures** What will I do to acknowledge adherence to rules and procedures? **37. Acknowledging lack of adherence to rules and procedures** What will I do to acknowledge lack of adherence to rules and procedures?
	9. Building Relationships	Students feel welcome, accepted, and valued.	What strategies will I use to help students feel welcome, accepted, and valued?	**38. Using verbal and nonverbal behaviors that indicate affection for students** How will I use verbal and nonverbal behaviors that indicate affection for students? **39. Understanding students' backgrounds and interests** How will I demonstrate that I understand students' backgrounds and interests? **40. Displaying objectivity and control** How will I demonstrate objectivity and control?
	10. Communicating High Expectations	Typically reluctant students feel valued and do not hesitate to interact with the teacher or their peers.	What strategies will I use to help typically reluctant students feel valued and comfortable interacting with their peers or me?	**41. Demonstrating value and respect for reluctant learners** How will I demonstrate value and respect for reluctant learners? **42. Asking in-depth questions of reluctant learners** How will I ask in-depth questions of reluctant learners? **43. Probing incorrect answers with reluctant learners** How will I probe incorrect answers with reluctant learners?

Visit ***go.SolutionTree.com/instruction*** *for a free reproducible version of this figure.*

Appendix B
Orthography Exercises

Exercise 1: Spelling English Phonemes

1. How many ways are there to spell the /sh/ sound in English?

Most people can easily name several, such as sh (as in *ship*), ti (as in *motion*), and ch (as in *chef*). However, the same people can read *ocean*, *social*, *special*, *tension*, *session*, *mission*, *sure*, and *conscience* even though they didn't list ce, ci, si, ssi, s, or sci as spellings for the /sh/ sound. They "just know" how to pronounce those words because they've seen them in print and read them over and over and over again during the course of their reading lives.

2. How many ways are there to spell the short /ĕ/ sound in English?

Again, most people can list several: e (as in *bed*), ie (as in *friend*), and ea (as in *bread*). But without consciously being aware that the /ĕ/ sound can also appear as ae, ai, ay, ei, u, a, and eo, the same people can still read and properly pronounce *aesthetic*, *said*, *says*, *heifer*, *bury*, *many*, and *leopard*. Here again, most skilled readers have some conscious orthographic knowledge; however, it pales in comparison to what they know implicitly and unconsciously.

For a complete list of the forty-four English phonemes and various spellings for them, see appendix E. (Visit **go.SolutionTree.com/instruction** to access appendices E, F, and G.)

Exercise 2: Pronunciations

1. Pronounce the following words.

bite	*give*	*love*	*some*
come	*gone*	*melon*	*theme*
dine	*hate*	*none*	*there*
done	*have*	*one*	*were*
fate	*impede*	*open*	*where*

2. Explain why you pronounced each word the way you did.

In English, when a word ends in e, the preceding vowel sound is long (*hate*, *fate*, *theme*, *impede*, *dine*, *bite*); but there are many notable exceptions to this rule (*come*, *done*, *give*, *gone*, *have*, *love*, *none*, *one*, *some*, *there*, *were*, *where*). In some cases, there aren't any rules at all; in multisyllabic English words with vowel-consonant-vowel patterns, such as *open* or *melon*, the syllables may legally split before the consonant (*o-pen*) or after the consonant (*mel-on*). Most skilled readers can easily pronounce the list of words, even if they cannot articulate the rules. They simply know how each word should be said.

Exercise 3: Plurals

1. Make each of the following words plural.

baby ____________	*kiss* ____________
bus ____________	*loaf* ____________
cargo ____________	*opportunity* ____________
church ____________	*reply* ____________
cross ____________	*school* ____________
day ____________	*smile* ____________
ear ____________	*thief* ____________
echo ____________	*tomato* ____________
guess ____________	*town* ____________
hero ____________	*wife* ____________

2. Write down the rule or rules you used to make the previous list of words plural.

Most skilled readers will properly form plurals with little trouble. However, they typically find it more difficult to articulate the rule they used to do it.

Add -s to make a word plural, unless the word ends in ch, s, or o (then add -es), in a consonant plus y (change the y to i and add -es), or in -f (change the -f to a v and add -es).

And forming plurals of the following words, although they are all exceptions to this rule, does not typically prove to be very challenging for skilled readers.

belief	*goose*	*photo*	*thief*
child	*man*	*piano*	*tooth*
cliff	*memo*	*reply*	*town*
deer	*mouse*	*roof*	*video*
fish	*opportunity*	*sheep*	*wife*
foot	*ox*	*smile*	*woman*

Exercise 4: Suffixes

1. Add the suffix on the left side of the following table to the words on the right.

Add the Suffix . . .	To the Words . . .	To Make . . .
-ing	admit find forget meet upset	________ ________ ________ ________ ________
-ed	export insist lift persist prefer rain repeat transmit	________ ________ ________ ________ ________ ________ ________ ________
-en	weak	________
-er	train	________
-ence	occur	________

2. Explain your decision to double or not double the final consonant of each word.

Most likely, you correctly suffixed at least 80 percent of the words in the table. But were you able to explain the following?

*When adding a suffix to a word with more than one syllable, double the consonant only when the word ends in a stressed syllable (*admitting, forgetting, occurrence, preferred, transmitted, *and* upsetting, *but* visiting *and* entered*), but not if the word ends in two written consonants (*exported, finding, insisted, lifted, persisted*) or if there are two written vowels together in the word (*meeting, rained, weaken, trainer, repeated*).*

Exercise 5: Permissible Spelling Patterns

1. List all the rules you can think of that govern permissible spelling patterns in English (for example, U always follows Q).

2. The following table displays four sets of words. In each set, only one of the words is an actual English word. The other three are nonwords; they contain spelling patterns that are not permissible in English. Select the real word in each group by examining the spelling patterns. (See page 175 for answers.)

Set 1	Set 2
alcazav	absqquatulate
zeugma	lexxicomanc
cabotaj	tristesse
mistigriv	majjolica
Set 3	**Set 4**
ulotrichous	penneeck
anglliform	sixsain
mpignorate	exeqies
inspssate	mumpsimus

Most skilled readers can correctly identify the real word in two or three of the sets. But very rarely can a person articulate the rule that helped them identify the real word. To say it differently, the knowledge that allows a reader to select the actual English word is implicit and unconscious; it operates below the level of conscious attention and recall.

Answers:

The rule for set 1 is "words do not end in V or J," and the real word is *zeugma* (which means to apply two different senses of a word to a single object, as in "She opened the door and her heart to the little boy").

The rule for set 2 is "J, Q, and X are never doubled," and the real word is *tristesse* (which means melancholy or sorrow).

The rule for set 3 is "every syllable must have a written vowel," and the real word is *ulotrichous* (which means to have crisp or woolly hair).

The rule for set 4 is "S never follows X, U always follows Q, and CK is always used after a single short vowel," and the real word is *mumpsimus* (which describes a person who insists that he or she is right when he or she is, in fact, wrong).

Appendix C
Reading in the Disciplines

Reading in the content areas (particularly social studies, science, and mathematics) requires a nuanced approach to comprehension. This is because experts in different disciplines approach texts differently (Shanahan, Shanahan, & Misischia, 2006). Knowing how experts in a specific discipline think about and interact with texts can help students better comprehend texts in that content area. Cynthia Shanahan (2017) explains:

> Expert readers read within a disciplinary framework. It is not simply a matter of calling on topic knowledge. Rather, expert readers use *disciplinary knowledge* to guide their reading —knowledge of the way individuals create, represent, and evaluate information—and this knowledge can guide reading even when topic knowledge is low. (p. 493)

Table C.1 (page 178) summarizes how people typically create, represent, and evaluate information in social studies, science, and mathematics.

Table C.1: Discipline-Specific Approaches to Texts

	Social Studies	Science	Mathematics
Why Do Authors Create Texts?	Synthesizing evidence to answer a question or analyze a historical problem	Reasoning from the particular to the general or abstract	Reasoning logically to identify universal principles and theorems
How Do Authors Represent Information?	Argumentation structures Narrative or descriptive structures in textbooks	Argumentation structures Experimental article structure Narrative or descriptive structures in textbooks Mathematical expressions and graphical displays often incorporated with written text	Argumentation structures Descriptive structure with worked examples in textbooks Charts, graphs, formulae, and linguistic explanations
How Should Readers Evaluate Texts?	Readers should read everything critically.	Readers should read scholarly work critically. Readers should read textbooks less critically (to learn).	Readers should evaluate arguments for precision, simplicity, and clarity. Readers regard textbooks as authoritative.
Discipline-Specific Reading Strategies	Sourcing Identification Contextualization Corroboration Interpretation	Sourcing Selecting Translating	Previewing Close reading Logical verification Summarizing Predicting
Potential Problems for Students	Antiquated vocabulary and language Failure of students to recognize interpretations as such	High lexical density and technical vocabulary Failure of students to recognize varying levels of confidence	Technical notation (equations, symbols, diagrams) Failure of students to recognize different meanings of the same symbol depending on context

Source: Adapted from Moje, Stockdill, Kim, & Kim, 2011; Phillips & Yarden, 2017; Shanahan, 2017.
Visit ***go.SolutionTree.com/instruction*** *for a free reproducible version of this table.*

As table C.1 indicates, the primary reason for creating texts in social studies is synthesizing evidence to answer a question or analyze a historical problem. The evidence is usually primary sources, which encompass a wide variety of text types: personal letters, legal documents, newspaper reports, editorials, interviews, pictures, paintings, political cartoons, films, and so on. Most scholarly social studies texts use an argumentative structure in which a visible author explains how evidence and reasoning support a specific claim; in particular, historians tend to make claims about cause-effect relationships. However, most social studies textbooks have an invisible author and use a narrative or descriptive structure (which tends to have an authoritative tone). For example, a social studies textbook might state, "There were three causes of World War II . . ." rather than "The author considers the following three events to be the primary causes of World War II for the following reasons . . ." These features of textbooks (invisible author, authoritative tone) can actually discourage students from engaging in the critical reading strategies that social scientists value. Elizabeth Birr Moje, and colleagues (2011) explain that "students reading anonymous texts seemed less likely to think about the author as a historical source, less likely to make evaluations of possible author bias, and demonstrated a lack of critical reading in written responses to questions" (p. 462). Expert historians believe that all readers should critically read all texts, including textbooks. Therefore, they use reading strategies that reflect that belief.

- **Sourcing:** Ask questions about the *author* of a text, including determining the author's social, cultural, and political position.

- **Identification:** Classify a text by its *genre* (letter, newspaper account, commentary, commission report, and so on) and determine the *purpose* for which the writer originally wrote it.
- **Contextualization:** Pay attention to the *time period* in which the writer produced the text, including the political, social, economic, and cultural conditions of that time.
- **Corroboration:** Compare one account with other accounts from a historical period and look for *agreement and disagreement* across multiple texts and between a text and one's own views.
- **Interpretation:** Read a text from a particular philosophical *perspective* (feminist, Marxist, and so on).

Working with primary sources can help to remind students that all texts have authors and are interpretations, but primary sources pose potential problems due to antiquated vocabulary and language, depending on the date of the source.

In science, the primary reason for creating texts is to use specific results (such as those from a lab experiment) and reasoning to arrive at general or abstract principles. As in social studies, many scientific texts employ an argumentation structure (evidence + reasoning = conclusion) and incorporate mathematical expressions and graphical displays along with written text. Journal articles use a well-defined structure consisting of an abstract, introduction, literature review, methods section, report of results or findings, discussion section, and conclusions section. Textbooks, however, usually have narrative or descriptive structures. Expert scientists tend to adopt a critical stance toward scholarly work but acknowledge that students should read textbooks as authoritative in order to learn proven principles. Expert scientists engage in some of the same reading strategies as historians, such as *sourcing*, but also use unique reading strategies such as *selecting* and *translating*.

- **Sourcing:** Ask questions about the *author* of a text, including determining the reputation and expertise of the author or research group, the source of funding for research, and the prestige of associated universities.
- **Selecting:** Jump around in articles to find *information* that relates to one's work or interests (and only take time to critique information that might be useful).
- **Translating:** Transfer information between *forms*, such as converting the information in a chart or graph to text and vice versa.

The most obvious challenge for students is the high lexical density of scientific texts; there are more content terms per phrase in scientific texts than in any other discipline. Additionally, the content terms tend to be technical and *polysemous*, meaning they have specialized disciplinary meanings that differ from their common meanings (for example, terms such as *energy* and *force* have common meanings that are different from their specialized science meanings; Nagy & Hiebert, 2011). A less obvious, but still significant, challenge for students reading scientific texts is that students often fail to recognize words and phrases that signal varying levels of confidence. Phillips and Yarden (2017) explain, "Students consistently assume that *could be* is certain, they fail to see it as a hedge, as is also the case with the word *may*" (p. 432). Teaching students to look for words that signal tentativeness or uncertainty, such as *possibly*, *could be*, *because*, *conclude*, *might*, *if–then*, *support for*, *therefore*, *since*, *assume*, *generally considered*, *believe*, *likely impossible*, and *tend*, can help them overcome this obstacle.

Finally, writers typically create mathematics texts to show how mathematicians have used logical reasoning to identify principles and theorems that apply across time and space. While scholarly work in mathematics often utilizes an argumentation structure, textbooks typically use a descriptive structure (with worked examples) and an authoritative tone. Interestingly, Moje and colleagues (2011) find:

> A lower-level math textbook tended to present definitions as a one-to-one relationship between a word and a concept, presented as absolute, unchallengeable fact. In higher-level texts, on the other hand, the treatment of definitions seemed much more complex. Words and concepts were open to multiple definitions, where choice of definition was driven by author's purpose; definitions did more than just name concepts, functioning as key elements of the mathematical rhetoric. (p. 470)

When evaluating texts, expert mathematicians tend to look for precision, simplicity, and clarity; they place far less emphasis on who wrote a text or when he or she wrote it than do historians or scientists. Also, unlike the scientists who skip around to find ideas that interest them, mathematicians tend to note the overall structure and thread of the argument the writer is presenting in a text before settling down to read the text line by line, verifying that each statement follows formal logic (Weber, 2008). Expert mathematicians use the following strategies as they read.

- **Previewing:** Note the *overall structure* and gist of the argument a text makes.
- **Close reading:** Pay special attention to *details and nuances* in the text.
- **Logical verification:** Carefully examine *reasoning* to see if it follows the rules of formal logic.
- **Summarizing:** Asking oneself, "*What do I know now*, based on what I have read so far?"
- **Predicting:** Ask oneself, "*What will happen* if I try this solution?"

As one might expect, the technical notation (such as equations, symbols, and diagrams) in mathematical texts makes them potentially challenging for students. Additionally, the same symbol can often take on different meanings depending on context (for example, *x* can indicate multiplication or a variable, + can indicate addition or a positive number, and – can indicate subtraction or a negative number), creating the potential for confusion if students are not reading carefully.

Appendix D
List of Figures and Tables

Visit **go.SolutionTree.com/instruction** for free reproducible versions of figures and tables with an asterisk.

References and Resources

Adams, M. J. (1990). *Beginning to read: Thinking and learning about print.* Cambridge, MA: MIT Press.

Adams, M. J., & Bruck, M. (1993). Word recognition: The interface of educational policies and scientific research. *Reading and Writing, 5*(2), 113–139.

Adler, M. J., & Van Doren, C. (1972). *How to read a book: The classic guide to intelligent reading.* New York: Touchstone.

Afflerbach, P., Pearson, P. D., & Paris, S. G. (2008). Clarifying differences between reading skills and reading strategies. *The Reading Teacher, 61*(5), 364–373.

Allington, R. L. (1983). Fluency: The neglected reading goal. *The Reading Teacher, 37*(6), 556–561.

Allington, R. L., & McGill-Franzen, A. (2017). Comprehension difficulties and struggling readers. In S. E. Israel (Ed.), *Handbook of research on reading comprehension* (2nd ed., pp. 271–292). New York: Guilford Press.

Anderson, J. R. (2010). *Cognitive psychology and its implications* (7th ed.). New York: Worth.

Anderson, J. R., & Reder, L. M. (1979). An elaborative processing explanation of depth of processing. In L. S. Cermak & F. I. M. Craik (Eds.), *Levels of processing in human memory* (pp. 385–404). Hillsdale, NJ: Erlbaum.

Anderson, R. C. (1984). Role of readers' schema in comprehension, learning, and memory. In R. C. Anderson, J. Osbourne, & R. J. Tierney (Eds.), *Learning to read in American schools: Basal readers and content text* (pp. 243–258). Hillsdale, NJ: Erlbaum.

Anderson, R. C., Hiebert, E.H., Scott, J.A., & Wilkinson, I.A.G. (1985). *Becoming a nation of readers: The report of the Commission on Reading.* Champaign, IL: Center for the Study of Reading.

Appleman, D. (2009). *Critical encounters in high school English: Teaching literary theory to adolescents* (2nd ed.). New York: Teachers College Press.

Associated Press. (2017). Environmentalists are not in favor of government-planned fish farms. *Newsela.* Accessed at https://newsela.com/read/hungry-planet-fish-farms/id/25500 on January 18, 2018.

Atwell, N. (1987). *In the middle: Writing, reading, and learning with adolescents.* Portsmouth, NH: Heinemann.

Au, K. H., & Raphael, T. E. (1998). Curriculum and teaching in literature-based programs. In T. E. Raphael & K. H. Au (Eds.), *Literature-based instruction: Reshaping the curriculum* (pp. 123–148). Norwood, MA: Christopher-Gordon.

August, D., & Shanahan, T. (Eds.). (2006). *Developing literacy in second-language learners: Report of the National Literacy Panel on Language-Minority Children and Youth.* Mahwah, NJ: Erlbaum.

Baird, B., Smallwood, J., & Schooler, J. W. (2011). Back to the future: Autobiographical planning and the functionality of mind-wandering. *Consciousness and Cognition, 20*(4), 1604–1611.

Beck, I. L., McKeown, M. G., & Kucan, L. (2002). *Bringing words to life: Robust vocabulary instruction.* New York: Guilford Press.

Beck, I. L., Perfetti, C. A., & McKeown, M. G. (1982). Effects of long-term vocabulary instruction on lexical access and reading comprehension. *Journal of Educational Psychology, 74*(4), 506–521.

Benjamin, R. G., & Schwanenflugel, P. J. (2010). Text complexity and oral reading prosody in young readers. *Reading Research Quarterly, 45*(4), 388–404.

Bennett, A. (2006). *The history boys: A play.* New York: Farrar, Straus and Giroux.

Berenhaus, M., Oakhill, J., & Rusted, J. (2015). When kids act out: A comparison of embodied methods to improve children's memory for a story. *Journal of Research in Reading, 38*(4), 331–343.

Biemiller, A. (2005). Size and sequence in vocabulary development: Implications for choosing words for primary grade vocabulary instruction. In E. H. Hiebert & M. L. Kamil (Eds.), *Teaching and learning vocabulary: Bringing research to practice* (pp. 223–242). Mahwah, NJ: Erlbaum.

Biemiller, A. (2012). Teaching vocabulary in the primary grades: Vocabulary instruction needed. In E. J. Kame'enui & J. F. Baumann (Eds.), *Vocabulary instruction: Research to practice* (2nd ed., pp. 34–50). New York: Guilford Press.

Biemiller, A., & Slonim, N. (2001). Estimating root word vocabulary growth in normative and advantaged populations: Evidence for a common sequence of vocabulary acquisition. *Journal of Educational Psychology, 93*(3), 498–520.

Blachowicz, C. L. Z., & Fisher, P. (2008). Attentional vocabulary instruction: Read-alouds, word play, and other motivating strategies for fostering informal word learning. In A. E. Farstrup & S. J. Samuels (Eds.), *What research has to say about vocabulary instruction* (pp. 32–55). Newark, DE: International Reading Association.

Blachowicz, C. L. Z., & Fisher, P. (2012). Keep the "fun" in fundamental: Encouraging word consciousness and incidental word learning in the classroom through word play. In E. J. Kame'enui & J. F. Baumann (Eds.), *Vocabulary instruction: Research to practice* (2nd ed., pp. 189–209). New York: Guilford Press.

Booth, A. E. (2009). Causal supports for early word learning. *Child Development, 80*(4), 1243–1250.

Boulenger, V., Hauk, O., & Pulvermüller, F. (2009). Grasping ideas with the motor system: Semantic somatotopy in idiom comprehension. *Cerebral Cortex, 19*(8), 1905–1914.

Bowey, J. A., & Muller, D. (2005). Phonological recoding and rapid orthographic learning in third-graders' silent reading: A critical test of the self-teaching hypothesis. *Journal of Experimental Child Psychology, 92*(3), 203–219.

Bowman, B. T., Donovan, M. S., & Burns, M. S. (Eds.). (2001). *Eager to learn: Educating our preschoolers.* Washington, DC: National Academies Press.

Bowman, M., & Treiman, R. (2002). Relating print and speech: The effects of letter names and word position on reading and spelling performance. *Journal of Experimental Child Psychology, 82*(4), 305–340.

Boyles, N. (2012). Closing in on close reading. *Educational Leadership, 70*(4), 36–41.

Brabham, E. G., & Villaume, S. K. (2001). Questions and answers—Building walls of words. *The Reading Teacher, 54*(7), 700–703.

Bradbury, R. (1953). *Fahrenheit 451.* New York: Ballantine Books.

Branscombe, M. (2015). Showing, not telling: Tableau as an embodied text. *The Reading Teacher, 69*(3), 321–329.

Brophy, J. E., & Good, T. L. (1986). Teacher behavior and student achievement. In M. C. Wittrock (Ed.), *Handbook of research on teaching* (3rd ed., pp. 328–375). New York: Macmillan.

Byrne, B. (1992). Studies in the acquisition procedure for reading: Rationale, hypotheses, and data. In P. B. Gough, L. Ehri, & R. Treiman (Eds.), *Reading acquisition* (pp. 1–34). Hillsdale, NJ: Erlbaum.

Calvino, I. (1986). *The uses of literature* (W. Weaver, Trans.). New York: Harcourt Brace .

Carle, E. (1969). *The very hungry caterpillar.* New York: Philomel Books.

Carleton, L., & Marzano, R. J. (2010). *Vocabulary games for the classroom.* Bloomington, IN: Marzano Resources.

Carpenter, R. D., & Paris, S. G. (2005). Issues of validity and reliability in early reading achievement. In S. G. Paris & S. A. Stahl (Eds.), *Children's reading comprehension and assessment* (pp. 279–304). Mahwah, NJ: Erlbaum.

Casale, U. P. (1985). Motor imaging: A reading-vocabulary strategy. *Journal of Reading, 28*(7), 619–621.

Cattell, J. M. (1886). The time it takes to see and name objects. *Mind, 11*(41), 63–65.

Chall, J. S. (1983). *Learning to read: The great debate.* New York: McGraw-Hill Education.

Chard, D. J., Ketterlin-Geller, L. R., Baker, S. K., Doabler, C., & Apichatabutra, C. (2009). Repeated reading interventions for students with learning disabilities: Status of the evidence. *Exceptional Children, 75*(3), 263–281.

Cheatham, J. P., & Allor, J. H. (2012). The influence of decodability in early reading text on reading achievement: A review of the evidence. *Reading and Writing: An Interdisciplinary Journal, 25*(9), 2223–2246.

Cheryan, S., Ziegler, S. A., Plaut, V. C., & Meltzoff, A. N. (2014). Designing classrooms to maximize student achievement. *Policy Insights From the Behavioral and Brain Sciences, 1*(1), 4–12.

Chi, M. T., & Koeske, R. D. (1983). Network representation of a child's dinosaur knowledge. *Developmental Psychology, 19*(1), 29–39.

Chin, C., Brown, D. E., & Bruce, B. C. (2002). Student-generated questions: A meaningful aspect of learning in science. *International Journal of Science Education, 24*(5), 521–549.

Cho, B.-Y., & Afflerbach, P. (2017). An evolving perspective of constructively responsive reading comprehension strategies in multilayered digital text environments. In S. E. Israel (Ed.), *Handbook of research on reading comprehension* (2nd ed., pp. 109–134). New York: Guilford Press.

Chouinard, M. M., Harris, P. L., & Maratsos, M. P. (2007). Children's questions: A mechanism for cognitive development. *Monographs of the Society for Research in Child Development, 72*(1), vii–ix, 1–129.

Clay, M. M. (2000). *Concepts about print: What have children learned about printed language?* Portsmouth, NH: Heinemann.

Clay, M. M. (2013). *An observation study of early literacy achievement* (3rd ed.). Portsmouth, NH: Heinemann.

Cole, S. (2013, January 29). *The key sounds of English: 44 phonemes and 4 blends* [Blog post]. Accessed at https://readaboutreading.wordpress.com/2013/01/29/2013129the-key-sounds-of-english-44-phonemes-and-4-blends on January 18, 2018.

Compton-Lilly, C. (2003). *Reading families: The literate lives of urban children.* New York: Teachers College Press.

Conley, M. W. (2017). Improving reading comprehension: Developing comprehension strategies in the content areas. In S. E. Israel (Ed.), *Handbook of research on reading comprehension* (2nd ed., pp. 406–427). New York: Guilford Press.

Connor, C. M., & Morrison, F. J. (2016). Individualizing student instruction in reading: Implications for policy and practice. *Policy Insights From the Behavioral and Brain Sciences, 3*(1), 54–61.

Connor, C. M., Morrison, F. J., & Katch, L. E. (2004). Beyond the reading wars: Exploring the effect of child-instruction interactions on growth in early reading. *Scientific Studies of Reading, 8*(4), 305–336.

Connor, C. M., Morrison, F. J., & Petrella, J. N. (2004). Effective reading comprehension instruction: Examining child × instruction interactions. *Journal of Educational Psychology, 96*(4), 682–698.

Connor, C. M., Morrison, F. J., & Slominski, L. (2006). Preschool instruction and children's literacy skill growth. *Journal of Educational Psychology, 98*(4), 665–689.

Connor, C. M., Morrison, F. J., & Underwood, P. (2007). A second change in second grade: The independent and cumulative impact of first- and second-grade reading instruction and students' letter-word reading skill growth. *Scientific Studies of Reading, 11*(3), 199–233.

Connor, C. M., Piasta, S. B., Fishman, B., Glasney, S., Schatschneider, C., Crowe, E., et al. (2009). Individualizing student instruction precisely: Effects of child × instruction interactions on first graders' literacy development. *Child Development, 80*(1), 77–100.

Cook, S. W., Mitchell, Z., & Goldin-Meadow, S. (2008). Gesturing makes learning last. *Cognition, 106*(2), 1047–1058.

Cunningham, A. E. (2006). Accounting for children's orthographic learning while reading text: Do children self-teach? *Journal of Experimental Child Psychology, 95*(1), 56–77.

Cunningham, A. E., Nathan, R. G., & Raher, K. S. (2011). Orthographic processing in models of word recognition. In M. L. Kamil, P. D. Pearson, E. B. Moje, & P. P. Afflerbach (Eds.), *Handbook of reading research* (Vol. 4, pp. 259–285). New York: Routledge.

Cunningham, A. E., Perry, K. E., Stanovich, K. E., & Share, D. L. (2002). Orthographic learning during reading: Examining the role of self-teaching. *Journal of Experimental Child Psychology, 82*(3), 185–199.

Cutica, I., Ianì, F., & Bucciarelli, M. (2014). Learning from text benefits from enactment. *Memory and Cognition, 25*(2), 261–287.

Dalton, B., & Grisham, D. L. (2011). eVoc strategies: 10 ways to use technology to build vocabulary. *The Reading Teacher, 64*(5), 306–317.

Daniels, M. (1994). The effect of sign language on hearing children's language development. *Communication Education, 43*(4), 291–298.

Daniels, M. (1996). Bilingual, bimodal education for hearing kindergarten students. *Sign Language Studies, 90*, 25–37.

Davey, B., & McBride, S. (1986). Effects of question-generation training on reading comprehension. *Journal of Educational Psychology, 78*(4), 256–262.

de Abreu, M. D., & Cardoso-Martins, C. (1998). Alphabetic access route in beginning reading acquisition in Portuguese: The role of letter-name knowledge. *Reading and Writing, 10*(2), 85–104.

de Jong, P. F., & Share, D. L. (2007). Orthographic learning during oral and silent reading. *Scientific Studies of Reading, 11*(1), 55–71.

Delgado-Gaitan, C. (1990). *Literacy for empowerment: The role of parents in children's education.* New York: Falmer Press.

DeNeen, J. (2012). 30 storytelling tips for educators: How to capture your student's attention. *InformED.* Accessed at https://opencolleges.edu.au/informed/features/30-storytelling-tips-for-educators/#ixzz2CsiaXoIj on January 18, 2018.

Di Teodoro, S., Donders, S., Kemp-Davidson, J., Robertson, P., & Schuyler, L. (2011). Asking good questions: Promoting greater understanding of mathematics through purposeful teacher and student questioning. *Canadian Journal of Action Research, 12*(2), 18–29.

Dole, J. A., Duffy, G. G., Roehler, L. R., & Pearson, P. D. (1991). Moving from the old to the new: Research on reading comprehension instruction. *Review of Educational Research, 61*(2), 239–264.

Dole, J. A., Sloan, C., & Trathen, W. (1995). Teaching vocabulary within the context of literature. *Journal of Reading, 38*(6), 452–460.

Dr. Seuss. (1978). *I can read with my eyes shut!* New York: Beginner Books.

DSF Literacy Resources. (n.d.). *The 44 sounds (phonemes) of English*. Accessed at www.dyslexia-reading-well.com/support-files/the-44-phonemes-of-english.pdf on January 18, 2018.

Duke, N. K., & Carlisle, J. (2011). The development of comprehension. In M. L. Kamil, P. D. Pearson, E. B. Moje, & P. P. Afflerbach (Eds.), *Handbook of reading research* (Vol. 4, pp. 199–228). New York: Routledge.

Duke, N. K., & Pearson, P. D. (2002). Effective practices for developing reading comprehension. In A. E. Farstrup & S. J. Samuels (Eds.), *What research has to say about reading instruction* (3rd ed., pp. 205–242). Newark, DE: International Reading Association.

Dunlosky, J., Rawson, K. A., Marsh, E. J., Nathan, M. J., & Willingham, D. T. (2013). Improving students' learning with effective learning techniques: Promising directions from cognitive and educational psychology. *Psychological Science in the Public Interest, 14*(1), 4–58.

Durkin, D. (1978/1979). What classroom observations reveal about reading comprehension instruction. *Reading Research Quarterly, 14*(4), 481–533.

Eccleshare, J., Hope, J., Smith, S., & Woodfine, K. (2014). Diverse voices: The 50 best culturally diverse children's books. *Guardian News*. Accessed at https://theguardian.com/childrens-books-site/2014/oct/13/50-best-culturally-diverse-childrens-books on January 18, 2018.

Ehri, L. C. (1992). Reconceptualizing the development of sight word reading and its relationship to recoding. In P. Gough, L. C. Ehri, & R. Treiman (Eds.), *Reading acquisition* (pp. 107–143). Hillsdale, NJ: Erlbaum.

Ehri, L. C. (1997). Sight word learning in normal readers and dyslexia. In B. Blachman (Ed.), *Foundations of reading intervention and dyslexia: Implications for early intervention* (pp. 163–189). Mahwah, NJ: Erlbaum.

Ehri, L. C. (1998). Grapheme-phoneme knowledge is essential for learning to read words in English. In J. Metsala & L. C. Ehri (Eds.), *Word recognition in beginning literacy* (pp. 3–40). Mahwah, NJ: Erlbaum.

Ehri, L. C. (1999). Phases of development in learning to read words. In J. V. Oakhill & R. Beard (Eds.), *Reading development and the teaching of reading: A psychological perspective* (pp. 79–108). Oxford, England: Blackwell.

Ehri, L. C. (2002). Phases of acquisition in learning to read words and implications for teaching. *British Journal of Educational Psychology: Monograph Series, 1*, 7–28.

Ehri, L. C. (2005). Development of sight word reading: Phases and findings. In M. J. Snowling & C. Hulme (Eds.), *The science of reading: A handbook* (pp. 135–154). Oxford, England: Blackwell.

Ehri, L. C., & Wilce, L. S. (1983). Development of word identification speed in skilled and less skilled beginning readers. *Journal of Educational Psychology, 75*(1), 3–18.

Ehri, L. C., & Wilce, L. S. (1985). Movement into reading: Is the first stage of printed word learning visual or phonetic? *Reading Research Quarterly, 20*(2), 163–179.

El-Dinary, P. B., & Schuder, T. (1993). Seven teachers' acceptance of transactional strategies instruction during their first year using it. *Elementary School Journal, 94*(2), 207–219.

Elementary and Secondary Education Act (ESEA) of 1965: An Act to strengthen and improve educational quality and educational opportunities in the Nations [sic] elementary and secondary schools, Pub. L. No. 89–10, H. R. 2362. Accessed at https://govtrack.us/congress/bills/89/hr2362 on January 8, 2017.

Elkonin, D. B. (1973). Methods of teaching reading. In J. Downing (Ed.), *Comparative reading* (pp. 551–579). New York: Macmillan.

Elson, W. H., & Gray, W. S. (1936). *Elson-Gray basic readers: Curriculum foundation series*. Chicago: Foresman.

Engelkamp, J., & Zimmer, H. (2001). Categorical and order information in free recall of action phrases. *Psicológica, 22*, 71–96.

Entwisle, D. R. (1966). *Word associations of young children.* Baltimore: Johns Hopkins University Press.

Ezell, H. K., & Justice, L. M. (2000). Increasing the print focus of adult-child shared book reading through observational learning. *American Journal of Speech-Language Pathology, 9*(1), 36–47.

Faulkner, W. (1984). *The sound and the fury.* New York: Vintage Books. (original work published 1929)

Flesch, R. F. (1955). *Why Johnny can't read—And what you can do about it.* New York: Harper.

Fletcher, J. M., Lyon, G. R., Fuchs, L. S., & Barnes, M. A. (2007). *Learning disabilities: From identification to intervention.* New York: Guilford Press.

Foorman, B., Beyler, N., Borradaile, K., Coyne, M., Denton, C. A., Dimino, J., et al. (2016). *Foundational skills to support reading for understanding in kindergarten through 3rd grade* (NCEE 2016–4008). Washington, DC: National Center for Education Evaluation and Regional Assistance, Institute of Education Sciences, U.S. Department of Education.

Foorman, B. R., & Connor, C. M. (2011). Primary grade reading. In M. L. Kamil, P. D. Pearson, E. B. Moje, & P. P. Afflerbach (Eds.), *Handbook of reading research* (Vol. 4, pp. 136–156). New York: Routledge.

Frazier, B. N., Gelman, S. A., & Wellman, H. M. (2009). Preschoolers search for explanatory information within adult–child conversation. *Child Development, 80*(6), 1592–1611.

Frazier, L., Carlson, K., & Clifton, C., Jr. (2006). Prosodic phrasing is central to language comprehension. *Trends in Cognitive Sciences, 10*(6), 244–249.

Freeman, D. (1976). *Corduroy.* New York: Puffin Books.

Frith, U. (1985). Beneath the surface of developmental dyslexia. In K. E. Patterson, J. C. Marshall, & M. Coltheart (Eds.), *Surface dyslexia: Neuropsychological and cognitive studies of phonological reading* (pp. 301–330). London: Erlbaum.

Fulmer, S. M., & Frijters, J. C. (2011). Motivation during an excessively challenging reading task: The buffering role of relative topic interest. *Journal of Experimental Education, 79*(2), 185–208.

Gambrell, L. B., & Bales, R. J. (1986). Mental imagery and the comprehension-monitoring performance of fourth- and fifth-grade poor readers. *Reading Research Quarterly, 21*(4), 454–464.

Gambrell, L. B., Wilson, R. M., & Gnatt, W. N. (1981). Classroom observations of task-attending behaviors of good and poor readers. *Journal of Educational Research, 74*(6), 400–404.

Giambra, L. M. (1995). A laboratory method for investigating influences on switching attention to task-unrelated imagery and thought. *Consciousness and Cognition, 4*(1), 1–21.

Gibbons, G. (1997). *The moon book.* New York: Holiday House.

Gillies, R. M., Nicols, K., Burgh, G., & Haynes, M. (2013). Primary students' scientific reasoning and discourse during cooperative inquiry-based science activities. *International Journal of Educational Research, 63*, 127–140.

Glaser, R. (1984). Education and thinking: The role of knowledge. *American Psychologist, 39*(2), 93–104.

Glenberg, A. M., Gutierrez, T., Levin, J. R., Japuntich, S., & Kaschak, M. P. (2004). Activity and imagined activity can enhance young children's reading comprehension. *Journal of Educational Psychology, 96*(3), 424–436.

Goldenberg, C. (2011). Reading instruction for English language learners. In M. L. Kamil, P. D. Pearson, E. B. Moje, & P. P. Afflerbach (Eds.), *Handbook of reading research* (Vol. 4, pp. 684–710). New York: Routledge.

Goodman, K. S. (1965). A linguistic study of cues and miscues in reading. *Elementary English, 42*(6), 639–643.

Goodman, K. S. (1967). Reading: A psycholinguistic guessing game. *Journal of the Reading Specialist, 6*(4), 126–135.

Goodman, K. S., & Goodman, Y. (1985). A whole language comprehension centered view of reading development. *Gnosis, 7*, 2–8.

Gough, P. B. (1996). *A pox on both your houses* [Presentation]. Paper presented at the Symposium on Integrated Direct Instruction in Reading, sponsored by the Language Arts Foundation of America and Oklahoma City Schools, Oklahoma City, OK.

Gough, P. B., & Hillinger, M. L. (1980). Learning to read: An unnatural act. *Bulletin of the Orton Society, 30*, 179–196.

Gough, P. B., Juel, C., & Griffith, P. L. (1992). Reading, spelling, and the orthographic cipher. In P. B. Gough, L. C. Ehri, & R. Treiman (Eds.), *Reading acquisition* (pp. 35–48). Hillsdale, NJ: Erlbaum.

Gough, P. B., & Walsh, M. A. (1991). Chinese, Phoenicians, and the orthographic cipher of English. In S. A. Brady & D. Shankweiler (Eds.), *Phonological processes in literacy: A tribute to Isabelle Y. Liberman* (pp. 199–209). Hillsdale, NJ: Erlbaum.

Graesser, A. C., McNamara, D. S., & Louwerse, M. M. (2011). Methods of automated text analysis. In M. L. Kamil, P. D. Pearson, E. B. Moje, & P. P. Afflerbach (Eds.), *Handbook of reading research* (Vol. 4, pp. 34–53). New York: Routledge.

Graves, M. F. (2000). A vocabulary program to complement and bolster a middle-grade comprehension program. In B. M. Taylor, M. F. Graves, & P. van den Broek (Eds.), *Reading for meaning: Fostering comprehension in the middle grades* (pp. 116–135). Newark, DE: International Reading Association.

Graves, M. F. (2006). *The vocabulary book: Learning and instruction.* New York: Teachers College Press.

Haller, E. P., Child, D. A., & Walberg, H. J. (1988). Can comprehension be taught? A quantitative synthesis of "metacognitive" studies. *Educational Researcher, 17*(9), 5–8.

Harm, M. W., & Seidenberg, M. S. (1999). Phonology, reading acquisition, and dyslexia: Insights from connectionist models. *Psychological Review, 106*(3), 491–528.

Hauk, O., Johnsrude, I., & Pulvermüller, F. (2004). Somatotopic representation of action words in human motor and premotor cortex. *Neuron, 41*(2), 301–307.

Heath, S. B. (1983). *Ways with words: Language, life, and work in communities and classrooms.* New York: Cambridge University Press.

Hilden, K. R., & Pressley, M. (2007). Self-regulation through transactional strategies instruction. *Reading and Writing Quarterly, 23*(1), 51–75.

Hoffman, J. V. (1987). Rethinking the role of oral reading in basal instruction. *Elementary School Journal, 87*(3), 367–373.

Hoffman, J. V. (1991). Teacher and school effects in learning to read. In R. Barr, M. L. Kamil, P. Mosenthal, & P. D. Pearson (Eds.), *Handbook of reading research* (Vol. 2, pp. 911–950). Mahwah, NJ: Erlbaum.

Hoffman, J. V. (2017). Comprehension is *not* simple: Considering the persisting dangers in the simple view of reading comprehension. In S. E. Israel (Ed.), *Handbook of research on reading comprehension* (2nd ed., pp. 57–69). New York: Guilford Press.

Hoffman, J. V., & Segel, K. (1983). *Oral reading instruction: A century of controversy (1880–1980)* [Presentation]. Paper presented at the annual meeting of the International Reading Association, Anaheim, CA. (ERIC Document Reproduction Service No. ED239237).

Hudson, R. F., Lane, H. B., & Pullen, P. C. (2005). Reading fluency assessment and instruction: What, why, and how? *The Reading Teacher, 58*(8), 702–714.

Huey, E. B. (1908). *The psychology and pedagogy of reading, with a review of the history of reading and writing and of methods, texts, and hygiene in reading.* New York: Macmillan.

Hulme, C., Snowling, M. J., & Quinlan, P. (1991). Connectionism and learning to read: Steps towards a phonologically plausible model. *Reading and Writing, 3*(2), 159–168.

Hung, P.-H., Hwang, G.-J., Lee, Y.-H., Wu, T.-H., Vogel, B., Milrad, M., et al. (2014). A problem-based ubiquitous learning approach to improving the questioning abilities of elementary school students. *Journal of Educational Technology & Society, 17*(4), 316–334.

Hyatt, A. V. (1943). *The place of oral reading in the school program: Its history and development from 1880–1941.* New York: Teachers College Press.

Iberlin, J. M. (2017). *Cultivating mindfulness in the classroom.* Bloomington, IN: Marzano Resources.

James, W. (1892). *Psychology.* New York: Holt.

Jones, C. D., & Reutzel, D. R. (2012). Enhanced alphabet knowledge instruction: Exploring a change of frequency, focus, and distributed cycles of review. *Reading Psychology: An International Journal, 33*(5), 448–464.

Jorm, A. F. (1979). The cognitive and neurological basis of developmental dyslexia: A theoretical framework and review. *Cognition, 7*(1), 19–33.

Jorm, A. F., & Share, D. L. (1983). An invited article: Phonological recoding and reading acquisition. *Applied Psycholinguistics, 4*(2), 103–147.

Juel, C. (1991). Beginning reading. In R. Barr, M. L. Kamil, P. B. Mosenthal, & P. D. Pearson (Eds.), *Handbook of reading research* (Vol. 2, pp. 759–788). White Plains, NY: Longman.

Justice, L. M., & Ezell, H. K. (2002). Use of storybook reading to increase print awareness in at-risk children. *American Journal of Speech-Language Pathology, 11*(1), 17–29.

Justice, L. M., & Ezell, H. K. (2004). Print referencing: An emergent literacy enhancement strategy and its clinical applications. *Language, Speech, and Hearing Services in Schools, 35*(2), 185–193.

Justice, L. M., Kaderavek, J. N., Fan, X., Sofka, A., & Hunt, A. (2009). Accelerating preschoolers' early literacy development through classroom-based teacher-child storybook reading and explicit print referencing. *Language, Speech, and Hearing Services in Schools, 40*(1), 67–85.

Justice, L. M., & Pullen, P. C. (2003). Promising interventions for promoting emergent literacy skills: Three evidence-based approaches. *Topics in Early Childhood Special Education, 23*(3), 99–113.

Kaschak, M. P., Connor, C. M., & Dombek, J. L. (2017). Enacted reading comprehension: Using bodily movement to aid the comprehension of abstract text content. *PLOS One, 12*(1), e0169711.

Killingsworth, M. A., & Gilbert, D. T. (2010). A wandering mind is an unhappy mind. *Science, 330*(6006), 932.

King, A., & Rosenshine, B. (1993). Effects of guided cooperative questioning on children's knowledge construction. *Journal of Experimental Education, 61*(2), 127–148.

Kintsch, W. (1983). *Text structure and inference* (Technical Report No. 123). Boulder: Institute of Cognitive Science, University of Colorado.

Kipling, R. (2008). *Just so stories.* New York: Puffin Books. (Original work published 1902)

Klingner, J., Brownell, M., Mason, L. H., Sindelar, P. T., Benedict, A., Griffin, C., et al. (2016). Teaching students with special needs in the new millennium. In D. H. Gitomer & C. A. Bell (Eds.), *Handbook of research on teaching* (5th ed., pp. 639–716). Washington, DC: American Educational Research Association.

Klingner, J. K., Vaughn, S., Arguelles, M. E., Hughes, M. T., & Leftwich, S. A. (2004). Collaborative strategic reading: "Real-world" lessons from classroom teachers. *Remedial and Special Education, 25*(5), 291–302.

Klingner, J. K., Vaughn, S., Hughes, M. T., & Arguelles, M. E. (1999). Sustaining research-based practices in reading: A 3-year follow-up. *Remedial and Special Education, 20*(5), 263–274.

Kucan, L., & Palincsar, A. S. (2011). Locating struggling readers in a reconfigured landscape. In M. L. Kamil, P. D. Pearson, E. B. Moje, & P. P. Afflerbach (Eds.), *Handbook of reading research* (Vol. 4, pp. 341–358). New York: Routledge.

Kuhn, M. R. (2000). *A comparative study of small group fluency instruction*. Unpublished doctoral dissertation, University of Georgia, Athens.

Kuhn, M. R. (2004). Helping students become accurate, expressive readers: Fluency instruction for small groups. *The Reading Teacher, 58*(4), 338–344.

Kuhn, M. R. (2005). A comparative study of small group fluency instruction. *Reading Psychology, 26*(2), 127–146.

Kuhn, M. R., & Schwanenflugel, P. J. (2017). Reconsidering fluency's role in reading comprehension. In S. E. Israel (Ed.), *Handbook of research on reading comprehension* (2nd ed., pp. 316–331). New York: Guilford Press.

Kuhn, M. R., Schwanenflugel, P. J., Meisinger, E. B., Levy, B. A., & Rasinski, T. V. (2010). Aligning theory and assessment of reading fluency: Automaticity, prosody, and definitions of fluency. *Reading Research Quarterly, 45*(2), 230–251.

Kuhn, M. R., Schwanenflugel, P. J., Morris, R. D., Morrow, L. M., Woo, D. G., Meisinger, E. B., et al. (2006). Teaching children to become fluent and automatic readers. *Journal of Literacy Research, 38*(4), 357–387.

Kyte, C. S., & Johnson, C. J. (2006). The role of phonological recoding in orthographic learning. *Journal of Experimental Child Psychology, 93*(2), 166–185.

LaBerge, D., & Samuels, S. J. (1974). Toward a theory of automatic information processing in reading. *Cognitive Psychology, 6*(2), 293–323.

Landow, G. P. (2006). *Hypertext 3.0: Critical theory and new media in an era of globalization* (3rd ed.). Baltimore: Johns Hopkins University Press.

Latu, I. M., Mast, M. S., Lammers, J., & Bombari, D. (2013). Successful female leaders empower women's behavior in leadership tasks. *Journal of Experimental Social Psychology, 49*(3), 444–448.

Lawrence, J. F., & Snow, C. E. (2011). Oral discourse and reading. In M. L. Kamil, P. D. Pearson, E. B. Moje, & P. P. Afflerbach (Eds.), *Handbook of reading research* (Vol. 4, pp. 320–337). New York: Routledge.

Lee, H. (1960). *To kill a mockingbird*. Philadelphia: Lippincott.

Leu, D. J., Zawilinski, L., Castek, J., Banerjee, M., Housand, B., Liu, Y., et al. (2008). What is new about the new literacies of online reading comprehension? In L. S. Rush, A. J. Eakle, & A. Berger (Eds.), *Secondary school literacy: What research reveals for classroom practice* (pp. 37–68). Chicago: National Council of Teachers of English.

Leung, C. B. (1992). Effects of word-related variables on vocabulary growth through repeated read-aloud events. In C. K. Kinzer & D. J. Leu (Eds.), *Literacy research, theory, and practice: Views from many perspectives* (pp. 491–498). Chicago: National Reading Conference.

Levelt, W. J. M., Roelofs, A., & Meyer, A. S. (1999). A theory of lexical access in speech production. *Behavioral and Brain Sciences, 22*(1), 1–38.

Li, G. (2002). *"East is east, west is west"? Home literacy, culture, and schooling*. New York: Lang.

Li, G. (Ed.). (2009). *Multicultural families, home literacies, and mainstream schooling*. Charlotte, NC: Information Age.

Li, G. (2011). The role of culture in literacy, learning, and teaching. In M. L. Kamil, P. D. Pearson, E. B. Moje, & P. P. Afflerbach (Eds.), *Handbook of reading research* (Vol. 4, pp. 515–538). New York: Routledge.

Lind, A., Hall., L., Breidegard, B., Balkenius, C., & Johansson, P. (2014). Speakers' acceptance of real-time speech exchange indicates that we use auditory feedback to specify the meaning of what we say. *Psychological Science, 25*(6), 1198–1205.

Lindgren, R., & Johnson-Glenberg, M. (2013). Emboldened by embodiment: Six precepts for research on embodied learning and mixed reality. *Educational Researcher, 42*(8), 445–452.

Logan, G. D. (1997). Automaticity and reading: Perspectives from the instance theory of automatization. *Reading and Writing Quarterly, 13*(2), 123–146.

Mahdavi, J. N., & Tensfeldt, L. (2013). Untangling reading comprehension strategy instruction: Assisting struggling readers in the primary grades. *Preventing School Failure, 57*(2), 77–92.

Mann, H. (1891). Second annual report of the secretary of the board of education, 1838. In M. Mann (Ed.), *Life and works of Horace Mann* (Vol. 2, pp. 531–532). Boston: Lee and Shephard.

Manzo, U. C., & Manzo, A. V. (2008). Teaching vocabulary-learning strategies: Word consciousness, word connection, and word prediction. In A. E. Farstrup & S. J. Samuels (Eds.), *What research has to say about vocabulary instruction* (pp. 80–105). Newark, DE: International Reading Association.

Markus, H. R., & Nurius, P. (1986). Possible selves. *American Psychologist, 41*(9), 954–969.

Marsh, G., Friedman, M., Welch, V., & Desberg. P., (1981). A cognitive-developmental theory of reading acquisition. In G. MacKinnon & T. Waller (Eds.), *Reading research: Advances in theory and practice* (pp. 199–221). San Diego, CA: Academic Press.

Marzano Resources. (n.d.). *The Marzano compendium of instructional strategies.* Centennial, CO: Author. Accessed at www.marzanoresources.com/online-compendium/intro on May 3, 2018.

Marzano Resources. (2016). Developmental scales for elements. In *Marzano Compendium of Instructional Strategies.* Centennial, CO: Author.

Marzano, R. J. (2004). *Building background knowledge for academic achievement: Research on what works in schools.* Alexandria, VA: Association for Supervision and Curriculum Development.

Marzano, R. J. (2006). *Classroom assessment and grading that work.* Alexandria, VA: Association for Supervision and Curriculum Development.

Marzano, R. J. (2007). *The art and science of teaching: A comprehensive framework for effective instruction.* Alexandria, VA: Association for Supervision and Curriculum Development.

Marzano, R. J. (2010a). *Formative assessment and standards-based grading.* Bloomington, IN: Marzano Resources.

Marzano, R. J. (2010b). *Teaching basic and advanced vocabulary: A framework for direct instruction.* Boston: Cengage ELT.

Marzano, R. J. (2017). *The new art and science of teaching.* Bloomington, IN: Solution Tree Press.

Marzano, R. J. (2018). *Making classroom assessments reliable and valid.* Bloomington, IN: Solution Tree Press.

Marzano, R. J., Marzano, J. S., & Pickering, D. J. (2003). *Classroom management that works: Research-based strategies for every teacher.* Alexandria, VA: Association for Supervision and Curriculum Development.

Marzano, R. J., & Pickering, D. J. (1997). *Dimensions of learning: Teacher's manual* (2nd ed.). Alexandria, VA: Association for Supervision and Curriculum Development.

Marzano, R. J., & Pickering, D. J. (2005). *Building academic vocabulary: Teacher's manual.* Alexandria, VA: Association for Supervision and Curriculum Development.

Marzano, R. J., Pickering, D. J., & Pollock, J. E. (2001). *Classroom instruction that works: Research-based strategies for increasing student achievement.* Alexandria, VA: Association for Supervision and Curriculum Development.

Marzano, R. J., Rogers, K., & Simms, J. A. (2015). *Vocabulary for the new science standards.* Bloomington, IN: Marzano Resources.

Marzano, R. J., & Simms, J. A. (2013). *Vocabulary for the Common Core.* Bloomington, IN: Marzano Resources.

Marzano, R. J., & Simms, J. A. (2014). *Questioning sequences in the classroom.* Bloomington, IN: Marzano Resources.

Mason, J. (1980). When do children begin to read: An exploration of four year old children's letter and word reading competencies. *Reading Research Quarterly, 15*(2), 203–227.

Mason, L. H. (2004). Explicit self-regulated strategy development versus reciprocal questioning: Effects on expository reading comprehension among struggling readers. *Journal of Educational Psychology, 96*(2), 283–296.

Masonheimer, P. E., Drum, P. A., & Ehri, L. C. (1984). Does environmental print identification lead children into word reading? *Journal of Reading Behavior, 16*(4), 257–271.

Mayer, R. E. (2001). *Multimedia learning.* New York: Cambridge University Press.

Mayer, R. E., & Moreno, R. (2002). Animation as an aid to multimedia learning. *Educational Psychology Review, 14*(1), 87–99.

McGuffey, W. H. (1879). *McGuffey's second eclectic reader.* New York: American Book.

McKenna, M. C., & Picard, M. C. (2006). Revisiting the role of miscue analysis in effective teaching. *The Reading Teacher, 60*(4), 378–380.

McKeown, M. G., Beck, I. L., Omanson, R. C., & Pople, M. T. (1985). Some effects of the nature and frequency of vocabulary instruction on the knowledge and use of words. *Reading Research Quarterly, 20*(5), 522–535.

McKeown, M. G., Beck, I. L., & Sandora, C. (2012). Direct and rich vocabulary instruction needs to start early. In E. J. Kame'enui & J. F. Baumann (Eds.), *Vocabulary instruction: Research to practice* (2nd ed., pp. 17–33). New York: Guilford Press.

McNamara, D. S., Graesser, A. C., McCarthy, P. M., & Cai, Z. (2014). *Automated evaluation of text and discourse with Coh-Metrix.* New York: Cambridge University Press.

Merga, M. K. (2017). What motivates avid readers to maintain a regular reading habit in adulthood? *Australian Journal of Language and Literacy, 40*(2), 146–156.

Meyer, B. J. F. (1971). *Idea units recalled from prose in relation to their position in the logical structure, importance, stability, and order in the passage.* Unpublished master's thesis, Cornell University, Ithaca, New York.

Meyer, B. J. F. (1975). *The organization of prose and its effects on memory.* Amsterdam: Elsevier Science.

Meyer, B. J. F., Brandt, D. M., & Bluth, G. J. (1980). Use of the top-level structure in text: Key for reading comprehension of ninth-grade students. *Reading Research Quarterly, 16*(1), 72–103.

Meyer, B. J. F., & Freedle, R. O. (1979). *Effects of discourse type on recall* (Prose Learning Series Research Report No. 6). Tempe: Arizona State University.

Meyer, B. J. F., & Freedle, R. O. (1984). Effects of discourse type on recall. *American Educational Research Journal, 21*(1), 121–143.

Meyer, B. J. F., & Poon, L. W. (2001). Effects of structure strategy training and signaling on recall of text. *Journal of Educational Psychology, 93*(1), 141–159.

Meyer, B. J. F., & Ray, M. N. (2011). Structure strategy interventions: Increasing reading comprehension of expository text. *International Electronic Journal of Elementary Education, 4*(1), 127–152.

Meyer, B. J. F., & Rice, G. E. (1982). The interaction of reader strategies and the organization of text. *Text and Talk: Interdisciplinary Journal for the Study of Discourse and Communications Studies, 2*(1–3), 155–192.

Meyer, B. J. F., Wijekumar, K., Middlemiss, W., Higley, K., Lei, P. W., Meier, C., et al. (2010). Web-based tutoring of the structure strategy with or without elaborated feedback or choice for fifth- and seventh-grade readers. *Reading Research Quarterly, 45*(1), 62–92.

Meyer, B. J. F., Young, C. J., & Bartlett, B. J. (1989). *Memory improved: Reading and memory enhancement across the life span through strategic text structures*. Hillsdale, NJ: Erlbaum.

Michaels, S., O'Connor, C., & Resnick, L. B. (2008). Deliberative discourse idealized and realized: Accountable talk in the classroom and in civic life. *Studies in Philosophy and Education*, *27*(4), 283–297.

Michaels, S., O'Connor, M. C., & Hall, M. W. (2013). *Accountable Talk sourcebook: For classroom conversation that works*. Pittsburgh, PA: Institute for Learning, University of Pittsburgh.

Miller, J., & Schwanenflugel, P. J. (2006). Prosody of syntactically complex sentences in the oral reading of young children. *Journal of Educational Psychology*, *98*(4), 839–853.

Mochizuki, K. (1993). *Baseball saved us*. New York: Lee & Low.

Moje, E. B., Stockdill, D., Kim, K., & Kim, H.-J. (2011). The role of text in disciplinary learning. In M. L. Kamil, P. D. Pearson, E. B. Moje, & P. P. Afflerbach (Eds.), *Handbook of reading research* (Vol. 4, pp. 453–486). New York: Routledge.

Moss, L. (1995). *Zin! Zin! Zin! A violin*. New York: Simon & Schuster Books for Young Readers.

Mrazek, M. D., Franklin, M. S., Phillips, D. T., Baird, B., & Schooler, J. W. (2013). Mindfulness training improves working memory capacity and GRE performance while reducing mind wandering. *Psychological Science*, *24*(5), 776–781.

Murphy, P. K., Wilkinson, I. A. G., Soter, A. O., Hennessey, M. N., & Alexander, J. F. (2009). Examining the effects of classroom discussion on students' comprehension of text: A meta-analysis. *Journal of Educational Psychology*, *101*(3), 740–764.

Murray, C., & Greenberg, M. T. (2001). Relationships with teachers and bonds with school: Social emotional adjustment correlates for children with and without disabilities. *Psychology in the Schools*, *38*(1), 25–41.

Murray, C., & Greenberg, M. T. (2006). Examining the importance of social relationships and social contexts in the lives of children with high-incidence disabilities. *Journal of Special Education*, *39*(4), 220–233.

Nagy, W. (2005). Why vocabulary instruction needs to be long-term and comprehensive. In E. H. Hiebert & M. L. Kamil (Eds.), *Teaching and learning vocabulary: Bringing research to practice* (pp. 27–44). Mahwah, NJ: Erlbaum.

Nagy, W. E., & Hiebert, E. H. (2011). Toward a theory of word selection. In M. L. Kamil, P. D. Pearson, E. B. Moje, & P. P. Afflerbach (Eds.), *Handbook of reading research* (Vol. 4, pp. 388–404). New York: Routledge.

National Commission on Excellence in Education. (1983). *A nation at risk: The imperative for educational reform—A report to the nation and the Secretary of Education, United States Department of Education*. Washington, DC: Author.

National Early Literacy Panel. (2008). *Developing early literacy: Report of the National Early Literacy Panel*. Washington, DC: National Institute for Literacy.

National Educational Psychological Service. (2016). *Shared/paired reading at home*. Accessed at https://education.ie/en/Schools-Colleges/Services/National-Educational-Psychological-Service-NEPS-/NEPS-Guides/Reading-and-Dyslexia/Reading-and-Dyslexia-Shared-Paired-Reading-At-Home.pdf on January 18, 2018.

National Governors Association Center for Best Practices & Council of Chief State School Officers. (2010a). *Common Core State Standards for English language arts and literacy in history/social studies, science, and technical subjects*. Washington, DC: Authors. Accessed at www.corestandards.org/assets/CCSSI_ELA%20Standards.pdf on March 30, 2018.

National Governors Association Center for Best Practices & Council of Chief State School Officers. (2010b). *Common Core State Standards for mathematics*. Washington, DC: Authors. Accessed at www.corestandards.org/assets/CCSSI_Math%20Standards.pdf on March 30, 2018.

National Institute of Child Health and Human Development. (2000). *Report of the National Reading Panel—Teaching children to read: An evidence-based assessment of the scientific research literature on reading and its implications for reading instruction* (NIH Publication No. 00-4769). Washington, DC: U.S. Government Printing Office.

Ness, M. (2016). When readers ask questions: Inquiry-based reading instruction. *The Reading Teacher, 70*(2), 189–196.

Neuman, S. B., Newman, E. H., & Dwyer, J. (2011). Educational effects of a vocabulary intervention on preschoolers' word knowledge and conceptual development: A cluster-randomized trial. *Reading Research Quarterly, 46*(3), 249–272.

Newsela. (2016). Should Washington, D.C., become a state? Its mayor says yes. Accessed at https://newsela.com/read/dc-statehood/id/17488 on January 18, 2018.

Noice, H., & Noice, T. (2001). Learning dialogue with and without movement. *Memory and Cognition, 29*(6), 820–827.

Noice, H., & Noice, T. (2006). What studies of actors and acting can tell us about memory and cognitive functioning. *Current Directions in Psychological Science, 15*(1), 14–18.

Nolte, R. Y., & Singer, H. (1985). Active comprehension: Teaching a process of reading comprehension and its effects on reading achievement. *The Reading Teacher, 39*(1), 24–31.

Ogbu, J. U. (1982). Cultural discontinuities and schooling. *Anthropology and Education Quarterly, 13*(4), 290–307.

Orthography. (n.d.). In *Merriam-Webster Dictionary*. Accessed at https://merriam-webster.com/dictionary/orthography on January 8, 2018.

Paas, F., Renkl, A., & Sweller, J. (2003). Cognitive load theory and instructional design: Recent developments. *Educational Psychologist, 38*(1), 1–4.

Pachai, A. A., Acai, A., LoGiudice, A. B., & Kim, J. A. (2016). The mind that wanders: Challenges and potential benefits of mind wandering in education. *Scholarship of Teaching and Learning in Psychology, 2*(2), 134–146.

Palincsar, A. S., & Brown, A. L. (1984). Reciprocal teaching of comprehension-fostering and comprehension-monitoring activities. *Cognition and Instruction, 1*(2), 117–175.

Paratore, J. R., Cassano, C. M., & Schickedanz, J. A. (2011). Supporting early (and later) literacy development at home and at school. In M. L. Kamil, P. D. Pearson, E. B. Moje, & P. P. Afflerbach (Eds.), *Handbook of reading research* (Vol. 4, pp. 107–135). New York: Routledge.

Paris, S. G. (2005). Reinterpreting the development of reading skills. *Reading Research Quarterly, 40*(2), 184–202.

Paris, S. G. (2008, December). *Constrained skills—So what?* Oscar Causey address presented at the National Reading Conference, Orlando, FL.

Paris, S. G., Carpenter, R. D., Paris, A. H., & Hamilton, E. E. (2005). Spurious and genuine correlates of children's reading comprehension. In S. G. Paris & S. A. Stahl (Eds.), *Children's reading comprehension and assessment* (pp. 131–160). Mahwah, NJ: Erlbaum.

Paris, S. G., & Luo, S. W. (2010). Confounded statistical analyses hinder interpretation of the NELP report. *Educational Researcher, 39*(4), 316–322.

Park, L. S. (2001). *A single shard*. New York: Clarion.

Pearson, P. D., & Cervetti, G. N. (2017). The roots of reading comprehension instruction. In S. E. Israel (Ed.), *Handbook of research on reading comprehension* (2nd ed., pp. 12–56). New York: Guilford Press.

Pearson, P. D., & Gallagher, M. C. (1983). The instruction of reading comprehension. *Contemporary Educational Psychology, 8*(3), 317–344.

Pennac, D. (2006). *The rights of the reader* (S. A. Adams, Trans.). London: Walker Books.

Perfetti, C. A. (1992). The representation problem in reading acquisition. In P. Gough, L. Ehri, & R. Treiman (Eds.), *Reading acquisition* (pp. 107–143). Hillsdale, NJ: Erlbaum.

Perfetti, C. A., & Hogaboam, T. (1975). The relationship between single word decoding and reading comprehension skill. *Journal of Educational Psychology, 67*(4), 461–469.

Peterson, D. S., & Taylor, B. M. (2012). Using higher order questioning to accelerate students' growth in reading. *The Reading Teacher, 65*(5), 295–304.

Phillips, B. M., & Piasta, S. B. (2013). Phonological awareness and alphabet knowledge: Key precursors and instructional targets to promote reading success. In T. Shanahan & C. J. Lonigan (Eds.), *Early childhood literacy: The National Early Literacy Panel and beyond* (pp. 95–116). Baltimore: Brookes.

Phillips, L. M., & Yarden, A. (2017). Structure, epistemology, and metalanguage foundations of reading comprehension in scientific texts. In S. E. Israel (Ed.), *Handbook of research on reading comprehension* (2nd ed., pp. 428–441). New York: Guilford Press.

Phonemic Chart. (n.d.). *Phonemic chart keyboard.* Accessed at http://phonemicchart.com on January 18, 2018.

Posner, M. I., & Snyder, C. R. R. (1975). Attention and cognitive control. In R. L. Solso (Ed.), *Information processing and cognition: The Loyola symposium* (pp. 669–681). Hillsdale, NJ: Erlbaum.

Pressley, M. (2002). Metacognition and self-regulated comprehension. In A. E. Farstrup & S. J. Samuels (Eds.), *What research has to say about reading instruction* (3rd ed., pp. 291–309). Newark, DE: International Reading Association.

Pressley, M. (2006). *Reading instruction that works: The case for balanced teaching* (3rd ed.). New York: Guilford Press.

Pressley, M., Allington, R. L., Wharton-McDonald, R., Block, C. C., & Morrow, L. M. (2001). *Learning to read: Lessons from exemplary first-grade classrooms.* New York: Guilford Press.

Pressley, M., El-Dinary, P. B., Gaskins, I., Schuder, T., Bergman, J. L., Almasi, J., et al. (1992). Beyond direct explanation: Transactional instruction of reading comprehension strategies. *Elementary School Journal, 92*(5), 513–555.

Pressley, M., Wharton-McDonald, R., Mistretta-Hampton, J. M., & Echevarria, M. (1998). The nature of literacy instruction in ten fourth- and fifth-grade classrooms in upstate New York. *Scientific Studies of Reading, 2,* 159–194.

Purcell-Gates, V., Duke, N., & Stouffer, J. (2016). Teaching literacy: Reading. In D. H. Gitomer & C. A. Bell (Eds.), *Handbook of research on teaching* (5th ed., pp. 1217–1267). Washington, DC: American Educational Research Association.

RAND Reading Study Group. (2002). *Reading for understanding: Toward an R&D program in reading comprehension.* Santa Monica, CA: RAND.

Rasinski, T., Blachowicz, C., & Lems, K. (Eds.). (2006). *Fluency instruction: Research-based best practices.* New York: Guilford Press.

Rasinski, T. V., & Hoffman, J. V. (2005). Theory and research into practice: Oral reading in the school literacy curriculum. *Reading Research Quarterly, 11,* 65–73.

Rasinski, T. V., Reutzel, D. R., Chard, D., & Linan-Thompson, S. (2011). Reading fluency. In M. L. Kamil, P. D. Pearson, E. B. Moje, & P. P. Afflerbach (Eds.), *Handbook of reading research* (Vol. 4, pp. 286–319). New York: Routledge.

Rayner, K. (1998). Eye movements in reading and information processing: 20 years of research. *Psychological Bulletin, 124*(3), 372–422.

Reithaug, D. (2002). *The 44* phonemes.* Accessed at www.boardman.k12.oh.us/userfiles/363/Phonological%20 Awareness/44Phonemes.pdf on January 18, 2018.

Roberts, T. A. (2003). Effects of alphabet letter instruction on young children's word recognition. *Journal of Educational Psychology, 95*(1), 41–51.

Roberts, T. A., Christo, C., & Shefelbine, J. A. (2011). Word recognition. In M. L. Kamil, P. D. Pearson, E. B. Moje, & P. P. Afflerbach (Eds.), *Handbook of reading research* (Vol. 4, pp. 229–258). New York: Routledge.

Roediger, H. L., III, & Karpicke, J. D. (2006). Test-enhanced learning: Taking memory tests improves long-term retention. *Psychological Science, 17*(3), 249–255.

Rogers, K., & Simms, J. A. (2015). *Teaching argumentation: Activities and games for the classroom.* Bloomington, IN: Marzano Resources.

Rosenblatt, L. M. (1978). *The reader, the text, the poem: The transactional theory of the literary work.* Carbondale: Southern Illinois University Press.

Rosenshine, B., Meister, C., & Chapman, C. (1996). Teaching students to generate questions: A review of the intervention studies. *Review of Educational Research, 66*(2), 181–221.

Rosenshine, B. V. (1986). Synthesis of research on explicit teaching. *Educational Leadership, 43*(7), 60–69.

Rueda, R. (2011). Cultural perspectives in reading: Theory and research. In M. L. Kamil, P. D. Pearson, E. B. Moje, & P. P. Afflerbach (Eds.), *Handbook of reading research* (Vol. 4, pp. 84–103). New York: Routledge.

Sadoski, M., & Paivio, A. (2001). *Imagery and text: A dual coding theory of reading and writing.* Mahwah, NJ: Erlbaum.

Sansone, C., & Thoman, D. B. (2005). Interest as the missing motivator in self-regulation. *European Psychologist, 10*(3), 175–186.

Sansone, C., Thoman, D. B., & Smith, J. L. (2000). Interest and self-regulation: Understanding individual variability in choices, efforts, and persistence over time. In R. H. Hoyle (Ed.), *Handbook of personality and self-regulation* (pp. 192–217). Chichester, England: Wiley-Blackwell.

Schiefele, U., Schaffner, E., Möller, J., & Wigfield, A. (2012). Dimensions of reading motivation and their relation to reading behavior and competence. *Reading Research Quarterly, 47*(4), 427–463.

Schrieber, P. A. (1980). On the acquisition of reading fluency. *Journal of Reading Behavior, 12*(3), 177–186.

Schrieber, P. A. (1987). Prosody and structure in children's syntactic processing. In R. Horowitz & S. J. Samuels (Eds.), *Comprehending oral and written language* (pp. 243–270). San Diego, CA: Academic Press.

Scott, D., & Marzano, R. J. (2014). *Awaken the learner: Finding the source of effective education.* Bloomington, IN: Marzano Resources.

Scott, J. A., & Ehri, L. C. (1990). Sight word reading in prereaders: Use of logographic vs. alphabetic access routes. *Journal of Reading Behavior, 22*(2), 149–166.

Scott, J. A., Jamieson-Noel, D., & Asselin, M. (2003). Vocabulary instruction throughout the day in twenty-three Canadian upper-elementary classrooms. *Elementary School Journal, 103*(3), 269–286.

Scott, J. A., Miller, T. F., & Flinspach, S. L. (2012). Developing word consciousness: Lessons from highly diverse fourth-grade classrooms. In E. J. Kame'enui & J. F. Baumann (Eds.), *Vocabulary instruction: Research to practice* (2nd ed., pp. 169–188). New York: Guilford Press.

Sendak, M. (1963). *Where the wild things are.* New York: Harper & Row.

Sénéchal, M. (1997). The differential effect of storybook reading on preschoolers' acquisition of expressive and receptive vocabulary. *Journal of Child Language, 24*(1), 123–138.

Seymour, P. H. K., & Duncan, L. G. (2001). Learning to read in English. *Psychology: The Journal of the Hellenic Psychological Society, 8*(3), 281–299.

Shanahan, C. (2017). Comprehension in the disciplines. In S. E. Israel (Ed.), *Handbook of research on reading comprehension* (2nd ed., pp. 479–499). New York: Guilford Press.

Shanahan, T., Callison, K., Carriere, C., Duke, N. K., Pearson, P. D., Schatschneider, C., et al. (2010). *Improving reading comprehension in kindergarten through 3rd grade: A practice guide* (NCEE 2010–4038). Washington, DC: National Center for Education Evaluation and Regional Assistance, Institute of Education Sciences, U.S. Department of Education.

Shanahan, C., Shanahan, T., & Misischia, C. (2006, December). *Frameworks for literacy in three disciplines* [Presentation]. Paper presented at the annual meeting of the National Reading Conference, Los Angeles, CA.

Share, D. L. (1995). Phonological recoding and self-teaching: *Sine qua non* of reading acquisition. *Cognition, 55*(2), 151–218.

Share, D. L. (1999). Phonological recoding and orthographic learning: A direct test of the self-teaching hypothesis. *Journal of Experimental Child Psychology, 72*(2), 95–129.

Share, D. L. (2004). Orthographic learning at a glance: On the time course and developmental onset of self-teaching. *Journal of Experimental Child Psychology, 87*(4), 267–298.

Share, D. L. (2008). Orthographic learning, phonological recoding, and self-teaching. In R. V. Kail (Ed.), *Advances in child behavior and development* (Vol. 36, pp. 31–82). San Diego, CA: Elsevier Academic Press.

Sim, S., & Berthelsen, D. (2014). Shared book reading by parents with young children: Evidence-based practice. *Australasian Journal of Early Childhood, 39*(1), 50–55.

Simms, J. A. (2016, August). *The critical concepts (Final version: English language arts, mathematics, and science)*. Centennial, CO: Marzano Resources.

Simms, J. A., & Marzano, R. J. (2018). *Knowledge maps* [video series]. Accessed at www.marzanoresources.com/online-compendium/additional-resources on May 7, 2018.

Smagorinsky, P. (2001). If meaning is constructed, what is it made from? Toward a cultural theory of reading. *Review of Educational Research, 71*(1), 133–169.

Smallwood, J., & Schooler, J. W. (2006). The restless mind. *Psychological Bulletin, 132*(6), 946–958.

Smith, N. B. (1965). *American reading instruction: Its development and its significance in gaining a perspective on current practices in reading*. Newark, DE: International Reading Association.

Snow, C. E., Burns, M. S., & Griffin, P. (Eds.). (1998). *Preventing reading difficulties in young children* (Report of the Committee of Reading Difficulties in Young Children, National Research Council). Washington, DC: National Academies Press.

Snow, C. E., & Juel, C. (2005). Teaching children to read: What do we know about how to do it? In M. J. Snowling & C. Hulme (Eds.), *The science of reading: A handbook* (pp. 501–520). Oxford, England: Blackwell.

Snow, C. E., Porche, M. V., Tabors, P. O., & Harris, S. R. (2007). *Is literacy enough? Pathways to academic success for adolescents*. Baltimore: Brookes.

Spiro, R. J., Vispoel, W. P., Schmitz, J. G., Samarapungavan, A., & Boerger, A. E. (1987). Knowledge acquisition for application: Cognitive flexibility and transfer in complex content domains. In B. C. Britton & S. Glynn (Eds.), *Executive control processes in reading* (pp. 177–200). Hillsdale, NJ: Erlbaum.

Sprenger-Charolles, L., Siegel, L. S., & Bonnet, P. (1998). Reading and spelling acquisition in French: The role of phonological mediation and orthographic factors. *Journal of Experimental Child Psychology, 68*(2), 134–165.

Springer, S. E., Dole, J. A., & Hacker, D. J. (2017). The role of interest in reading comprehension. In S. E. Israel (Ed.), *Handbook of research on reading comprehension* (2nd ed., pp. 519–542). New York: Guilford Press.

Stahl, K. A. D., & Bravo, M. A. (2010). Contemporary classroom vocabulary assessment for content areas. *The Reading Teacher, 63*(7), 566–578.

Stahl, K. A. D., & Stahl, S. A. (2012). Young word wizards! Fostering vocabulary development in preschool and primary education. In E. J. Kame'enui & J. F. Baumann (Eds.), *Vocabulary instruction: Research to practice* (2nd ed., pp. 72–92). New York: Guilford Press.

Stahl, S. A. (2004). What do we know about fluency? In P. McCardle & V. Chhabra (Eds.), *The voice of evidence in reading research* (pp. 187–211). Baltimore: Brookes.

Stahl, S. A. (2005). Four problems with teaching word meanings (and what to do to make vocabulary an integral part of instruction). In E. H. Hiebert & M. L. Kamil (Eds.), *Teaching and learning vocabulary: Bringing research to practice* (pp. 95–114). Mahwah, NJ: Erlbaum.

Stahl, S. A., & Clark, C. H. (1987). The effects of participatory expectations in classroom discussion on the learning of science vocabulary. *American Educational Research Journal, 24*(4), 541–555.

Stahl, S. A., & Fairbanks, M. M. (1986). The effects of vocabulary instruction: A model-based meta-analysis. *Review of Educational Research, 56*(1), 72–110.

Stahl, S. A., & Murray, B. A. (1994). Defining phonological awareness and its relationship to early reading. *Journal of Educational Psychology, 86*(2), 221–234.

Stahl, S. A., & Nagy, W. E. (2006). *Teaching word meanings*. Mahwah, NJ: Erlbaum.

Stahl, S. A., & Vancil, S. J. (1986). Discussion is what makes semantic maps work in vocabulary instruction. *The Reading Teacher, 40*(1), 62–67.

Stanovich, K. E. (1990). Concepts in developmental theories of reading skill: Cognitive recourses, automaticity, and modularity. *Developmental Review, 10*(1), 72–100.

Stone, T. L. (2015). *The house that Jane built: A story about Jane Addams*. New York: Holt.

Strauss, R. (2004). *Tree of life: The incredible biodiversity of life on earth*. Tonawanda, NY: Kids Can Press.

Stroop, J. R. (1935). Studies of interference in serial verbal reactions. *Journal of Experimental Psychology, 18*(6), 643–662.

Stuart, M., & Coltheart, M. (1988). Does reading develop in a sequence of stages? *Cognition, 30*(2), 139–181.

Sturm, B. W. (1999). The enchanted imagination: Storytelling's power to entrance listeners. *School Library Media Research, 2*, 1–21.

Taboada, A., & Guthrie, J. T. (2006). Contributions of student questioning and prior knowledge to construction of knowledge from reading informational text. *Journal of Literacy Research, 38*(1), 1–35.

Taylor, B. M., Pearson, P. D., Clark, K., & Walpole, S. (2000). Effective schools and accomplished teachers: Lessons about primary-grade reading instruction in low-income schools. *Elementary School Journal, 101*(2), 121–165.

Taylor, B. M., Pearson, P. D., Peterson, D. S., & Rodriguez, M. C. (2003). Reading growth in high-poverty classrooms: The influence of teacher practices that encourage cognitive engagement in literacy learning. *Elementary School Journal, 104*(1), 3–28.

Taylor, B. M., Pearson, P. D., Peterson, D. S., & Rodriguez, M. C. (2005). The CIERA school change framework: An evidence-based approach to professional development and school reading improvement. *Reading Research Quarterly, 40*(1), 40–69.

Taylor, D., & Dorsey-Gaines, C. (1988). *Growing up literate: Learning from inner-city families*. Portsmouth, NH: Heinemann.

Taylor, L. K., Alber, S. R., & Walker, D. W. (2002). The comparative effects of a modified self-questioning strategy and story mapping on the reading comprehension of elementary students with learning disabilities. *Journal of Behavioral Education, 11*(2), 69–87.

Teachers College Reading and Writing Project. (2006). *Concepts about print assessment.* Accessed at https://connect.readingandwritingproject.org/file/download?google_drive_document_id=0B3yKjAsMtuECVXFvM1NVZ1BJenc on January 15, 2018.

Therrien, W. J., & Hughes, C. (2008). Comparison of repeated reading and question generation on students' reading fluency and comprehension. *Learning Disabilities, 6*(1), 1–16.

Thompson, G. B., Fletcher-Flinn, C. M., & Cottrell, D. S. (1999). Learning correspondences between letters and phonemes without explicit instruction. *Applied Psycholinguistics, 20*(1), 21–50.

Thorndike, E. L. (1917). Reading as reasoning: A study of mistakes in paragraph reading. *Journal of Educational Psychology, 8*(6), 323–332.

Tinkham, T. (1997). The effects of semantic and thematic clustering on the learning of second language vocabulary. *Second Language Research, 13*(2), 138–163.

Tortello, R. (2004). Tableaux vivants in the literature classroom. *The Reading Teacher, 58*(2), 206–208.

Trabasso, T., & Bouchard, E. (2002). Teaching readers how to comprehend text strategically. In C. C. Block & M. Pressley (Eds.), *Comprehension instruction: Research-based best practices* (pp. 176–200). New York: Guilford Press.

Treiman, R., & Rodriguez, K. (1999). Young children use letter names in learning to read words. *Psychological Science, 10*(4), 334–338.

Tunmer, W. E., & Chapman, J. W. (1998). Language prediction skill, phonological recoding ability and beginning reading. In C. Hulme & R. M. Joshi (Eds.), *Reading and spelling: Development and disorders* (pp. 33–67). Hillsdale, NJ: Erlbaum.

Tunmer, W. E., & Chapman, J. W. (2006). Metalinguistic abilities, phonological recoding skills, and the use of sentence context in beginning reading development: A longitudinal study. In R. M. Joshi & P. G. Aaron (Eds.), *Handbook of orthography and literacy* (pp. 617–635). Mahwah, NJ: Erlbaum.

Tunmer, W. E., & Nicholson, T. (2011). The development and teaching of word recognition skill. In M. L. Kamil, P. D. Pearson, E. B. Moje, & P. P. Afflerbach (Eds.), *Handbook of reading research* (Vol. 4, pp. 405–431). New York: Routledge.

Tyler, K. M., Uqdah, A. L., Dillihunt, M. L., Beatty-Hazelbaker, R., Connor, T., Gadson, N., et al. (2008). Cultural discontinuity: Toward a quantitative investigation of a major hypothesis in education. *Educational Researcher, 37*(5), 280–297.

Valdés, G. (1996). *Con respeto: Bridging the distances between culturally diverse families and schools: An ethnographic portrait.* New York: Teachers College Press.

Varao Sousa, T. L., Carriere, J. S. A., & Smilek, D. (2013). The way we encounter reading material influences how frequently we mind wander. *Frontiers in Psychology, 4*, 892.

Varoufakis, Y. (2017). Opinion: Should we tax robots that take our jobs? *Newsela.* Accessed at https://newsela.com/read/robot-tax/id/27665 on January 18, 2018.

Vellutino, F. R., Fletcher, J. M., Snowling, M. J., & Scanlon, D. M. (2004). Specific reading disability (dyslexia): What have we learned in the past four decades? *Journal of Child Psychology and Psychiatry, 45*(1), 2–40.

Vintinner, J. P., Harmon, J., Wood, K., & Stover, K. (2015). Inquiry into the efficacy of interactive word walls with older adolescent learners. *High School Journal, 98*(3), 250–261.

Viorst, J. (1972). *Alexander and the terrible, horrible, no good, very bad day.* New York: Aladdin.

Vogel, E. (2003). Using informational text to build children's knowledge of the world around them. In N. K. Duke & V. S. Bennett-Armistead (Eds.), *Reading and writing informational text in the primary grades: Research-based practices* (pp. 157–198). New York: Scholastic.

Walczyk, J. J., & Griffith-Ross, D. A. (2007). How important is reading skill fluency for comprehension? *The Reading Teacher*, *60*(6), 560–569.

Weber, K. (2008). How mathematicians determine if an argument is a valid proof. *Journal for Research in Mathematics Education*, *39*(4), 431–459.

Wessling, R., & Reitsma, P. (2000). The transient role of explicit phonological recoding for reading acquisition. *Reading and Writing*, *13*(3–4), 313–336.

Wharton-McDonald, R., & Erickson, J. (2017). Reading comprehension in the middle grades: Characteristics, challenges, and effective supports. In S. E. Israel (Ed.), *Handbook of research on reading comprehension* (2nd ed., pp. 353–376). New York: Guilford Press.

Wharton-McDonald, R., Pressley, M., & Hampston, J. M. (1998). Literacy instruction in nine first-grade classrooms: Teacher characteristics and student achievement. *Elementary School Journal*, *99*(2), 101–128.

White, T. G., Sowell, J., & Yanagihara, A. (1989). Teaching elementary students to use word-part clues. *The Reading Teacher*, *42*(4), 302–308.

Wilkinson, I. A. G., & Son, E. H. (2011). A dialogic turn in research on learning and teaching to comprehend. In M. L. Kamil, P. D. Pearson, E. B. Moje, & P. P. Afflerbach (Eds.), *Handbook of reading research* (Vol. 4, pp. 359–387). New York: Routledge.

Willems, M. (2003). *Don't let the pigeon drive the bus!* New York: Hyperion Books for Children.

Wilson, G. P. (2003). Supporting young children's thinking through tableau. *Language Arts*, *80*(5), 375–383.

Wolf, M. K., Crosson, A. C., & Resnick, L. B. (2005). Classroom talk for rigorous reading comprehension instruction. *Reading Psychology*, *26*(1), 27–53.

Wong, B., & Jones, W. (1982). Increasing metacomprehension in learning disabled and normally achieving students through self-questioning training. *Learning Disability Quarterly*, *5*(3), 228–240.

Zucker, T. A., Ward, A. E., & Justice, L. M. (2009). Print referencing during read-alouds: A technique for increasing emergent readers' print knowledge. *The Reading Teacher*, *63*(1), 62–72.

Index

Solution Tree

Solution Tree's mission is to advance the work of our authors. By working with the best researchers and educators worldwide, we strive to be the premier provider of innovative publishing, in-demand events, and inspired professional development designed to transform education to ensure that all students learn.

ASCD®

LEARN. TEACH. LEAD.

ASCD is a global nonprofit association dedicated to the whole child approach that supports educators, families, community members, and policy makers. We provide expert and innovative solutions to facilitate professional development through print and digital publishing, on-site learning services, and conferences and events that empower educators to support the success of each child.